Gluing & Clamping:
A Woodworker's Handbook

Patrick Spielman

Sterling Publishing Co., Inc. New York

Photo Credits

The illustrations in this book display the products, creations, and photography of many people and business organizations. Represented among them are: Bingham Projects, 175, 516–518; Ekstrom, Carlson, and Co., 283; Fine Wood and Tool Store, Inc., 324; Gougeon Brothers, 244 and 245; Lee Valley Tools, 38 and 148; Peterson Builders, 277; and Scan Furniture, 428 and 476.

Edited by Michael Cea

Library of Congress Cataloging-in-Publication Data

Spielman, Patrick E.
   Gluing and clamping: a woodworker's handbook.

   Includes index.
   1. Woodwork.   2. Gluing.   3. Clamps (Engineering)
I. Title.
TT180.S64   1986   684'.08   86-903
ISBN 0-8069-6274-7 (pbk.)

Second Printing, 1986

Table of Contents

Acknowledgments

Many companies and private individuals provided a healthy measure of assistance in this work. Those that generously supplied photos or drawings or provided sample materials or tools include the following:

Adjustable Clamp Company
Adwood Corp.
Aircraft Spruce & Specialty Co.
Albert Constantine & Son, Inc.
Bahco Record Tools Limited
Bob Morgan Woodworking Supplies, Co.
Borden Inc., Adhesives Div.
Bostik Consumer Div., USM Corp.
Brinks and Cotton Mfg. Co.
California Redwood Association
Chem Tech, Inc.
Ciba Geigy (UK) Ltd.
Cincinnati Tool Co.
Craft Supplies USA
Cushman Mfg. Co.
Ekstrom, Carlson, and Co.
Fine Wood and Tool Store
Forest Products Laboratory
Formica Corp.
Freeman Mfg. and Supply Co.
Franklin Chemical Industries, Inc.
Garrett Wade Co., Inc.
Gougeon Bros., Inc.
Griset Industries
Hartford Clamp Co.
Helikon Furniture
Lee Valley Tools
Loctite Corp.
Peterson Builders
Riverside Woodworks
Scan Furniture
Stanley Tools
Shopsmith, Inc.
Universal Clamp Co.
Wetzler Clamp Co.
Wilsonart Plastic Co.
Woodgrain, Inc.
Woodworker's Store
Workrite Products Co.

Some individuals and companies granted the author extra privileges or special assistance for which sincere gratitude is hereby expressed. Special thanks to: Jeff Cowie of the Adjustable Clamp Company for the generous supply of excellent photos and project plans, and to David Drake of Shopsmith, Inc. for the photos of their various clamping systems. For valuable and up-dated information about epoxies, I extend my appreciation to Jerry Schindler of Chem Tech, Inc., and to Pat Gougeon of Gougeon Bros., Inc., for their help. Laura Bell, Lucille Foy, and Susan Lewin of the Formica Corp. came up with many good photos for the chapter on plastic laminates. Thanks to Darrel Nish of Craft Supplies USA, and to Leonard Lee of Lee Valley Tools for their special photos. Thank you Mathew Heitzke of the Fine Wood and Tool Store for the information and samples of "biscuit" joinery. Thanks to Elmont Bingham, Bingham Projects, Inc., for the use of laminating illustrations, and to Bob Webb of Bob Morgan Woodworking Supplies for some photos in the veneering chapter. Alan E. Fitchett of Albert Constantine & Son, Inc., provided information about veneering and photos of inlay work. Bryan River and The Forest Products Laboratory was the source for a wealth of technical assistance. Thanks to Roger Lautenbach for his "leads" and to Mark Obernberger and Bob Spielman for their helpful efforts. I would like to recognize some superior work by former students, Robert Cuellar, David Goetz, Dan Jischke, Lars Johnson, Kevin Mueller, Steve Mueller, and Marty Orsted, whose projects appear in this book. Thanks to Julie Kiehnau for her efficient and speedy typing talents. And finally, thanks to all of those other individuals or concerns that have in one way or another affected, influenced, or contributed to the pages of this book.

Patrick Spielman

Introduction

The gluing of wood is an amazing phenomenon. It is quite spectacular when two pieces of wood are easily joined together with the resulting bond so complete the joint is stronger than the wood itself. (See Illus. 1.) However, at times the woodworker may wonder if he has made a good enough joint. If the joint fails, its quality is clearly visible and the woodworker will experience a great deal of disappointment, and sometimes embarrassment. If the joint doesn't fail, he may still wonder if he made all the correct decisions and used the proper gluing methods to ensure that the joint is of high quality and is durable.

This book is an attempt to clarify the mystery associated with the gluing and clamping of wood. Most of us, professionals and amateurs alike, lack confidence in this area. After all, we know that wood itself is an organic and unstable material that exhibits many different and variable properties. Every piece of wood is unique with its own grain, density, weight, moisture content, and overall structure. We also realize that wood can actually change dimensionally—sometimes quite drastically—under certain conditions.

All fundamentals of gluing and clamping will be discussed. This includes what glues to use, what wood is best for a particular job,

Illus. 1. The objective: a good glue joint that is stronger than the wood itself. Note the desirable effect of high "wood failure," which is preferred over glue failure.

ways to control the variables involved in the gluing process, the clamps and other tools needed, safety factors, and many other important considerations. Then the entire range of gluing techniques is explored. Edge-to-edge (Illus. 2 and 3), face-to-face (Illus. 4–7), and end-to-end gluing (Illus. 8) are all important techniques that will be discussed separately and in a thorough manner. Other extremely useful gluing techniques are explored. These include veneering (a way of decorating and conserving rare woods [Illus. 9]), applying plastic laminates (Illus. 10), and curved wood lamination, in which layers of wood are glued together while bent over a mould or form to produce very strong members (Illus. 11 and 12). The final chapter shows how to make some essential repairs and supplies projects on which the craftsman can apply the gluing and clamping techniques he has just learned.

Illus. 2. Building a desk similar to this one, made by the Cushman Mfg. Co., requires many gluing jobs, including making edge-to-edge panels and gluing various structural joints.

Illus. 3. Decorative edge-to-edge glue joints are perfect for cutting boards, a job which also requires using the appropriate glue. (See page 105 for details.)

Illus. 4. Large turning stock is commonly made by gluing boards face to face to increase thickness and width dimensions.

Illus. 5. Carving blanks often need gluing to achieve sufficient sizes.

Illus. 6. This laminated lamp base is 5½" square at the base and 18" high. It is an unusual piece in that end grain is exposed on all four sides. This is achieved by cutting each piece at 45° to the grain.

Illus. 7. This authentic butcher block table by Lars Johnson consists entirely of maple glued face to face, creating the entire top in end grain.

Illus. 8. This ready-to-be glued scarf joint can be employed to increase the length of wood. This is an important process commonly used in boat building. (See Chapter 8 for more information.)

Illus. 9. A veneered buffet by Scan Furnishings has solid edgings and legs.

Illus. 10. This four-foot expandable dining room table involved face-to-face gluing for the base, forming the curved apron, and "putting down" the wood grain plastic laminate on the top.

Illus. 11. A laminated dining chair of beech and oak veneers produced by Scan Furnishings.

Illus. 12. This veneer-laminated table leg is easy to make. See Chapter 11 for plans and how-to information for this and other projects that can be made from the same easy-to-make mould.

With a knowledge of the gluing and clamping techniques presented in this book, the average craftsman will become a much more creative and skillful woodworker. He will be able to conserve material by removing (ripping out) defects from lumber and regluing the pieces together. (See Illus. 13–15.) He will be able to relieve the internal stresses in boards, consequently reducing the problems of warpage and distortion, as well as strengthen baseball bats, beams, and other objects. He will even be able to use the narrow edgings and wood scraps that normally clutter up his workshop to make useable panels (Illus. 16). These panels can in turn be used to make clocks (Illus. 17) and other projects, and as shelving, drawer sides, etc. If he is a woodworker involved in a specialized craft like model-making (Illus. 18) or musical-instrument making, these techniques will prove to be just as valuable. (See Illus. 19.)

Illus. 13. Glue-ups of any size can be made with all defects removed.

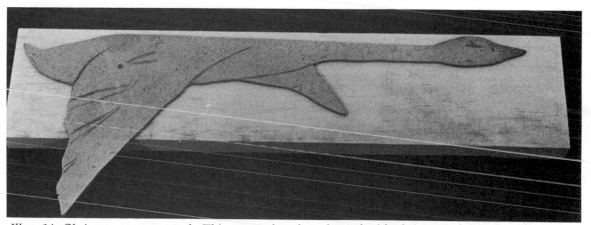

Illus. 14. Gluing to conserve stock. This narrow board can be used with gluing, as shown in Illus. 15, to make this project.

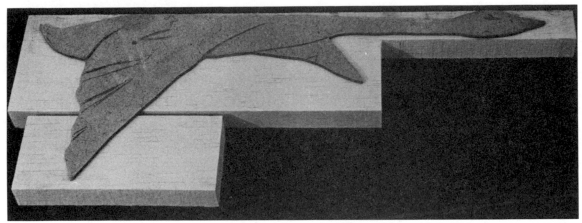

Illus. 15. Cutting away extra waste and then gluing solves the problem of insufficient width and saves material.

Illus. 16. Narrow scrap edgings can be glued together to make useful panels such as drawer slides or shelving.

Illus. 17. Very narrow waste strips of random sizes were combined to make this interesting clock face that measures $\frac{3}{4} \times 11 \times 11$ inches.

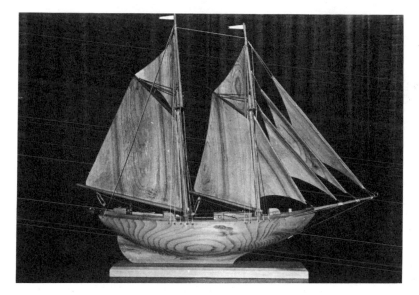

Illus. 18. Modelmakers have their preferred glues. This all-wood ship by Bill Herbst even has carved wood sails.

Illus. 19. This wood mail box must be assembled with exterior glue. See my book, Making Country-Rustic Furniture, *for more on this and other exterior projects.*

The adhesive manufacturing industry is monumental. *Adhesives Age,* a magazine devoted to the field, recently listed in their annual directory over 650 adhesive companies and over 1,000 plants. Many of these companies, intending to set their products apart from the others, have only succeeded in confusing consumers with misleading and exaggerated advertisements.

There is little that is "new" about gluing wood. It still presents the same problems to woodworkers it did decades ago. And despite the onslaught of glues on the market, there are only about a dozen types that are very important to the woodworker. Some of the highly advertised new additives or special formulations of common standbys are hardly worth noting. (However, there are some interesting exceptions, like the new epoxies, which are discussed in Chapter 2.)

Clamping techniques have changed very little over the years. Holding joints together until the glue sets or cures is still the principal purpose of clamping. Sometimes certain jobs call for some imaginative ideas or self-made devices. Many of the old tools and old clamping techniques are still unchanged, and remain the best. Included in the project section are some plans and ideas for self-made clamping devices.

Wood today is too expensive and your investment in labor too great for you to depend on unreliable gluing and clamping techniques. Hopefully, this book will make you more knowledgeable, confident, and successful, and give you a better understanding of this essential and very comprehensive woodworking subject.

Pat Spielman

Chapter 1
Selecting Wood for Gluing

At first glance, wood gluing appears to be a simple, straightforward process, in which the ·basic procedures are: apply the glue, spread it, clamp the wood, and allow the glue to dry. However, many factors determine the success of the glue bond. One of the most important ones is the type of wood used. (See Illus. 20)

To determine which species of wood to use, for a specific job, the craftsman has to take into account the following characteristics of wood: its density; its shrinkage and expansion capabilities; and its moisture content. These factors are interrelated.

Density

Two pieces of wood can have equal dimensions, size, volume, and moisture content and still vary greatly in weight. This is because the denser woods, which are the heavier woods, have less air space in their structures.

Illus. 21 and 22 compare the percentages of air space and actual wood substance in species that have two distinctly different densities. (The magnification is the same in each photo.) Illus. 21 shows a section of sugar maple, a very dense, heavy, hard wood. Illus. 22

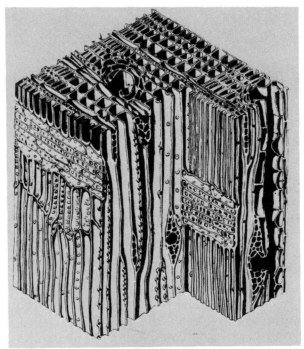

Illus. 20. This enlarged drawing shows the porous, sponge-like structure of wood that is good for gluing. This is actually a microscopic view of softwood measuring about ¼" on a side.

Illus. 21. A similar look at a cross-section of an actual sample of sugar maple drastically enlarged. Air space is only about 58% and the wood substance is about 42% of the total volume.

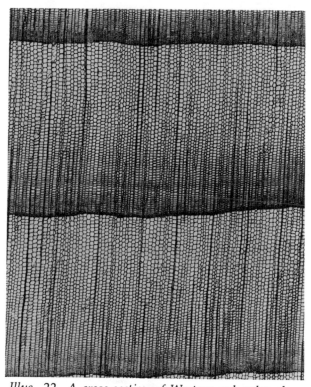

Illus. 22. A cross-section of Western red cedar also enlarged the same amount as the cross-section shown in Illus. 21. Air space comprises about 78% with actual wood substance amounting to about only 22% of the whole volume.

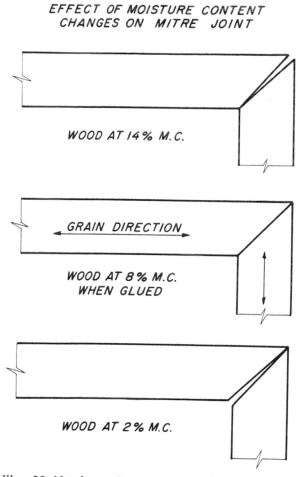

EFFECT OF MOISTURE CONTENT CHANGES ON MITRE JOINT

WOOD AT 14% M.C.

GRAIN DIRECTION

WOOD AT 8% M.C. WHEN GLUED

WOOD AT 2% M.C.

Illus. 23. Note how mitre joints react when made with wood that has a high tendency to shrink or swell. Using dried, quarter-sawed wood and some sort of glued reinforcing spline or feather also reduces the possibility of opened mitre joints. Above: Open joint that results from the wood swelling, increasing the width of the parts. Below: Open joint that results from shrinking, reducing the widths of the parts.

shows a section of Western red cedar, which is a highly porous, lightweight soft wood. The cedar has considerably more air (pore) space, and only about 20 percent is wood substance. Hickory, one of the densest and heaviest woods, is about half air space and half wood substance.

Soft woods are easier to glue than hard woods. Gluing the heavier, denser woods generally requires high-quality adhesives and better control of the other variables. Within the species of the wood itself, the sapwood is more easily glued than the denser heartwood.

Shrinkage and Expansion

Wood shrinks in a dry atmosphere and expands in environments with higher humidities. (See Illus. 23.) The shrinkage that results during the drying of fresh-sawn lumber often unleashes internal stresses in the form of cracks, splits, or sets up new forces that cause distortions; these distortions are known as warpage. Warped surfaces do not make good gluing surfaces. They make it difficult to get tight, closely fitting joints, or to apply even, uniform pressure over the entire joint.

Several factors determine the shrinkage and expansion capabilities of wood. The way boards have been cut is one of the major factors. Boards are cut in two distinct ways: They are either plain-sawed or quarter-

15

sawed. (See Illus. 24 and 25.) Plain-sawed and quarter-sawed boards have different shrinkage and expansion capabilities. It's important that the craftsman understand these capabilities.

Table 1 gives a good indication of shrinkage tendencies for most domestic and some imported woods in the United States. The figures indicated have been prepared by Forest Products Laboratory and are the percentage that quarter-sawed and plain-sawed boards shrink when they are dried all the way from a green (wet wood) state to a complete oven-dry condition with all of the moisture removed.

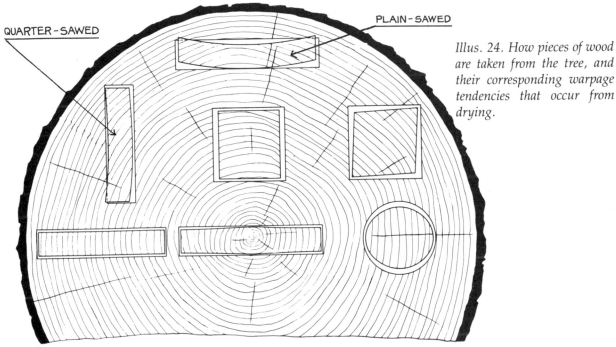

QUARTER-SAWED

PLAIN-SAWED

Illus. 24. How pieces of wood are taken from the tree, and their corresponding warpage tendencies that occur from drying.

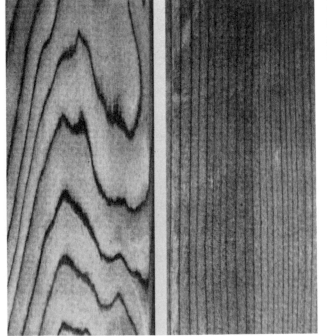

Illus. 25. The grain pattern on the face of a board identifies how it was cut from the tree. At left is a plain-sawed board; compare it to the straight lines of the quarter-sawed board at the right.

Table 1.

Hardwoods

	Quarter-Sawed Pct.	Plain-Sawed Pct.		Quarter-Sawed Pct.	Plain-Sawed Pct.
Alder, red	4.4	7.3	Holly, American	4.8	9.9
Ash:			Honeylocust	4.2	6.6
Black	5.0	7.8	Locust, black	4.6	7.2
Green	4.6	7.1	Magnolia:		
White	4.9	7.8	Southern	5.4	6.6
Aspen:			Maple:		
Bigtooth	3.3	7.9	Bigleaf	3.7	7.1
Quaking	3.5	6.7	Red	4.0	8.2
Basswood,			Silver	3.0	7.2
American	6.6	9.3	Sugar	4.8	9.9
Beech, American	5.5	11.9	Oak, red:		
Birch:			Black	4.4	11.1
Paper	6.3	8.6	Northern red	4.0	8.6
Sweet	6.5	9.0	Southern red	4.7	11.3
Yellow	7.3	9.5	Willow	5.0	9.6
Buckeye, yellow	3.6	8.1	Oak:		
Butternut	3.4	6.4	Bur	4.4	8.8
Cherry, black	3.7	7.1	Swamp	5.2	10.8
Chestnut, American	3.4	6.7	White	5.6	10.5
Cottonwood:			Persimmon, common	7.9	11.2
Balsam poplar	3.0	7.1	Sassafras	4.0	6.2
Black	3.6	8.6	Sweetgum	5.3	10.2
Eastern	3.9	9.2	Sycamore,		
Elm:			American	5.0	8.4
American	4.2	7.2	Tanoak	4.9	11.7
Rock	4.8	8.1	Tupelo:		
Slippery	4.9	8.9	Black	5.1	8.7
Hackberry	4.8	8.9	Water	4.2	7.6
Hickory, Pecan	4.9	8.9	Walnut, black	5.5	7.8
Hickory, True:			Willow, black	3.3	8.7
Shagbark	7.0	10.5	Yellow poplar	4.6	8.2

Imported Woods

	Quarter-Sawed Pct.	Plain-Sawed Pct.		Quarter-Sawed Pct.	Plain-Sawed Pct.
Andiroba	4.0	7.8	Lupuna	3.5	6.3
Angelique	5.2	8.8	Mahogany	3.7	5.1
Apitong	5.2	10.9	Nogal	2.8	5.5
Avodire	3.7	6.5	Obeche	3.1	5.3
Balsa	3.0	7.6	Okoume	5.6	6.1
Banak	4.6	8.8	"Parana pine"	4.0	7.9

Imported Woods

Cativo	2.3	5.3	Primavera	3.1	5.2
Greenheart	8.2	9.0	Ramin	3.9	8.7
Ishpingo	2.7	4.4	Santa Maria	5.4	7.9
Khaya	4.1	5.8	Spanish-cedar	4.1	6.3
Kokrodua	3.2	6.3	Teak	2.2	4.0
Lauan	3.8	8.0	"Virola"	5.3	9.6
Limba	4.4	5.4	Walnut, European	4.3	6.4

Softwoods

	Quarter-Sawed Pct.	Plain-Sawed Pct.		Quarter-Sawed Pct.	Plain-Sawed Pct.
Bald cypress	3.8	6.2	Pine (cont.)		
Cedar:			Loblolly	4.8	7.4
Atlantic white	2.9	5.4	Lodgepole	4.3	6.7
Northern white	2.2	4.9	Longleaf	5.1	7.5
Port-Orford	4.6	6.9	Ponderosa	3.9	6.2
Western red cedar	2.4	5.0	Red	3.8	7.2
Douglas-fir:			Shortleaf	4.6	7.7
Coast	4.8	7.6	Sugar	2.9	5.6
Interior north	3.8	6.9	Virginia	4.2	7.2
Fir:			Western white	4.1	7.4
White	3.3	7.0	Redwood:		
Hemlock:			Old-growth	2.6	4.4
Western	4.2	7.8	Young-growth	2.2	4.9
Larch, western	4.5	9.1	Spruce:		
Pine:			Engelmann	3.8	7.1
Eastern white	2.1	6.1	Sitka	4.3	7.5
Jack	3.7	6.6	Tamarack	3.7	7.4

As a general rule, shrinkage is usually 1½ to 2 times as great across the width of a plain-sawed board as across the width of a quarter-sawed board. Wood is essentially stable along the length (grain) of the board.

The density of wood also affects the amount of shrinkage. As the density increases, the amount of shrinkage becomes greater. Beech, for example, shrinks .54 percent for one percent reduction in moisture content. At this rate, a panel 25 inches wide that changes in moisture content from 5 to 8 percent can result in a dimensional change across the width of the panel ¼ inch. However, under the same conditions a piece of mahogany, which is less dense, swells only half as much.

Moisture content is probably the most important factor in the swelling and shrinking of wood. (See Illus. 26.) Moisture is always present in wood, even in properly seasoned wood. Wood intended for use in most parts of the United States should be conditioned or dried to within a range of 6 to 8 percent moisture content. (See Illus. 27.) Wood to be exposed to exterior conditions should be dried to within a range of 10 to 14 percent moisture content. Remember, however, wood this high in moisture content is just too wet to be successfully glued with some adhesives. In fact, green wood is almost impossible to glue. The water in the wood dilutes the adhesive after it spreads. This causes excessive penetration and results in very poor joint quality. Moist woods can, however, be glued with some types of epoxies. (See Chapter 2.)

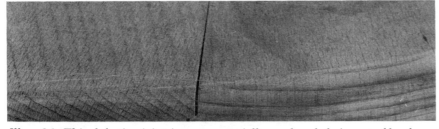

Illus. 26. This defective joint in a commercially produced chair seat of beech can be traced to the moisture content of the wood at the time of gluing, which was above the range required for the environment in which the chair was used. Note the growth rings in the members of the joint. The piece at the right has a greater tendency to shrink than the one at the left.

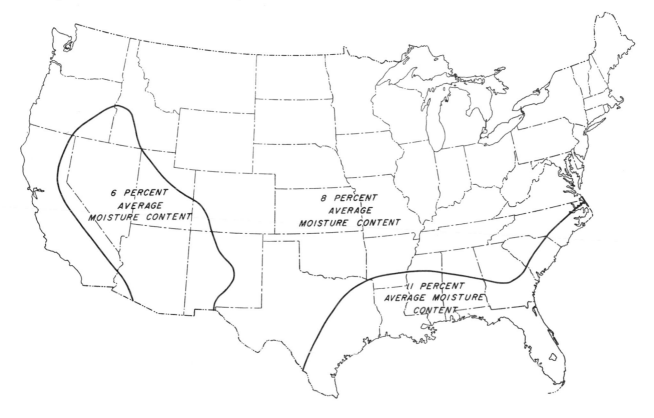

Illus. 27. Recommended moisture content quantities for interior wood usage for various regions of the United States.

Since wood loses and gains moisture from the air, it is subject to dimensional change on a long-term (seasonal) and short-term (daily) basis. When wood is neither gaining nor losing moisture to the surrounding air, it is at its equilibrium moisture content (E.M.C.). Plywood, hardboard, and particle boards have lower E.M.C. values because their fibres have been modified in some way during their manufacture. However, when a project calls for the use of these sheet materials or a combination of solid woods bonded to them (and/or bonded to each other), they should be conditioned before bonding in an environment that has a humidity and temperature similar to the environment where the object will be used. (See Illus. 28 and 29.)

Illus. 28. Sheet materials and solid woods such as this pine edge on particle board should be glued together only after both pieces have been conditioned in temperature and relative humidity similar to that expected in use.

Illus. 29. A moisture meter gives exact readings of the moisture content in wood.

Bonding Recommendations

Try not to glue different wood species together into one unit; because of their different expansion and shrinkage rates, problems may arise. (See Illus. 30.) Even if these problems don't break the glue bond completely, the finished product will still suffer in quality or in visual appeal. If you do bond wood material with different expansion and shrinkage characteristics, it may be necessary to design or devise a method to restrain warpage. Methods include "balanced" cross-grained glue-ups similar to the alternating layers of plywood, and various mechanical restraints like steel bolts.

Illus. 30. Making critical glue-ups using pieces of different species of wood can cause problems—even joint failure—due to their different coefficients of dimensional change. Environmental moisture changes will set up different stresses within the panel.

The most stress-free gluing occurs when the component pieces in the glue-up are of the same species (uniform in density), of similar cuts (all quarter-sawed or all plain-sawed), and all have a moisture content that is best suited for the environment in which they will be used (Illus. 31). Remember, however, that gluing wood pieces of different moisture content or plain-sawed and quarter-sawed board together can cause serious problems in the assembly. (See Illus. 32 and 33.)

It's almost impossible to keep the dimensions of wood totally stable unless the wood is chemically treated. An earlier book of mine, *Working Green Wood with PEG* (Sterling Publishing Co., Inc., 1980), discusses this topic at length. It is possible, however, that with some wise planning and foresight the wood could contract or expand without serious consequences.

It is actually possible to take advantage of wood's instability. For example, some craftsmen put a very dry dowel or tenon into wood of normal dryness. The drier dowel or tenon increases in size, making the joint tighter than when done normally.

Comparing Wood Species

The Forest Products Laboratory has categorized various hardwood and softwood species according to properties that will affect their abilities to be glued. (See Table 2.) This information is derived from numerous tests of side-to-side grain glue joints bonded with basic woodworking glues that include animal glues, urea resins, and resorcinols.

Illus. 31. The most stress-free glue-ups result when the component pieces are of the same species (uniform density), of similar cuts (all quarter-sawed is best), and are uniform in moisture content.

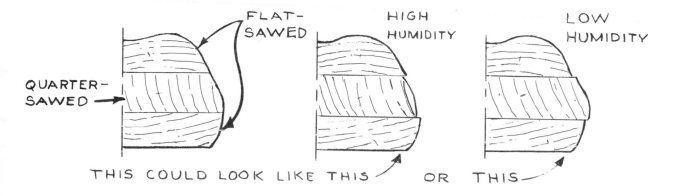

Illus. 32. Here is what can happen when plain-sawed and quarter-sawed boards are used in the same glue-up.

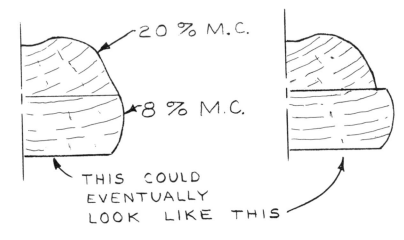

THIS COULD
EVENTUALLY
LOOK LIKE THIS

Illus. 33. An example of a potential problem created in carving stock made by gluing woods together that are not equal in moisture content.

Group 1	Group 2	Group 3	Group 4
(Glue very easily with glues of wide range in properties and under wide range of gluing conditions)	(Glue well with glues of fairly wide range in properties under a moderately wide range of gluing conditions)	(Glue satisfactorily with good quality glue, under well-controlled gluing conditions)	(Require very close control of glue and gluing conditions, or special treatment to obtain best results)
HARDWOODS			

Aspen
Chestnut, American
Cottonwood
Willow, black
Yellow-poplar
	Alder, red
	Basswood [1]
	Butternut [1] [2]
	Elm:
	   American [2]
	   Rock [1] [2]
	Hackberry
	Magnolia [1] [2]
	Mahogany [2]
	Sweetgum [1]
		Ash, white [2]
		Cherry, black [1] [2]
		Dogwood [2]
		Maple, soft [1] [2]
		Oak:
		   Red [2]
		   White
		Pecan
		Sycamore [1] [2]
		Tupelo:
		   Black [1]
		   Water [1] [2]
		Walnut, black
			Beech, American
			Birch, sweet and yellow [2]
			Hickory [2]
			Maple, hard
			Osage-orange
			Persimmon

SOFTWOODS			

Baldcypress
Fir:
   White
   Grand
   Noble
   Pacific silver
   California red
Larch, western
Redcedar, western [3]
Redwood
Spruce, Sitka
	Douglas-fir
	Hemlock
	   Western [3]
	Pine:
	   Eastern white [3]
	   Southern [1]
	   Ponderosa
	Redcedar, eastern [2]
		Alaska-cedar [2]	

[1] Species is more subject to starved joints, particularly with animal glue, than the classification would otherwise indicate.

[2] Bonds more easily with resin adhesives than with nonresins.

[3] Bonds more easily with nonresin adhesives than with resin.

Table 2. Table prepared by Forest Products Laboratory that classifies the relative gluing properties of various hardwoods and softwoods.

Chapter 2
Woodworking Glues

Store shelves and mail order catalogues abound with an overwhelming array of adhesive and gluing products. Most of these products are not used at all to glue wood. Of the rest, the average woodworker only has to concern himself with about six different types.

Some of the adhesives used to bond wood are not available to the home craftsman. For example, casein resin glues—which became popular during World War I, when they were used to manufacture wooden airplanes—have lost favor among woodworkers because they are difficult to mix, have a short working life, and have poor resistance to moisture. Woodworkers now prefer easier-to-use resin glues, and as a result manufac-turers have stopped marketing casein resin glues for consumer use. They can be found, however, in wood-using industries, where factory conditions are conducive to their use.

Woodworking glues or adhesives are considered good bonding agents only if they fulfill certain requirements. They must provide a strong bond during all the seasons of the year. They have to be able to withstand one or a combination of the four basic stress factors that occur in most woodworking applications. (See Illus. 34.) Also, a proper glue joint should have a high percentage of "wood failure," which means the glue joint is stronger than the wood surrounding the glue line (See Illus. 35.)

Illus. 34. Four basic stresses required of wood-glued joints.

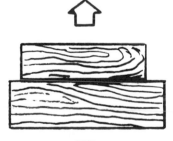

TENSILE

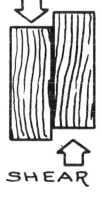

SHEAR

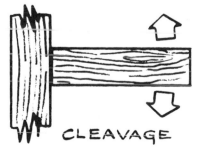

CLEAVAGE

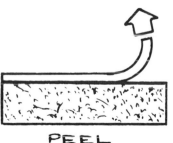

PEEL

Illus. 35. A close-up look at a successful joint in oak. Note that the pieces exhibit high wood failure, not failure or separation at the glue line.

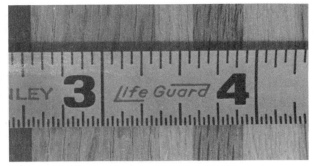

Illus. 36. The optimum glue line thickness is very thin, ranging from .002 to .005 inch in thickness.

Glue Line

Before discussing the various types of glues available on the market, we should stop to discuss glue lines. Glue lines are one factor that will be mentioned frequently. They are the layers of adhesive between two adjoining pieces of wood. The optimum glue line thickness between two pieces of wood (for conventional work) ranges from .002 to .005 in thickness. (See Illus. 36.) Tentacles of cured glue extending from this layer help to provide an interlocking action of the glue joint. Modern research has pretty well proven that the glue-holding process is a combination of this mechanical action coupled with a chemical reaction that takes place between the glue film and the chemical substances of the wood. Glue lines are important because they help determine how closely two pieces of wood fit together; the closer those pieces fit together, the stronger the joint.

Animal Adhesives

Woodworking glues can be divided into two basic groups: (1) those formulated from materials of natural origin, such as animal or hide glues, and (2) those synthetic (manmade) adhesives that are chemically made (see page 26). Animal adhesives—commonly referred to as animal or hide glues—are part of a group of natural adhesives. As the name implies, these are adhesives that have their major ingredient derived from natural sources.

Natural adhesives have been used since early man. The Ancient Egyptians made veneer casein glues from sour milk and lime. During World War I, the first practical water-resistant casein and blood glues were developed for commercial use. Vegetable, starch, and soybean glues also served industrial needs for some time, but they have generally been replaced by improved synthetic resin glues. Today, of all the natural glues only the animal or hide glues are important to the average woodworker. (See Illus. 37.)

Animal glues are the oldest type of glues still in use. Wood-instrument makers have been using hot animal glue for hundreds of years. In fact, the Stradivari string instruments made in the 17th century were assembled with animal glues.

Animal glues are prepared from the hides, bones, sinews, and hide fleshings of cattle. Essentially, they are by-products of the meat processing and tanning industries. There are different grades of animal glues that are sold in either a dry granular form or as ready-to-use liquids.

The one essential advantage of animal glue is that it allows joints to become undone, if desired. Carefully applied heat and moisture will soften the glue and separate the joint. This is especially important for those who repair and refinish antiques, older furniture, and other items assembled with animal glue.

Illus. 37. Two ready-to-use liquid hide glues, with granular type shown at the right.

Liquid Hide Glues

Liquid hide glues are nontoxic and have a slow drying time, which makes them a good choice when a long working time is required for complicated assemblies. They require a working temperature of between 70 and 90 °F, have excellent resistance to solvents, and are thicker than popular liquid white glues. Their glue lines are a soft tan or liquid color and sand very easily without gumming, especially when compared to the liquid white glues. (See Illus. 77.) Because of their poor water resistance, liquid hide glues should not be used on exterior projects.

Dry or Granular Animal Glue

Dry or granular animal glue must be mixed with water. This is not the easiest type of glue to use. It is used generally by those craftsmen who prefer traditional woodworking methods. Some claim that this type of glue has far greater holding power than its ready-to-use liquid counterpart.

Granular animal glue requires heating equipment. There are several companies that provide electric glue pots like the one from Lee Valley Tools of Ottawa, Canada, shown in Illus. 38. The "pot" is thermostatically controlled, so it keeps the temperature within the required 140 to 150 °F range. The inside pot is removable for portability and cleanup.

Illus. 38. Granular hide glue is mixed with water and heated in a pot for use.

Only as much glue as anticipated for a day or two's use should be prepared at one time. The dry-glue granules should be covered generously with cold water and allowed to soak. The glue will soften after several hours and become gelatinous. The excess water should then be poured off, and the glue heated to a temperature not exceeding 150 °F. The temperature should be maintained, and water should be added until a smooth, lump-free consistency is obtained.

To use the glue, apply with a stiff brush and bring pressure to the joint while the glue is still hot. A good-quality glue will thicken to the proper pressing consistency quicker than do lower grades of the same concentration. Some thickening must occur before pressure is applied. If the assembly is fairly complicated, and if you're working in a cold shop, it is best to warm your wood to at least 70 °F or above. Boards can be warmed by placing them on or near heat registers, or in a heat box (see Illus. 59 on page 37).

Obviously, one should not overheat the wood or the glue. Overheating robs the glue of its strength, as does repeated heatings. Do not reheat any one batch of glue more than four times. As the glue cools, it gels; it can be kept in this condition for extended periods in airtight containers. Thus, you should heat only the amount of glue you need.

Synthetic Adhesives

The majority of adhesives available on the market today are synthetic. They can be formulated to perform special gluing jobs, and are similar to typical commercial plastics. In fact, many of the adhesives today are manufactured by the plastics industry.

At this point, I should discuss some of the terms associated with synthetic adhesives. The term "synthetic resin" was first applied to indicate those chemical compounds that resembled the appearance of natural glues. As more and more synthetic resins became available, the term "synthetic" was omitted; adhesives of the modern chemical industry are now simply called "resin glues."

Resin glues are used today in the majority of all gluing jobs. Each type is capable of producing joints that are as strong as, or, in most cases, stronger than the wood itself. They are all very durable, and many types are inexpensive.

Nearly all the resin glues today develop their strength and durability in the joint by undergoing a chemical reaction called *curing*. The rate of curing, like that of all chemical reactions, depends on the temperature of the glue line. Increasing the temperature (to a point), speeds the rate of curing and strength development.

Resin glues can be either thermosetting or thermoplastic. Thermosetting resins are cured by chemical reaction through catalysts or heat. In use, they are transformed to a hard, infusible and insoluble state. The reaction is not reversible once the cure is achieved.

A number of thermosetting resins have qualities that make them more suitable for use where resistance to severe conditions of moisture, etc., is required. The resorcinol-formaldehyde resins, epoxies, and urea and plastic resins are the more common synthetic resin adhesive types available to the average woodworker.

Thermoplastic resins are reversible in that the glue line can be softened or reliquified by the application of heat or solvent actions. Hot-melts are thermoplastic. Thermoplastics are only used when the woodworker wants to physically change the glue; as for example, when the glue is melted, and then solidified upon cooling. Most thermoplastics do not perform well when subject to heat.

Polyvinyl Resin ("White") Glues

These glues are ready to use and do not require any mixing. (See Illus. 39.) Glues in this category are also called "polyvinyl acetate" or "PVA" glues. They are also sometimes referred to as polyvinyl-resin emulsion glues. For simplicity, they are sometimes referred to as polyvinyl resin, but more often as liquid white glues. Typical trade names include Elmer's Glue-All, Paxbond, 3C Company's Quick Tack Glue and All Purpose White Glue, Freeman's Cold Glue, Garrett Wade's Gap-Filling Glue, and Franklin's White Glue, plus many, many more! Some perform better than others. Some "off" brands are exceptionally watered down and virtually worthless.

Liquid white glues set when the water of the emulsion partially diffuses and is absorbed into the wood, whereupon the emulsified resin coagulates. There is no apparent chemical curing reaction, as happens with thermosetting glues. Setting action is primarily by drying and is fairly rapid at room temperature; on unstressed joints, it may be possible to release clamping pressure in as little as half an hour or less. However, leave the pressure on longer when it is convenient.

The advantages of liquid white glues include a long shelf life (storage) that's almost indefinite. Also, cured glue lines are nearly invisible, since the dried glue is transparent or very light in color. (See Illus. 40.) Glues of this type have little dulling effect on cutting tools.

However, sanding the liquid white glues is more difficult than with most other glues (see Illus. 77 on page 49). During sanding, the heat from friction softens squeeze-out; the squeeze-out becomes rubbery and gums the abrasive. Some other disadvantages include loss of strength at temperatures over 100 °F. White glues are also weakened somewhat by a relatively high humidity. Do not use them for outdoor projects or for any projects that are likely to be exposed to excessive moisture. The fact that they set fast limits assembly time to as little as 10 to 12 minutes

(with some brands) and requires quick pressure application at assembly. This may not be a disadvantage for less complicated jobs, but the "quick set" is a distinct problem with complicated or involved assemblies that require extra time.

Most white glues are made for use at room temperatures (70 °F). Use at lower temperatures is not recommended. The glue "chalks" and the result will be very poor, weak joints. (See Illus. 99 on page 58.) Improper low-temperature gluing can be easily identified by the dried squeeze-out, which takes on the very white appearance of chalk. Otherwise, the glue is nearly transparent.

PVA can be specially formulated for special applications. One company makes an exterior-grade PVA. It is catalyzed, with the catalyst being the waterproofing agent. Another version of PVA is a high-viscosity type that is called a "nonsag" adhesive, which is advantageous in many joint-type assemblies where the squeeze-out normally sags or runs onto surfaces.

Illus. 39. Liquid white (polyvinyl resin or PVA) glues are ready to use.

Illus. 40. The PVA glue line in this oak is nearly invisible.

Authorities pretty much agree that certain qualities of white glues are very useful in the assembly of some joints including dowel, mortise-and-tenon, and other corner joints. It seems that the white (PVA) glues have a certain elasticity or "cold flow," which means the glue sort of stretches along with the individual members of the joint as they shrink and swell due to day-to-day and season-to-season changes in moisture content of the wood. Consequently, PVA or white glues are not recommended where the joint will be highly stressed (as for example, the limb of a laminated archery bow where considerable pressure is required to close the joint). (As a point of interest, I have been using one of the major brands of liquid white glues for more than a quarter of a century. I've used it for all "normal" *interior* furniture and cabinet joinery without failure. I don't think it could ever be improved for this type of woodworking.) As long as one works within its prescribed limits, PVA or white glue should be one of the most popular and versatile glues in your workshop. They are nontoxic, and can be used on toys and other items children will use. The "wet" glue cleans up easily with water; I consider it economical when compared to its "younger brother," "yellow glue."

Aliphatic Resin (Liquid Yellow Glues)

Aliphatic resin or liquid yellow glues (Illus. 41) are essentially so-called improvements to the polyvinyl or white glues already described. They do possess certain qualities that might be regarded as better. First, they have greater heat resistance, which improves sanding jobs. They are heavier in consistency, so they run or drip less, which contributes a lot to the overall neatness of a good number of special gluing jobs.

Illus. 41. Aliphatic resin or "liquid yellow" glues.

Yellow glues also have greater resistance to moisture than the white glues, but they should in no way be used for exterior gluing of any kind. Most importantly, be aware that yellow glues set much faster than white glues, but their total cure takes longer. The yellow glues are thicker and somewhat more difficult to spread. Some of the popular brands include Elmer's Carpenter's Wood Glue, Franklin's Titebond, 3C Company's Super Wood Glue, and Garrett Wade's Slo-Set.

As with the white glues, some yellow glues are and some are not affected by freezing. However, for best results, the glue, materials, and room temperature should be well above freezing. Check specific glues for their minimum-use temperature. (See Illus. 99 on page 58, which shows a chalked joint glued with yellow glue.) Like the white glues, unset yellow glue can be cleaned up with water.

However, the squeeze-out sets rapidly, which makes it more difficult to wipe it up with a damp rag. Avoid using a very wet rag, as this will dilute the glue, weaken the glue line, increase penetration to the surface, and swell the wood fibres.

Hot-Melts

Hot-Melts (Illus. 42) are available to the home craftsman in stick and sheet forms. These adhesives require no particular preparation for use other than some means of melting and applying the hot glue to the material. Glue guns (Illus. 43 and 44) are the most common means to handle melting and apply the hot glue to the material.

Illus. 44. Hot-melts make quick repairs; they also glue a variety of materials to each other.

Hot-melts are applied to the wood in molten form at temperatures ranging from 250 ° to 450 °F. The joint must be mated within just a few seconds to obtain the best bond; the best bond, however, will be second rate at best. This glue, being a thermoplastic, sets by chilling or cooling, which happens very fast on the colder wood that's being bonded. Cold wood can chill the adhesive prematurely and give poor adhesion. Therefore, the best conditions are from room temperature up to 90 °F. Usually the adhesive is applied to only one of the two mating surfaces and pressure is immediately applied by hand. (See Illus. 45.) There is no time for

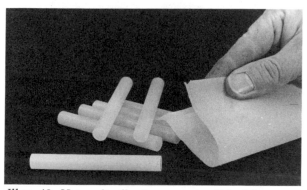

Illus. 42. Hot-melt adhesives come in sticks (glue gun cartridges) and sheets for veneering.

Illus. 43. Hot-melts are ideal for temporary gluing jobs. This small workpiece will be glued to a larger piece of plywood for edge-routing, and then removed.

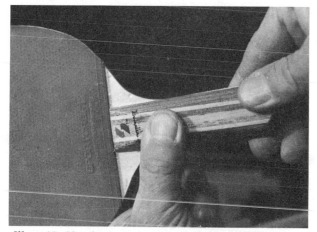

Illus. 45. Hand pressure with hot-melts is usually the only effective technique since the molten glue cools and sets too fast for common clamping techniques.

clamping unless the substrates are pre-heated, and even then the assembly must be very uncomplicated.

Hot-melts cool within 2 to 45 seconds. As a rule, the hot-melts produce much weaker and thicker glue lines than those generally accepted in fine woodworking projects. However, for many other jobs there isn't anything better. Hot-melts are perfect for temporary joints (Illus. 43), such as those needed for stack sawing, routing small parts, and split wood turnings.

Excess glue from hot-melts cannot be easily sanded off of surfaces. It's best cleaned up with a sharp knife or chisel. Hot-melt glues and glue guns (Illus. 42–46) are ideal for gluing many dissimilar materials, making quick repairs, and building models and mock-ups. They are widely used to glue on decorative trim, embossed carvings, and other surface bonds that are not subjected to stress or impact in normal use. Hot-melts achieve about 75 to 95% of their ultimate strength as soon as they cool.

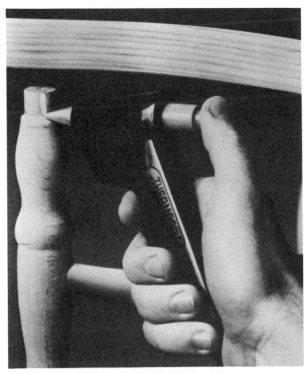

Illus. 46. A typical economy type of hot glue gun found in most hardware stores.

Hot-melts in sheet form are available by mail order from several suppliers. (See Illus. 42.) This material is heat-activated with an ordinary household iron. For veneering small- to medium-size projects with this glue, turn to page 182 for more information.

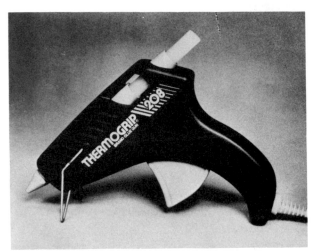

Illus. 47. A trigger-actuated hot glue gun is somewhat more expensive, but much easier and more convenient to handle.

Cyanoacrylate Adhesives

Cyanoacrylate adhesives (better known as the "super" or "krazy" glues) form bonds almost instantly on a variety of materials. (See Illus. 48 and 49.) These adhesives are very expensive, but the cost appears to be leveling off, and for some difficult-to-handle jobs, glues of this category are invaluable.

"Super" glues have the reputation for gluing everything; there are even stories about people who have accidentally glued their fingers together. In fact, most packaging carries the warning, "bonds skin instantly." Fortunately, special solvents are available to dissolve such bonds. Acetone and nail polish remover will also dissolve these "skin assemblies."

The cyanoacrylates are exceptionally fast setting. Most of the many, many brands on the market are primarily formulated for the bonding of nonporous surfaces such as metals, glass, plastics, rubber, and ceramics. Because these glues have poor viscosity, the

Illus. 48. An assortment of "super"glues. Not all such glues are formulated for gluing wood.

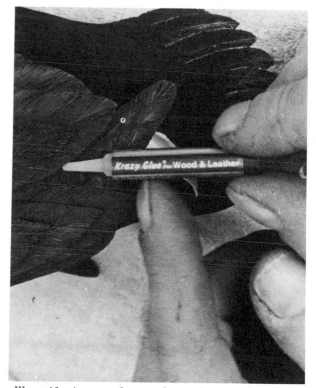

Illus. 49. A super glue can be used to attach a carved feather insert to a decoy. The work is hand-held in place for a few seconds. This glue sets quickly.

surfaces of the joint must mate very closely. In other words, these glues as a rule have very poor gap-filling qualities.

With most types of cyanoacrylates, too much glue applied to hard, nonporous surfaces lowers the bond quality. Soft, porous materials such as wood, leather, etc., require more glue. It may even be necessary to experiment with your specific species of wood. If the wood is exceptionally soft or porous, an initial "sealing" application may be necessary, followed by another application for joining the parts together.

Clamps are not needed when gluing with "super" glues. Parts can be held in place with light hand pressure. One company has come out with "super" glue in a gel form. This fills gaps and bonds both porous and nonporous materials. Naturally, you should be careful not to get any adhesive on your fingers or skin.

Of all of the cyanoacrylate adhesives available today, only a few are of any use for wood-to-wood joints. Because of their relatively high cost for very small volumes, use these glues only where others are less appropriate or less convenient. These glues are used in model building, making miniatures, in delicate carvings (Illus. 49), and similar type jobs.

Some glues in the cyanoacrylate category actually cure faster in the presence of moisture. One example, the "hot stuff" cyanoacrylate adhesive system marketed by Craft Supplies of Provo, Utah, is used to mount green-wood bowl blanks to a dry waste block for face-plate mountings on the turning lathe. (See Illus. 553 on page 222.) The hot stuff is of two types: "Original" and Super "T." The original is water-thin. This type is ideal for closing hairline cracks. Because of its penetrating qualities, it works well for hardening soft areas such as are commonly found in spalted wood. To use as a filler, pack dry sawdust in the crack and add a drop or two of "hot stuff" for a solidifying penetration. To speed the cure, a little "shot" of the spray accelerator will set everything hard in less than a minute.

The Super "T" hot stuff has a syrup-like consistency that gives it good gap-filling qualities. It will set in seconds. To use it for

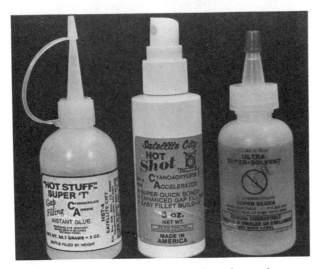

Illus. 50. These cyanoacrylate glues have the capabilities to mount green chunks of wood to dry waste blocks for lathe turning.

mounting green bowl blanks to a dry waste block, apply the Super "T" to the bowl blank and spray the accelerator onto the waste piece. Quickly position the block to the bowl blank; the bond will be complete in less than one minute. The accelerator spray causes the cyanoacrylate adhesive to cure instantly— even when applied to thick fillets made of the heavier Super "T."

Contact Cements

Contact cements (Illus. 51), are used primarily for veneering and to apply decorative plastic laminates and similar materials to panels. To use, spread them on both mating surfaces of the joint and let the surfaces partially dry. The mating surfaces will adhere instantly upon contact. The joined pieces cannot be repositioned after contact.

Contact cements are usually low-viscosity solutions that are either "solvent"-based or "water-based." Solvent-based contact cements contain dangerously volatile solvents. When these contacts are used, be aware of hazards like fire and explosion, and toxic-fume poisoning when they are used in confined work areas without adequate ventilation. Some of the newer solvent-based contact cements are nonflammable but still have harmful vapors.

Water-based contact cements can also present dangers of fume-inhalation; some can even be volatile as well. Use all contact cements in well-ventilated areas and always according to the manufacturer's instructions.

One distinct advantage of contacts is that because of the quick bond, machining and trimming of the final assembly can proceed almost immediately. Contact cements are ideal for nonstructural type joints and for bonding many dissimilar materials, but they are inadequate for highly stressed joints. Contact cements may be applied to small surfaces by brush, and onto larger surfaces by short nap rollers or a notched metal-spreading tool. (See pages 158 and 160 for more information about contact cements.)

Contact cements dry by the evaporation of their solvents. They develop considerable strength immediately upon contact with the surfaces to be bonded. The ultimate full-joint strength of contacts is overall much lower than other glues, so contacts should not be used for bonding conventional wood-to-wood joints.

Outside of factory situations, contact cements are the most widely used adhesives for bonding decorative laminates. Although other glues, including urea resins, liquid white, resorcinols and epoxies, can be used to bond decorative laminates, these glues require long-term pressure that involves some fairly involved clamping techniques or large presses. Contact cements require only short-term pressure, simplify bonding laminates to moderately curved surfaces, and do not require presses or clamps.

Bond failure in laminate work (if there is any) can be traced to improper glue spread, inadequate drying time, or inadequate pressure. At bonding, supplemental short-term pressure, in addition to the "laying down" hand pressure, is essential so that the two dried adhesive films are brought into intimate contact. At least 50 pounds of pressure per square inch is required. A small, narrow roller or pressure achieved from hammering against a small, flat scrap block is usually suf-

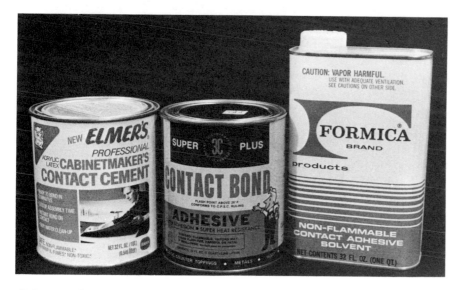

Illus. 51. Contact cements (adhesives) are most widely used for bonding decorative laminates. They require only brief, short-term pressure without conventional clamping tools.

ficient as long as the pressure is worked over the entire bonding area.

Contact cements satisfy two essential requirements important to the fabricating of counter tops with high-density plastic laminates. They can endure the heat of hot pans or utensils placed on the counter top without showing "delamination." They are also flexible enough to resist delamination at the edges when moisture conditions change. (See Chapter 10 for a thorough discussion of woodworking procedures for bonding and trimming plastic laminates with contact cements.)

Construction Mastics

Construction Mastics, adhesives with a heavy-bodied consistency, are used for a variety of jobs such as bonding floor systems to joists and applying wall panels of various types. Mastics are sold in typical cardboard tubes, usually for application with caulking guns. They are of various formulations consisting of rubber, resins, fillers, and solvents that evaporate to set the adhesive. Mastics are usually applied to only one surface. They are ideal for on-site bonding, and some can be used at temperatures near freezing if the adhesive itself has been previously conditioned at room temperature prior to use. (See Illus. 52.) They are not really used in the wood crafts.

Illus. 52. A mastic adhesive used in a floor system.

Resorcinol Resin Glues

Resorcinol resin glues are dark-red liquid resins to which a powdered catalyst is added before use. (See Illus. 53.) These adhesives are highly praised by many authorities because they are strong, waterproof, and generally very durable. Typical trade names for the do-it-yourselfer include Borden's Waterproof Glue, Wilhold's Waterproof Resorcinol, and U.S. Plywoods Resorcinol; in larger quantities, there is Kipper's Penacolite Resorcinol Adhesive, which is among glues manufactured for industrial use. Only the resorcinols are advertised as "waterproof"; however, some of the much less expensive urea resins or "plastic resin" glues have exceptionally high water resistance. These plastic resins can often be used where resorcinols are normally specified for use.

Illus. 53. Exterior glues (plastic [urea] resins, left and center) mixed with water have high moisture resistance. The resorcinol type, at right, is a liquid resin that mixes with a powdered catalyst for a totally waterproof bond.

Resorcinols cost approximately three times as much as the plastic resins, and they also give slightly more spread per volume. Once mixed, resorcinols have a working life that ranges from 20 minutes to nearly 2 hours, depending upon their formulation. They are applied by brush, roller, stick or spatula. Resorcinols apparently satisfy the need for a glue with a 100 percent waterproofing capability. (In fact, it's amusing that manufacturers advertise that joints glued with resorcinols will withstand without failure immersion in hot, boiling water. What projects do you make that are normally used in hot, boiling water? Certainly outdoor furniture, wood signs, or even wooden boats are not ever subjected to boiling water.) Resorcinols became popular in the early wood-laminating industries in the United States. However, some of the claims made about them for do-it-yourself woodcrafting are being questioned more and more.

In the early 1930s and prior to the development of resorcinols, the phenolic resin adhesives were the only suitable exterior adhesives available. These glues, however, needed high temperatures for proper curing and a durable bond.

Resorcinol-formaldehyde resins cured by room temperature played a vital part in the 1940s in the production of wooden aircraft and wooden naval vessels. Resorcinols are now used extensively in wood industries to bond or form large laminated timbers, for use in the construction of commercial buildings, exterior use, and for a variety of other products including boats, spiral staircases and even wood-laminated golf-club heads.

Today, glue lines made with resorcinols are very durable and strong, and have high resistance to solvents, acids, greases, and oils. The glue bond does not give or weaken from stresses caused by the shrinking and swelling of the wood, or, for that matter, just from hard use of the product. However, for the home craftsman to achieve good results, all of the gluing conditions must be near if not absolutely perfect. Successful bonding with resorcinols requires critical control of various important factors: There must be a minimum 70 °F temperature; the wood moisture content must be well under 12 percent; joints must have even pressure of 150 to 250 p.s.i. (pounds per square inch); and the fit of the joint must be precise. In fact, some specialists believe that glue lines thicker than

0.005 inch will result in an inferior bond. When resorcinols are used, the gluing of denser hardwoods may also be a problem. Precautionary measures such as double spreading the amount of glue covering each surface, substantially increasing the open assembly time (time of glue spread until clamping), and increasing temperatures help to reduce starved joints.

Probably one of the most distasteful qualities of a resorcinol glue joint is its appearance. (See Illus. 54.) It's wide and unusually reddish in color, and certainly not very becoming to a finely crafted piece of woodwork. Also, be careful when gluing thin materials—as, for example, in boat building, when thinner, flexible plywoods are glue-nailed or screwed to framing members. Since resorcinols require substantially more uniform and greater clamping pressure than other glues, it's highly probable that the only areas of adequate pressure are limited to those directly under the nail or screw.

Illus. 54. A resorcinol glue line is easy to identify. It is the most visible of all glue lines, typically reddish in color, wide and irregular in width, and just plain ugly in fine work.

Urea Resins

Urea Resins, or urea formaldehyde adhesives (Illus. 53), are also called plastic resin glues. They consist of dry powders that are mixed with water prior to use. They are best used on woods of 8 to 12 percent moisture content, best applied at room temperatures or slightly under 70 °F, and cure best at 70 °F. These glues are available to the wood crafter by mail order in one pound and larger quantity packages under such trade names as Wilhold's Marine-Grade Plastic Resin, and Weldwood's Plastic Resin Glues. They have good resistance to moisture and are quite durable under damp conditions. They tend to weaken some with temperatures in excess of 120 °F.

The glue cures to a light-tan color, which makes for good, inconspicuous glue lines on almost all species of wood. The cured glue also sands without gumming abrasives. This type of glue is an ideal general-purpose choice in that it can be used for many exterior jobs, common gluing jobs involving general furniture and cabinetry construction gluing, veneering, and can be glued with electronic equipment. (See page 91 for more information concerning electronic gluing equipment.) Depending upon room temperature, urea resins have a working life that ranges between 1 and 5 hours. However, pressure must be maintained at least 6 to 9 hours or until the squeezed-out glue is sufficiently cured and hard. When the glue is cured below 70 °F, the results are joints of erratic strength and durability. Consequently, the wood, as well as the room temperature, should be 70 °F or above for best results. Do not spread glue on cold wood from outside storage or on wood lying on a cold concrete floor even though they will be clamped in temperatures of 70 to 80 °F. Both air and wood temperature must be around 70 °F before starting the process.

Urea resin glues are also more difficult to use successfully in bonding woods of higher density such as oak and maple. However, for the lower-density soft woods such as fir, cedar and pine, urea resin glues are relatively easy to use and very durable indoors or out. Glues of this type do not make good gap fillers because they shrink considerably with curing. The "fit," or acceptable glue line thickness, is not nearly as critical as it is for resorcinol glues. However, as with most other glues, the best results are achieved with well-fitting joints that bring the mating pieces very close together. The excessive pressure required for resorcinols is not needed for urea resins. Complicated assemblies might be somewhat difficult on days of very warm weather, as the setting will be more rapid.

Special formulations or "additives" are often added to give urea resin glues certain properties for specific applications. Some glues are formulated to set faster at elevated temperatures, and some are formulated for high-frequency gluing (see page 91). Others have fillers or extenders added to reduce costs, while some are fortified with other adhesives that enhance properties like waterproofing. Most of these specialty products are not, however, available to the average woodworker.

Illus. 55. This two-part urea formaldehyde glue has some unusual methods for its mixing and clamping.

One unusual formulation of urea-formaldehhyde that is especially popular in Canada and England is sold under the trade name of Aerolite. (See Illus. 55.) This is a two-part urea resin that is somewhat unusual in its recommended application. One part is the powdered resin, and the other is a liquid hardener. In use, the resin is mixed with water and applied to one of the surfaces of the joint. The hardener is applied to the other surface of the joint. The curing process happens when the two surfaces of the joint are brought together rather than, as might be expected, mixing the hardener and glue together. Only light contact and "finger-tight" pressures are necessary.

The Aerolite glues can be used in temperatures as low as 50 °F. The actual setting rate depends upon the temperature. Artificial heat such as a heat box (see Illus. 59) or a flameless electric heat gun can be used to warm the assembly and to speed the cure. Otherwise, overnight cure at room temperature is satisfactory, with full strength and maximum water resistance attained after several days.

One advantage of Aerolite glues is that they have a shelf life of up to two years. The shelf life of other urea resin glues is limited. Always test "aged" glue.

Incidentally, Aerolite glues are widely used in the building of experimental aircraft and by amateur boat builders. Aerolite urea-formaldehyde resin glues are available in the United States from the Aircraft Spruce & Specialty Co. of Fullerton, California.

Clamping times for urea resins generally should be doubled for stressed joints, such as those involved when making laminated bends or curves. Water may be used to clean up glue drippings, brushes, etc., while the glue is still liquid. Once the urea resin begins to set, it is impervious to water.

One problem associated with the use of these glues is skin irritation caused by the emission of gases. Avoid breathing the powder or sanding dust if eyes, nose, or skin exhibit any signs of irritation. The shop should also be well-ventilated.

Epoxy Resins

Epoxies have two components: a resin and a hardener, which are combined and mixed just prior to use. (See Illus. 56–58.) Both the resin and the hardener are 100 percent solids.

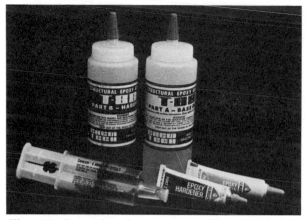

Illus. 56. Examples of epoxy glue with typical 1 to 1 resin and hardener mix ratio.

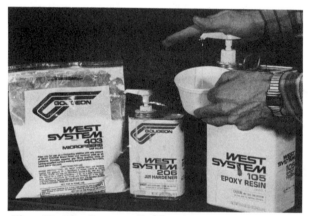

Illus. 57. The Gougeon Brothers' epoxy system meters the correct 5 to 1 resin hardener ratio with one stroke of each pump.

This means that epoxy resin systems carry no solvents at all. The mixture of resin and hardener tends to give off heat (an exotherm reaction) as the chemical reaction takes place. Consequently, mixing small quantities is advised when possible.

Epoxies are perhaps the most versatile of all adhesives because they are used to bond such a wide variety of materials under various conditions. In addition to successfully bonding all species and kinds of wood and all wood-panel materials, epoxies can bond metals, ceramics, and countless other porous or nonporous materials without much difficulty. The exceptions include some types of plastics. Some special epoxies require elevated temperatures to assure strong, enduring bonds of unlike materials to each other. One company, Bingham's Recreational Projects, assembles archery bows, water skis and other items with an epoxy that requires an overnight cure at temperatures of 150° to 180 °F. The temperature can be reached in a specially made curing chamber or a heat box (Illus. 59), with heat bulbs or regular light bulbs supplying the heat source. Temperatures can be somewhat controlled by either screwing bulbs in or out of the heat box or by propping the lid slightly open with sticks.

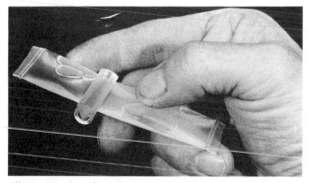

Illus. 58. Another epoxy system is this pouch or bi-package. Premeasured resin and hardener come in the same tube separated by a clamp that's removed to mix the two components together. This system is described on page 38.

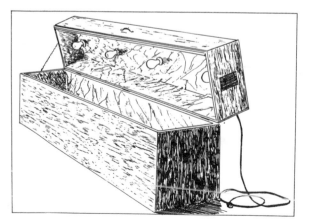

Illus. 59. This simple heat box for curing glues such as special epoxies is of foil-lined plywood construction with 250 watt light bulbs providing the heat source.

Epoxy does not shrink, which makes it a good gap filler. In fact, epoxies will fill the largest gaps. Some types of epoxies are even intended to be used as grouts or putty.

Many people believe that all epoxies are very thick or heavy in viscosity. This is true for most but not all epoxies; after all, they are formulated to serve various, particular requirements. One company makes an epoxy that is of thin consistency so it can penetrate deeply. Some epoxies are made to set fast, such as the five-minute epoxy (Illus. 56). Some are formulated to be very rigid, while others are designed to be flexible. The key is to match the exact type or brand to your specific needs. The following discussions of several different types and brands of epoxies that are currently popular should help you determine which one you need.

Epoxy as a fastening material for wood has only been around some 30 years or so. It was first used to bond less porous materials in the aircraft, automotive, electronic, and space industries. The major deficiencies of epoxy as a wood-bonding adhesive is its apparent high cost, the fact that many people do not know how to work with it, its reputation for being messy and its toxicity. Despite these disadvantages, epoxies are becoming very popular among amateur and professional woodworkers alike.

In general, epoxies should not be used to do the menial jobs that the older, established, and less expensive glues handle very effectively. Think of epoxies simply as opportunities to expand your woodworking capabilities. A woodworking colleague once said, "Epoxies now allow us to do all of the things in woodworking that we weren't allowed to do before." There is a lot of truth in this assessment. Epoxies have definitely opened the door for the creative woodworker.

Remember, one type of epoxy does not serve all needs. Some epoxies are better for specific jobs than others. Manufacturers have striven to make epoxies easier and more desirable to use. They are available in a broad range of sizes or volumes. They can be obtained in very small tubes or gallon and drum quantities. Buying larger quantities brings the unit cost down immensely. For the most part, epoxies have a good shelf life, so little goes to waste because of storage. Most consumer epoxies are 1 to 1 resin to hardener ratios. If this or other ratios are necessary (as per the manufacturer's instructions), be certain to measure very carefully. Manufacturers have recently come out with the double syringe system (Illus. 60). The twin nozzles dispense equal proportions which, as with the tube system, need to be mixed with a stick. One company has just made available a remarkable dual syringe dispensing system. The two epoxy components are accurately "metered" from a cartridge through a mixing nozzle so the system precisely measures and mixes the two-part adhesive and it is ready for use when applied. When the application is complete, the cartridge is simply resealed with a locking cap.

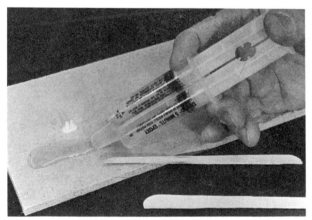

Illus. 60. A twin-nozzle system dispenses equal portions that must be mixed before use.

Another interesting epoxy "package" is the plastic tubular pouch or bi-package, as shown in Illus. 58. This has the hardener and resin in the same container, but they are separated by a leakproof clamp. When the clamp is removed, the premeasured resin and hardener can flow together and be blended with a kneading action, as shown in Illus. 61. Snipping a corner off the pouch makes a squeezable dispenser, as shown in Illus. 62. This system has a number of advantages in that it saves measuring time, there is no cleanup, mixing errors are absolutely eliminated, and there is little skin contact involved. The major disadvantage is that the entire contents must be mixed, which may be more than the amount needed.

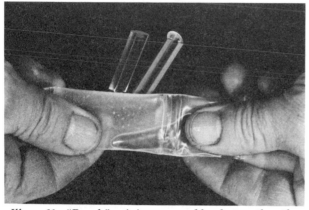

Illus. 61. "Pouch"-mixing epoxy blends together the previously separated resin and hardener.

Illus. 62. The pouch with a corner cut off becomes a dispenser for the mixed epoxy.

Amateur and professional boat builders and homemade aircraft builders are turning to epoxies in good numbers. There are several companies now serving these markets with some remarkably spectacular products. However, there are many, many uses for the epoxies that go far beyond the adventures of boat building. Epoxies have been used for the assembly of outdoor wood signs and outdoor furniture, making doors, and for many other outdoor projects and repairs of all sorts. I have also used epoxy systems when I wanted a job to hold tenaciously, when gap filling was required, and to repair and make all sorts of jigs and fixtures. One brand is even used as a finish for some special jobs, another brand is used to glue moist wood.

One can even mix epoxy to a heavy paste and use it somewhat like a mortar, that is, to "stick" pieces of wood together. Used as a wood sealer, epoxy helps protect surfaces against moisture gain and loss, providing a barrier that helps to preserve wood strength and dimensional stability. Epoxy can be used as a protective seal and a base for other finishes on green PEG-treated wood. (Refer to my book, Working Green Wood With PEG, Sterling Publishing Co., Inc., 1980.) Once you've used one of the new epoxy systems that are especially formulated for wood, you'll have difficulty working without it. A quantity of epoxy or an epoxy system is expensive, but considering its versatility, its superior qualities for special jobs, the amount of spread it has per volume, it can be a worthwhile investment for the serious woodworker.

An epoxy "system" usually consists of a resin and choices of one or more various types of hardeners, as well as compatible additives, fillers, coloring pigments, etc., that the woodworker can add or mix himself to get the precise working qualities he desires. Two well-known epoxy systems are those manufactured by the Gougeon Brothers, Inc., of Bay City, Michigan, and Chem Tech, Inc., of Chagrin Falls, Ohio. (See Illus. 56 and 57.) Both systems can be ordered directly from the manufacturers. Another epoxy system, which I use less, are the epoxies from the Allied Resin Corporation, East Weymouth, Massachusetts. Of the three epoxy systems, Gougeon Brothers and Chem Tech claim their epoxies are best-suited for the average woodworker.

The Chem Tech's epoxy product is called "T-88 Structural Epoxy." Introduced about 10 years ago, it was developed specifically for the amateur and professional wooden-boat builder and the home aircraft builder. Some of the major advantages of Chem Tech's epoxy system include: 1) it has an easy-to-mix, non-critical 1 to 1 mixing ratio (Illus. 63); 2) it cures without shrinking; 3) it is a good gap filler; 4) it can be applied to moist wood; 5) curing temperature is not critical and can be as low as 35 °F.; 6) it's nonstaining on wood and dries to transparent amber color that's almost invisible; 7) it's highly water resistant; 8) it needs minimum clamping pressure; and 9) its cure is nonbrittle but hard and may be worked in just a few hours. One disadvantage is that the adhesive on the surface makes the pieces very slippery and difficult at times to bring into precise alignment. (See Illus. 64 and 65.)

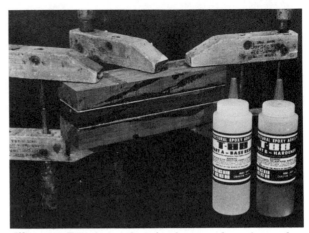

Illus. 65. Epoxies are best for dense and exotic woods. They require only minimal clamping pressure—just enough to hold the pieces in the desired position until the glue sets or cures.

Illus. 63. Chem-Tech's epoxy system features a non-critical 1 to 1 volume measure of resin and hardener, along with low-temperature gluing capabilities.

Illus. 64. Spreading Chem-Tech epoxy. Note the use of disposable gloves.

Gougeon Brothers' epoxy system is also known as the West System Brand Epoxy. (See Illus. 57 and 66.) Their products are essentially for the wooden-boat builders, but they are starting to branch off into other markets, like those for home-built aircrafts and structural laminates. The West System Brand resins and hardeners have the following features: 1) a thin consistency that can be thickened for conventional use and minimum penetration (Illus. 66–68); 2) a flexibility and an overall toughness; 3) nonshrinkage capacity; 4) an excellent moisture barrier, which allows them to be used as unthickened, penetrating sealers to restrict passage of moisture vapor into the wood; 5) they require minimal clamping pressure; 6) they can be thickened for use as an excellent gap filler; 7) they can be used as an interior flow on finish; and 8) slow or fast cure hardeners are available plus numerous fillers, thickening agents, fire retardants, coloring pigments and various strength-inducing fibres such as graphite and glass fabrics.

There are three distinct disadvantages. West System Brand products work best only with dried wood with 12 percent or less moisture content, with 7 to 10 percent ideal. Second, accurate mixing is very important (five parts of resin to one part hardener by weight). However, inexpensive pumps available from the company dispense the resin and hardener in proper ratios to alleviate the measuring problems. (See Illus. 57.) Third, this system is somewhat more difficult to use in temperatures below 65 °F. Depending upon room temperature, a tack-free partial cure requires 5 to 9 hours; do not sand work until at least 15 hours have passed. The total full cure requires as much as 7 days. However, when heating in a heating chamber (Illus. 59) or with an electric flameless gun to 140 to 150 °F, full cure requires just 2 hours. However, such heating should be done very cautiously and in full accordance with the directions of the manufacturer.

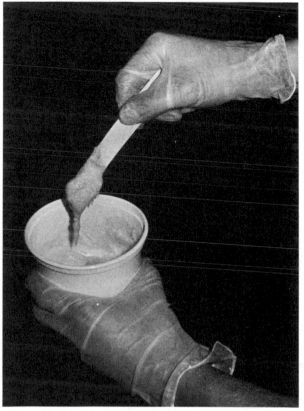

Illus. 68. Here the West System Brand Epoxy is thickened to a past consistency suitable for gap filling and filleting.

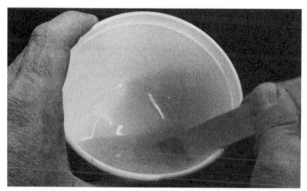

Illus. 66. The West System Brand Epoxy is normally very thin in consistency. The 5 to 1 resin to hardener ratio must be carefully measured and thoroughly mixed.

Illus. 67. The consistency of the West System Brand Epoxy can be thickened as desired with the addition of various fillers such as the fine cotton fibres shown here.

One of the unique features of the West System Brand Epoxy is its capability for use in "composite construction." Because the resins are of abnormally thin consistency, they penetrate deeply into the wood, encapsulate wood fibres and, thereby, considerably improve the wood's overall properties—especially its dimensional stability.

The best results for a moisture barrier are achieved with three or more applications of the resin. When used as a bonding adhesive, the West System Brand Epoxies are best applied in a two-step process. First apply a straight mixture (without any additives or fillers) to both surfaces of the joint. This wets out the surfaces with the epoxy and allows for maximum penetration into the wood fibres. Very porous woods such as cedar, balsa, and end grains can soak up more than the usual resin and may require recoating to assure that there is enough epoxy remaining on the mating surfaces for them to adhere properly. The second step is to thicken the resin with one of their recommended additives and apply it immediately over the previously "wetted-out" surfaces. Both surfaces should be coated so that a small quantity can be squeezed out of the joint with either light hand pressure or with very moderate clamping force, such as that provided by a staple gun, rubber bands, or filament tape.

Thickened epoxy can also be used to reinforce simple joints with a "fillet." (See Illus. 69 and 70.) A fillet is essentially a bead of thick epoxy used in much the same manner that glue blocks are used to reinforce conventional furniture joints.

Illus. 69. Making an epoxy fillet to strengthen a simple butt joint.

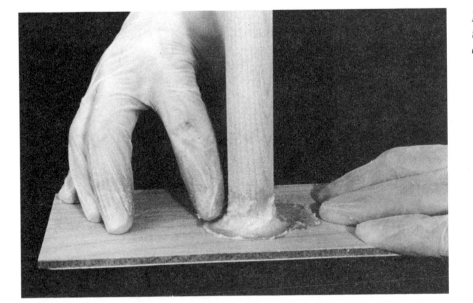

Illus. 70. Use an epoxy fillet to connect a large dowel securely to thin plywood.

Both the West System Brand products and Chem Tech's products are used with fibreglass cloth and other fabrics as surface-sheathing materials that add strength, stiffness, and reinforce various structures—particularly boat hulls. The epoxies saturate the woven fabric materials; when fully "wetted out," the cloth becomes transparent and virtually unnoticeable in the embedded matrix.

Technical manuals fully detailing these products and related products are available at a nominal price from Chem Tech and Gougeon Brothers. Both manuals are highly recommended, as is the book, *The Gougeon Brothers on Boat Building* (Gougeon Brothers, Inc., 1979). This book is for those contemplating or active in amateur boat building or similar projects. A new, revised edition is now available.

Other marine epoxy systems that might be worth looking into include: Hi-tech marine products of Marina del Rey, California; The Glen-L "Epoxy Encapsulation System" from Glen-L Marine Designs (of Bellflower, California); and System Three Resins of Seattle, Washington.

Polyester Resins

Polyester resins are recognizable as those thermoplastic resins commonly used to reinforce fibreglass. In all fibreglass constructions, such as all fibreglass boat hulls or snowmobile bodies, polyester resins are ideally suited for moulding and repair work. However, the common practice of using polyester resin reinforced fibreglass in a lay-up, where the fibreglass cloth is bonded directly to wood and/or plywood as a strengthening material, is really not used anymore by amateur and professional woodworkers or boat builders. The conventional fibreglassed wood-boat deck, lined plywood tanks and vats, etc., are much better sheathed with epoxy resins and other fabrics such as Dynel and polypropylene fabrics rather than polyester resin and fibreglass cloth. Polyester resins do not stick well to wood. Furthermore, they are brittle, subject to cracking, non-elastic, provide no flex for wood movements, shrink upon curing, and tend to blister when released from the wood substrate with impact because of their poor adhesion to wood. Because fibreglass-reinforced plastic bonded over wood substrates has checking and blistering tendencies, moisture collects in the voids and sets up conditions that can lead to rot. Boat repairs made with polyester resins used with fibreglass cloth over plywood have been known to peel away like a banana with little resistance.

Note: Table 3 on the following page summarizes the essential features of eleven commonly used wood glues.

Table 3.   # CHARACTERISTICS OF BASIC GLUES

Adhesive or Glue Type	Form	Mixing Requirements	Glue-Line Color	Major Use
Alipitatic (liquid yellow) glues	Liquid	None	Translucent, amber	General indoor wood projects
Animal glues (dry)	Granular	Mix with water, soak, heat to 145°F.	Tan-brown	Assembly, edge gluing and laminating
Animal glues (liquid)	Liquid ready to use	None	Amber-tan, dry color	Interior furniture, veneering construction & repairs
Contact cements (solvent-based)	Liquid	None	Yellow-tan	Bonding plastic laminates
Contact cements (water-based)	Liquid	None	Yellow-tan	Bonding plastic laminates
Polyvinyl glues (liquid white)	Liquid	None	Transparent	All assembly gluing, non-stressed joints
Resorcinol resins	Liquid	Mixed with powdered catalyst	Dark red	Laminations, exterior projects
Urea (urea-formaldehyde) plastic resins	Powder	Mix with water	Tan	All general woodworking interior and exterior projects
Thermoplastic hot-melts	Solid, stick, or sheet	None	Cream color	Noncritical joints, repairs, temporary joints
Epoxy resins	Liquid	Mix with liquid catalyst	Varies, mostly transparent	Special applications requiring high strength, marine, and non-porous materials
Cyanoacrylates (super or crazy glues)	Varies, usually liquids	None	Transparent	Modeling, repairs, special wood-bonding applications

CHARACTERISTICS OF BASIC GLUES

Adhesive or Glue Type	Advantages	Disadvantages	Service Durability	Clamping or Processing Conditions	Approx. Shelf and Working Life (Normal Conditions)
Alipitatic (liquid yellow) glues	Nontoxic; water cleanup	Sets fast; problematic for complicated assemblies	Very strong bonds; interior use; somewhat more moisture resistant than liquid white glues	60°–110°F	Fair, 9 months to 1 year
Animal glues (dry)	Very durable for interior use; quick setting	Poor moisture and heat resistance	Interior use	Clamp at room temperature	Indefinite; one day mixed
Animal glues (liquid)	Water cleanup; nontoxic solvent; excellent resistance; easily sanded	Low resistance to heat and moisture	Interior use	Room temperature	Good, one year
Contact Cements (solvent-based)	Permits quick bonds to large sheet laminates with minimum of equipment; unharmed by freezing; convenient to use	Fire hazard, hazardous odors	Resistant to water, heat, and humidity	Short-term contact pressure only	One year
Contact Cements (water-based)	Easy to apply; low hazard; low odors; nonflammable; water cleanup	Poor penetration on porous substrates; some are damaged by freezing	Generally lower in strength than other glues; water resistance varies	70°–75°F preferred	One year (unopened)
Polyvinyl glues (liquid white)	Colorless; odorless; quick green strength; nontoxic; no fire hazard; water cleanup	Not good under high stress; softens in presence of elevated temps. and humidity; clogs abrasives	Interior use only	Room temp. 5 mins. to 1 hour on nonstressed joints	One year (plus), indefinite in enclosed container
Resorcinol Resins	Very permanent; durable when used properly	Conditions must be perfect, bleeds and stains wood, expensive, not recommended under 70°F	Waterproof; marine usage	Room temp. and above required with substantial clamping pressure	One year unmixed; three hours mixed
Urea (urea-formaldehyde) plastic resins	High water resistance; sands easily	Poor gap filler, brittle, powder is strong sensitizer	Economical for exterior use	Room temperature	One year unmixed; three to five hours mixed
Thermo-plastic hot-melts	Rapid bonding; conveniently bonds variety of materials	Low penetration, low strength, sands poorly	Interior use	Hand pressure; cures upon cooling	Indefinite
Epoxy resins	Waterproof; sands easily; good gap filling	Expensive, toxic and messy	High water resistance	Varies—some require high temp., others cure over 35°F	Indefinite unmixed, 5 min. to several hours mixed
Cyanoacrylates (super or crazy glues)	Very fast; bonds with good strength (some bond green wood)	Only few formulated for wood, expensive, most are poor gap fillers (those formulated for nonporous surfaces)	High water resistance	Finger pressure only, room temperature	Pot life varies

Chapter 3
The Gluing Process

There are several different phases in the gluing and clamping process. They are as follows: selecting the glue, preparing the joint surface, mixing and spreading the adhesives, assembly, applying clamping pressure, cleanup, and testing the final assembly. Each phase is important and has a direct effect on the quality of the joint bond. I will take you through these phases step-by-step and discuss certain conditions that may crop up during the processes, and ways to correct these conditions.

Determining Which Glue to Use

There are many factors involved in the selection of the glue. However, there are several that should be of major concern to the woodworker and should be considered when he is determining which glue to use. They are : (1) the type of joint being glued, (2) how durable the joint should be, (3) cost of the glue, (4) working properties of the glue, and (5) moisture content of the wood.

The Type of Joint

Consideration should be given to the material dimensions and the species of wood involved, along with the particular grain directions of the respective parts. Flat surfaces glued together in face-to-face or edge-to-edge laminations are fairly easy to glue with a variety of adhesives. Other joints, such as right-angled or 90-degree butt and mitre joints, are very difficult to glue satisfactorily. Other joint strengtheners such as dowels and glue blocks may be required.

Some glues are of higher viscosity (thicker consistency), and these are generally best for the more-difficult-to-glue joints. (See Illus. 72 and 73.) Thinner glues may be desirable for some gluing assembly jobs where quick spreading and deeper penetration is required. White glues are generally thinner than yellow glues. Liquid hide glue can be thinned by increasing its temperature. Low-viscosity glues can also minimize squeeze-out and glue rundown in various joint assemblies.

Illus. 71. Selection of a good glue should be based on sound judgment more than package advertising.

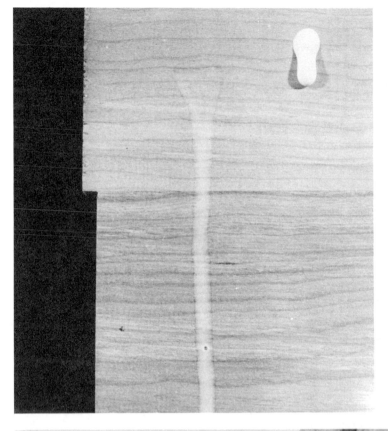

Illus. 72. The viscosity of glues can vary dramatically, as shown by these two off-the-shelf samples. High-viscosity glues, like the one on the right, are thicker.

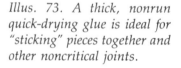

Illus. 73. A thick, nonrun quick-drying glue is ideal for "sticking" pieces together and other noncritical joints.

Some joints, like those used in model building, may require quick-tack or wet-tack properties. (See Illus. 74 and 75.) Glues with good tack qualities work best in situations where it seems likely that tightly fitting dowels or tenons will have the glue scraped off their surfaces as they are inserted into their holes or mortises. If joints don't fit "neatly" but have open spaces, then a gap-filling glue may be a better choice.

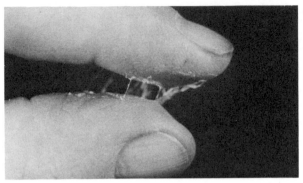

Illus. 74. This simple finger test helps to evaluate "wet-tack" qualities of a glue.

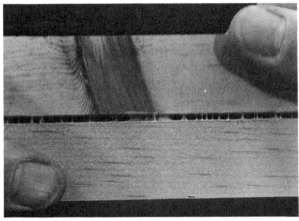

Illus. 75. Glues with high "wet-tack" are also good for holding corner blocks of furniture or parts of models in place without clamping.

Joint Durability

The durability desired of the glue joints is another consideration in the selection of glue. Almost all glues are fairly durable and long-lasting under normal dry conditions. However, durability varies from the relatively low-moisture resistance of animal glue to the higher all-around durability of resorcinols and epoxies.

Heat-resistance qualities may also be important when making cutting boards, kitchen counters, using heat-drying finishes, or using wooden products in elevated temperatures. Hot-melts, liquid white glues, yellow glues and animal hide glues are not the best choices when it comes to glue durability in moist and elevated temperatures. Resorcinols and epoxies are much better.

Cost

It's impossible to list exact, comparative figures on the costs of the different glues. Epoxies and resorcinol glues are, comparatively speaking, expensive. The lower-priced urea resins may work where these are recommended. What should be considered in the real cost is the cost per spread area and the cost of waste due to short pot life, mixing more glue than is needed, and the solvents needed for cleanup. (See Illus. 76.)

Illus. 76. Buying in larger quantities reduces cost. A gallon of white glue, which has an indefinite shelf life, will fill these plastic dispensers (from detergent soaps), cutting the cost to nearly half.

Working Properties

Working properties of the glue involve temperature requirements, pot life, shelf life, speed of set, assembly times (page 55), "sandability," heat and solvent resistance, cleanup requirements, and whether special tools or equipment are required for its use. The most important working properties are discussed here. Others will be discussed where applicable.

Temperature consideration is essential. Most glues work best at room temperatures or above. Be sure to check manufacturer's instructions regarding best temperatures. The temperature of the wood materials to be glued, the air temperature, and the temperature of the glue all must be carefully considered and evaluated according to the preferred conditions recommended for the glue chosen. If gluing below recommended temperatures, expect a much slower setting speed and, more importantly, a dramatic decrease in the glue's strength.

Some white (PVA) glues are formulated to resist freezing; others are formulated for use in temperatures below 70 °F. Some epoxies work at low temperatures; other glues, such as resorcinol, have a very specific recommended temperature.

Pot life is the working life of the glue once it is mixed or otherwise prepared for use. It usually ranges in time according to the variables (temperature, humidity, etc.) Some glues have a definite working life. Shelf life refers to the duration that glue or its components may be stored without degrading and still remain useable. Most manufacturers do not state the shelf life on the container. It's a good idea to mark the date of purchase on the container for future reference. Then you can determine the shelf life of the glue.

Solvent resistance is very important because you don't want the solvent to dissolve, deteriorate, or weaken your glue lines. Most glues are solvent resistant. Liquid animal-hide glues are good solvent-resistant glues, as are the polyvinyl (liquid white) glues. However, these glues do react to some organic solvents and oils. Also, be sure to check contact cements and veneer adhesives, which may be weakened by some finish solvents.

With some assemblies, it may be desirable to remove glue squeeze-out by sanding. White glues do not sand well; almost all other glues do. Animal hide and urea resin glues have exceptional sanding qualities, as do most cured epoxies. (See Illus. 77.)

Moisture Content

The moisture content of the wood at the time of gluing has much to do with the final

Illus. 77. Sandability is one important property for the home woodworker. This shows the superior sanding quality of animal hide glue on the left, verses the "gumming" of the liquid white glue on the right.

strength of joints, the amount of checks that will develop, and the amount of warpage in the glued members. Most glues will adhere to wood with any moisture content up to 12 percent, with some capable of gluing up to 15 percent. Water-resistant glues will adhere to wood with even higher moisture contents. Large changes in moisture content of the wood after gluing will cause shrinkage or swelling stresses that may seriously weaken both the wood and the joints, resulting in delamination. A moisture content of 5 to 6 percent is recommended for indoor projects. (See Illus. 27 on page 19.)

Preparing the Joint Surface

Wood surfaces that are being glued should be smooth, flat and true. They should also be free from machine marks, chipped or loosened grain, torn fibres or other irregularities. Surfaces should also be well fitted so the joint can be fitted closely without excessive force. It's definitely best when the machining is done just prior to gluing. If wood is machined days before bonding, changes in moisture content may result in warp, which destroys the nice flat surfaces you have carefully prepared.

Look carefully at Illus. 78 and 79. They illustrate some undesirable but often typical conditions that occur on wood surfaces to be glued. Their causes vary, but can be traced to poor machine or tool conditioning. To put it bluntly, they are caused by poor workmanship and lackadaisical craftsmanship. Erratic glue joints are guaranteed if these undesirable surface conditions are permitted.

Illus. 78. A close look at all gluing surfaces may reveal some potential problems.

Illus. 79. Surface conditions absolutely not suitable for gluing. Left to right: Rough band-sawn surface; burnished hardwood caused by a dull saw; softwood cut with a saw poorly "set"; a sanded edge; and last, a jointed surface that was fed too fast over the cutterhead.

Illus. 80. Best surfaces for gluing. Left: Surface made with a true and sharp hand plane. Right: True, flat surface properly fed through the jointer.

Illus. 81 illustrates four undesirable surface conditions that result from a wood planer. *Raised grain* can occur when wood with high moisture content is machined; it might be reduced with sharp knives. *Fuzzy grain* is often due to abnormal wood fibres that often occur in low-density woods like basswood, cottonwood, and willow. Sharp knives and slow feeds are the best corrective measures. *Chipped or torn grain* is a condition often found in denser hardwoods such as birch, cherry, and maple which have cross or swirly grain. Slower feeds and shallower cuts tend to reduce these problems. *Chip marks* are dents caused by shavings being pressed into the surface by outfeed rollers. A dust collector or vacuum to catch the shavings is the best prevention.

One factor affecting surface conditions that *can* be controlled is the *rate of feed*. Fast-feed rates reduce the number of knife cuts per inch of surface, and thus produce surfaces that are not as true or flat as those which are passed over the cutter with a slower feed rate. (See Illus. 82.) Slower feed rates increase the number of knife cuts; as a result, smoother cuts are made. Equally important

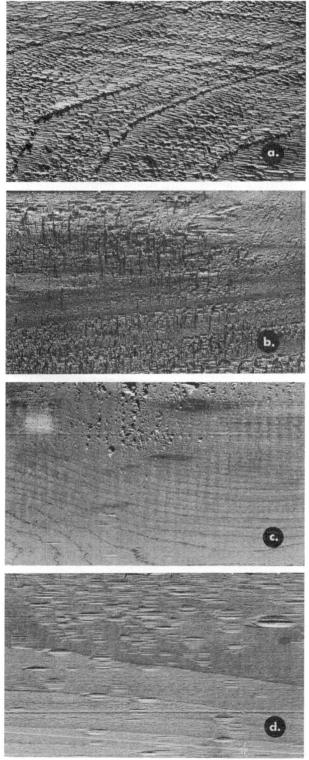

Illus. 82. Feed rates: A, fast rate of feed, which produces fewer knife marks per lineal inch and results in a rougher, "rippled" surface. B, same board cut with a slower feed rate.

is making sure that cutter heads are adjusted properly with all knife-cutting edges set equal-distance out from the center. Burnished surfaces resulting from improperly adjusted machines, dull knives, or excessively slow feeds produce very undesirable gluing surfaces, as shown in Illus. 83. Nicked knives or jointer tables not adjusted properly will also create surfaces unsuitable for gluing. (See Illus. 84 and 85.)

Illus. 81. More machine conditions that reduce gluing quality: A, raised grain; B, fuzzy grain; C, chipped or torn grain; and D, chip marks. These conditions are often found on stock machined on surfacers and planers.

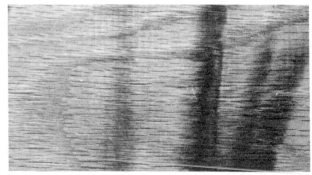

Illus. 83. Burnished surfaces, such as this, improperly cut on jointers and planers are case-hardened and will glue poorly because they are difficult to wet-out.

51

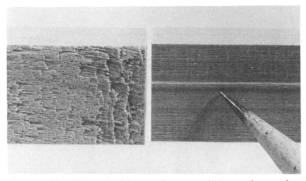

Illus. 84. Undesirable surface conditions from the jointer. Left: chipped grain resulting from the wrong feed direction. Right: a nick in the knife-cutting edges causes the bead to prohibit tight fit.

Illus. 85. Another very undesirable condition is these end "snips" caused from a jointer cut of adjustment with its out-feed table set too low.

Sanded surfaces as a rule do not make good surfaces. In edge-to-edge work, sanding rounds edges and removes more wood from the softer areas of the board than the dense areas. Consequently, a sanded surface is less uniform than a well-planed board. Also, sanding with coarse grits creates torn fibres that are likely to pull loose under stress. (See Illus. 79.)

Ideally, wood must be machined smooth and must be perfectly flat at the time of gluing. Surfaces should not have high and low areas. This condition increases the difficulty of distributing uniform pressure over the entire joint area and can also result in very thin adhesive areas on the high spots and a starved joint condition. The glue that fills in the low areas will develop poor strength and may shrink away from the surface during cure. Simply put: Inadequate contact results in poor adhesion.

Some species of wood like those with high extractive contents, such as "pitchy" pines, tend to undergo surface changes that are not completely understood. These surfaces are sometimes referred to as case-hardened, and they can be very difficult to wet with adhesives. Poor wetting characteristics reduce the actual adhesion and may result in weakened joints. All case-hardened lumber should be resurfaced just prior to gluing to ensure a high-quality bond. Undesirable gluing surfaces can be detected by observing the reaction of a drop of water placed on the surface. (See Illus. 86.)

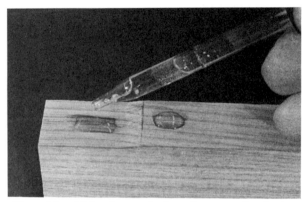

Illus. 86. This demonstrates the case-hardening effect of a wood surface allowed to age over a week after edge jointing. About 1 inch of the surface (under the dropper) was recut with a jointer, exposing new, freshly cut wood. Water drops were placed on both the new and old surfaces. As shown, the freshly cut surface is more conducive to good wetting, which is essential for good adhesion.

Almost any species of wood machined many days (to weeks) before bonding can exhibit surface characteristics similar to those of case hardening. Here again, a water-drop test will detect undesirable gluing. (See Illus. 87.)

Woods treated with preservatives and fire retardants may also be difficult to bond effectively. This is especially true of lumber treated with oil-based preservatives. Resurfacing or remachining just before bonding will remove the oily surface layer. Because the oil will diffuse back to the surface again,

52

Illus. 87. This experiment by technologist Bryan River shows water drops on aged yellow birch veneer. Left drop is on the untouched aged surface. Center drop is on the surface rubbed once with 320 grit abrasive. Drop at right is on the same surface, but rubbed twice with the same abrasive. This Illus. and Illus. 86 were taken within 30 seconds after the drops were applied.

the wood should be bonded immediately after resurfacing. Also, wipe the surfaces with clean rags and a volatile solvent such as mineral spirits just before bonding.

Many sheet materials such as plywood, hardboard, particle board, and plastic laminate are manufactured in hot presses. Thus, they have surfaces that make them difficult to wet with adhesives. These surface conditions are another form of case hardening. Sometimes light sanding is required on the backs of hardboard, particle board, and plastic laminate to expose fresh surfaces and get a good bond. Only light sanding is recommended in such cases. Avoid excessive sanding. This will only create irregular surfaces having high and low spots.

Mixing and Spreading Adhesives

When using glues that must be mixed, it is essential that you measure them accurately. The manufacturer's directions should be followed very closely. It's an economical practice not to mix more glue than needed at one time. Some adhesives require a "standing time," that is, the glue should not be used immediately after the initial mixing. Most adhesives recommend a second stir-mixing after they have been allowed to stand the recommended time. For many glues, metal-mixing containers should be avoided. Iron contamination may cause stains in the finished work. Plastic, polyethylene containers are best. Glue components that must be mixed by weight can be measured easily with an inexpensive scale. These are available in most drugstores.

When measuring volumes (Illus. 88 and 89), be sure that containers are not dented or lined with a film clinging to the container from a previous measurement. Scrape the edges or walls of measuring and mixing containers. Volumes are not directly proportional to weight. Consequently, powders should always be weighed because their density may change from batch to batch. Remember, when mixing glues on hot days the reactions will be much faster. Pot life will be shorter with setting, and curing more rapid.

Glue can be spread with a variety of devices, such as sticks and tongue depressors. (See Illus. 90 and 91.) These scrap or inexpensive devices can be simply thrown away after use. Bristle brushes, rollers (Illus. 92), trowels, squeegees, and notched, metal "comb"-type spreaders (Illus. 93) all require cleanup after use. Polyvinyl white and yellow liquid glues can be safely spread with your fingers—which are probably the most efficient spreading "tools." (See Illus. 94.)

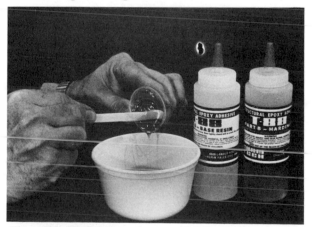

Illus. 88. Moderately deep, reusable plastic mixing pots are recommended over shallow pans, which make complete mixing difficult.

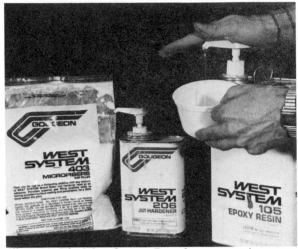

Illus. 89. *The West System Brand epoxy requires very accurate mixing. Components are best dispensed with their inexpensive minipumps.*

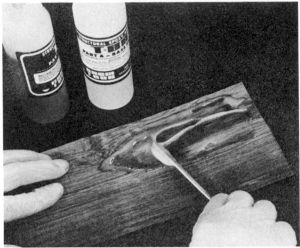

Illus. 90. *Scrap sticks work best to spread small areas with epoxy.*

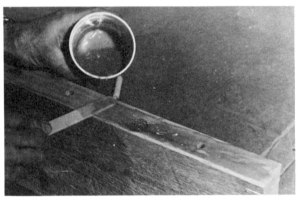

Illus. 91. *Spreading on a dowel edge joint. Here the dowels are only intended to aid in alignment of the adjoining pieces during assembly (not to make the joint stronger). In such situations, no effort is made to give the dowels or holes proper glue coverage.*

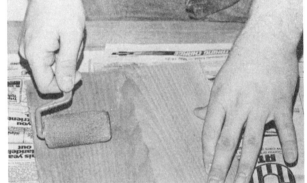

Illus. 92. *Larger surfaces are best and more quickly spread with short nap rollers. Here special veneer contact cement is applied to particle board.*

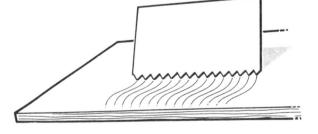

Illus. 93. *A notched spreading tool.*

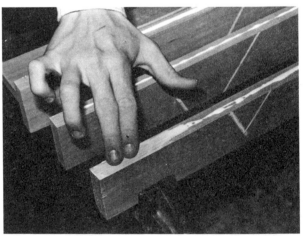

Illus. 94. *Spreading out a bead of white liquid glue with one's fingers.*

There is much controversy regarding single and double spreading, that is, applying glue to either one or both mating surfaces of the glue joint. With most glues, in normal circumstances, the glue should only be applied to one of the two mating surfaces. (See Illus. 95.) When double spreading is recommended, the adhesive is applied to uniform coverage on both substrates; because the solids in glues vary from type to type, the actual amount of wet-adhesive spread required varies. The manufacturer's instructions should be followed closely.

Illus. 95. Single spreading showing different quantities applied to each edge. Left: about the right amount of glue. Center: Not quite the right amount. Right: too much glue. Compare these glue spread amounts to their respective squeeze-outs shown in Illus. 96.

The amount of glue applied varies as well, but a good practical guide is to observe the squeeze-out when the clamping pressure is applied to the joint. If a sufficient amount of adhesive has been spread and pressure is applied, within the permissible time limit, a thin line of adhesive droplets will be visible all along the exposed joint. (See Illus. 96.) When excessive adhesive runs down from the joint, it indicates that either too much adhesive has been spread, the adhesive has been diluted too much, or that the pressure has been applied before the adhesive developed sufficient tack. When glue penetrates deeply into the wood, the result is a starved glue joint. Sanding dust should always be removed from gluing surfaces. The glue may not penetrate through this dust to the solid wood, and not wet-out properly. Air pressure and tack rags should be used to remove sanding dust.

Illus. 96. Observing squeeze-out is a guide to proper amount of glue applied, correct spread, and correct assembly period. Top joint: just the right amount of squeeze-out. Middle joint: barely enough. Bottom joint: excessive spread.

Double spreading is advised where long delays are anticipated in getting large assemblies spread, assembled, and under pressure. In such cases, the adhesive is likely to harden partially before pressure can be applied, and then will not adequately wet and adhere to the opposite uncoated surface, although it will adhere to an opposite, coated piece. Double spreading is always done when using contact cements, and it's a usual practice in many assembly joints—particularly with glued dowel, mortise-and-tenon, and mitre joints. (See pages 132 and 133.) Double spreading is often done when laminating wood to curved forms. (Page 92 shows some commercial glue-spreading devices.)

Assembly Periods

This is the time lapse between spreading the adhesive and applying full clamping pressure. (See Illus. 97.) *Open assembly time* refers to the time during which the two mating surfaces are spread but not in contact with each other. *Closed assembly time* refers to the time interval after the two spread surfaces are joined, but before they are pressed or clamped together. Generally, liquid animal-hide glues have longer assembly times than do the liquid white and yellow glues. A heavier glue spread will increase assembly time. Very dry woods and porous woods will decrease assembly times. This is because the adhesive solvents are either absorbed by the wood itself or evaporate into the air. Thus, the adhesive thickens during the assembly period; the thickening rate increases at higher temperatures. Avoid assembly periods that are too short or long. (See Illus. 98A and 98B.) The glue must be wet enough to transfer uniformly to the mating surface when pressure is applied. The speed of glue set is directly related to the moisture content of the wood. Since drier wood absorbs more, it should be allowed proportionally less assembly time.

Illus. 97. Open assembly time is that interval between spreading and bringing the parts of the joint into contact with each other.

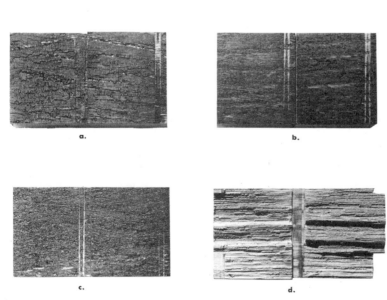

a.

b.

c.

d.

Illus. 98. Poor and good glue joints made under different gluing conditions. A: excessively thick glue line caused by too long of an open assembly period. B: too short of an assembly period; the joint was pressed before the glue had reached the desired viscosity. C: glue not adequately cured. D: a well-made joint that developed a high percentage of wood failure when broken.

Clamping Pressure

Clamping pressure on a glue joint should do three things: (1) smooth the glue and force the air out so the adhesive flows to a thin continuous film between the wood pieces; (2) bring the wood surfaces into direct and intimate contact with the glue; and (3) hold the joint steadily in this position during the setting or curing of the glue. Light pressure should be used with thin glues. Heavier pressure should be used with thicker glues. Clamping is done to bring the members close enough together so a thin glue line results.

Generally, the best joints are those made with glues of intermediate consistency, and clamped with moderately heavy pressures—that is, a range of 100 to 150 p.s.i. Most softwoods fall into this category. Dense hardwoods such as oak require, and will withstand without crushing, higher clamping pressure. For some jobs, as much as 300 p.s.i. may be necessary.

Craftsmen using average clamps and hand force can seldom create pressure exceeding the maximum p.s.i. recommendations. A heavy-duty bar clamp can exert about 2,000 pounds of force. A pipe clamp can deliver about 1,100 to 1,200 pounds. This force should be divided by the square inches of the glue joint surface to get the actual pounds of pressure distributed per square inch.

It is often more important to have uniform pressure over the entire joint area than it is to have an excessive amount of pressure. Uniformity of squeeze-out is a good indicator of correct pressure. Generally, heavier pressure is required for denser woods than for lower density softwoods.

Pressure also should be related according to the kind of glue, spread, assembly periods, type of joint, and quality of fit. Epoxy glues require less pressure than do urea and resorcinol resins. Some joints such as good-fitting "rubbed" glue blocks require practically no pressure at all. Also, remember that when bonding thin materials with mechanical clamps, it is desirable to use thicker lumber or other heavy "cauls" between the clamps and the work so the pressure is distributed evenly between the clamps.

It's very difficult to specify the number of clamps that should be used to produce acceptable pressure over a given amount of joint area. Some authorities say clamps should be placed every 16 to 20 inches apart; others suggest clamps every 8 to 10 inches. I favor the concept of using more clamps; it's more consistent with the idea of achieving uniformly distributed pressures. However, many variables need to be considered when determining the number of clamps required for a specific job. The kind and quality of clamps, the type of glue, species of wood, moisture content, temperature, joint fit, glue spread, etc., are some of these essential considerations.

Joint failure when contact cements are used can usually be traced to improper glue spread, inadequate drying time, or the lack of adequate pressure. At least 50 p.s.i. is required for most contact cements. Thus, besides initially flattening the material with your hands, you will also have to use a block and hammer or a narrow roller. Heavy pressure over the total joint area is necessary when contact cements are used.

If the joint has been clamped and the pressure released before the glue is set, such as when repositioning a misaligned board, all glue lines should be recoated with glue before being reclamped. If this is not done, a low-quality joint is sure to result. Respreading assures a properly wet surface.

Temperatures

Glue line temperatures are especially important to achieving strong, durable joints. Most glues are best used at 70 °F or slightly above. Always observe manufacturers' directions, as previously discussed. Even though the room temperature may be adequate for the glue, the wood itself may be of lower temperature. Wood does not warm up as fast as the surrounding air, and precautions should be taken when working in cold climates, unheated shops, or basements. Wood stored on a cold concrete floor or kept in an unheated garage and glued without temperature conditioning may produce some very erratic, inferior bonds. Illus. 99 shows the "chalky" look of the squeeze-out that results when liquid white and liquid yellow glues were used in cold temperatures. The squeeze-out of liquid white glue should appear almost transparent when gluing is performed at the optimum temperatures. Increasing the temperature speeds the set and cure of most adhesives, although there are some notable exceptions, such as hot-melts and some other thermoplastic adhesives. Some resorcinols and epoxies require elevated temperatures and/or special heating chambers. Temperatures can be elevated with infrared heat lamps or electric flameless heaters.

The duration of pressure periods or the time that the work must remain in clamps varies with different adhesives. Manufacturers' instructions should be consulted. Most adhesives continue to develop additional strength after the clamps have been removed. Wood should not be allowed to undergo large changes in moisture content immediately after pressure periods. Such changes induce dimensional changes, and the internal stresses may destroy the partially cured joints. If the joint is stressed or if it will be strained in use soon after removal from the clamps, it's best to double the clamping times. This is true for making projects with laminated bends and similar applications. Woods higher in moisture content will also dictate longer clamping or pressing periods.

Cleanup

Cleanup is the removal of glue-squeeze drippings; it is done often with a damp rag. The rag should not be too moist. Sometimes it's best to use a tool like a putty knife or stick to lift the beaded glue off of the surface shortly after the glue starts to set. This procedure minimizes the possibility of pushing glue into the pores, and reduces the amount of moisture applied to the glue joint area. *Tip:* Mixing in a little food coloring in glues that normally become transparent when dry will make them more visible, which makes their removal easier.

A variety of special cleanup problems can arise when veneering and working with plastic laminates. These are discussed in Chapters 10 and 11.

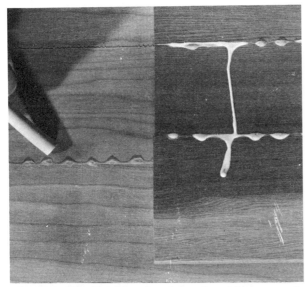

Illus. 99. Liquid white glue dries almost transparent at room temperatures, as shown by the squeeze-out of the joints on the left. The two joints at right were glued and cured in a cold workshop. Note how these joints exhibit a very white, chalk-like look on the squeeze-outs. Liquid yellow glue was used on the upper joint. The lower joint was made with liquid white glue. Cold gluing results in poor bond strength.

Testing the Glued Assembly

It is a good idea to test and check the glued pieces to evaluate the strength of your gluing procedures. Basically, this evaluation consists of nothing more than going through your scrap box, taking the cut-off of glued assemblies, and testing them for their breaking points. (See Illus. 100.) Some basic stresses can be evaluated by hitting the cut-offs with a hammer as they are held in a vise. (See Illus. 101.)

Sheer tests (Illus. 102) give indications of the surprising strength of glue joints. When the joint is glued properly, it is almost impossible to break it.

Illus. 103 shows how to test for tensile strength. Carefully study the surfaces of the broken joints. They can tell you a lot about your gluing practices. Study Illus. 104 and 105.

Illus. 101. This simple test will give you an idea of glue joint quality.

Illus. 100. Cut-offs of glued stock are ideal for simple breakage tests to evaluate your gluing techniques.

Illus. 102. Doing an impact sheer test will demonstrate the high strength glues provide in this stress mode if they are properly glued.

Illus. 103. Making an impact tensile strength test.

Illus. 104. A close-up look at the broken joint will tell a lot about overall joint strength.

Not all gluing is done to achieve initial high-joint strength. For example, contrary to first impressions, the strip canoe being made in Illus. 105 is at this point of construction only glued to hold the pieces together and

maintain the essential shape or form of the project. Little bending stresses are involved because the strips are narrow and thin, which makes them bend easily to form the shape of the canoe. Ultimate strength will be achieved when resin and a reinforcing sheathing material like fibreglass will be applied over the structure's surface. This forms a very strong, totally cohesive build-up that has a strength similar to that of a sheet of plywood. (See page 107 for more on strip canoe building.)

Illus. 105. Gluing in strip canoe building does not require high-stress joints to maintain the form or shape of the vessel. Resin-impregnated sheathing (such as fibreglass) applied over the glued and formed strips creates the ultimate end strength.

Problem Areas

Starved Glue Joints

Many failures in gluing can be attributed to "starved" joints. (See Illus. 106.) Starved joints are joints that do not have a film of glue between the mating surfaces. A low percentage of wood failure is a good indication of starved joints. Another indication is when glue is not continuously visible, as illustrated in the test sample shown in Illus. 106.

Starved joints are not necessarily the result of a lack of glue spread on the wood. Heavy spreads are just as likely to produce starved joints as light spreads. The cause is essentially the application of too much pressure to the joint while the glue is too fluid. Some woods simply absorb the glue because of their large percentage of open pores. Other woods containing too much moisture at the time of gluing dilute the glue solvents and retard the setup process. Light pressure should be used if conditions supporting starved joints are suspected.

Illus. 106. A starved glue joint is identified here by little or no wood failure. Also, there appears to be little if any glue visible on the surfaces.

End-Grain Glue Failure

End-grain gluing is best accomplished with a high-solid, fast-setting glue. Thinner, slower setting glues continue to penetrate by soaking into the end grain, leaving an insufficient quantity on the surfaces for an effective glue film. Thus, most end-grain glue failures can be traced to starved joint conditions. This condition can be alleviated somewhat by double coating, allowing maximum open-assembly time, and recoating again in an attempt to get the glue to remain in the joint without flowing away into the pores of the wood.

Thick Glue Lines

Thick glue lines should be avoided in almost all cases and situations. As a general rule, thicker glue lines produce weaker joints. This is especially true with adhesives containing water. Thick glue lines not only look bad, but with almost all of the commonly used adhesives, they are very weak as well. Many glues shrink upon drying (as they lose moisture); as a result, a void is left in the cured glue line. Urea or plastic resins simply are not acceptable as gap-filling glues because they will shrink, check, and crack. Epoxies are good gap fillers because their components are all solids without any solvents. Try one of the new gap-filling glues.

Glue Stains

Stains from glue that end up destroying the appearance of the finished product can happen from two basic causes. The most common problem occurs when the glue gets onto the surface of the wood and is not completely removed before the finish is applied. (See Illus. 107 and 108.) Since many glues are almost transparent when dry, it is difficult to detect glue on surfaces. To alleviate this problem, make sure the surfaces are planed and sanded well. Otherwise, the glue fills the pores and prevents the application of stain or top-coat finish from coloring the wood uniformly.

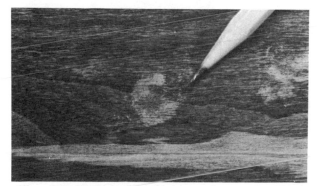

Illus. 107. Typical glue spotting under a stained surface. Note the finger prints and the light areas along the joint. Glue spotting is great advertisement for poor workmanship.

61

Illus. 108. This ugly light streak along the mitre joint is caused from the squeeze-out being wiped into the pores and then prematurely stained without being sanded adequately beforehand.

Illus. 109. A clean joint, without glue spotting under the stain, appears much more professional.

Nasty black stains can appear on raw wood as a result of an iron reaction. This condition, shown in Illus. 110, often occurs when bar clamps are used on oak, walnut, butternut, cherry, and some other woods. This problem occurs more with some particularly acidic glues. The stains are often deep and difficult to remove. To prevent this condition, place strips of wax paper or plastic film between the clamp and the work. Another preventive measure is to keep the clamp surfaces well waxed. (See Illus. 111.) This not only minimizes black stains, but it also prevents squeeze-out glue from adhering to the clamps and fouling up the jaw adjustment mechanisms. Wax also makes the clamps easier to clean up after repeated use. Do not coat too freely with the paste wax—buff it. If globs of wax remain on the clamp, they can transfer to and penetrate into the wood, which creates a new problem.

Illus. 110. Black stain resulting from glue and clamp iron reaction.

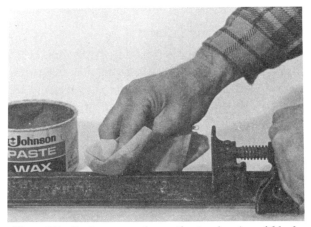

Illus. 111. Paste wax reduces the tendencies of black staining and improves overall clamp operation and cleanliness.

Sunken Joints

Sunken joints occur when cured glue joints are improperly conditioned before being machined or further worked. (See Illus. 112.) Sunken joints are especially obvious on projects with high-gloss finishes. This condition is less obvious with dull finishes, but they can still be detected by touch. If any moisture enters the joint from the glue, the moisture should be allowed to diffuse throughout the glued members. Furthermore, stresses set up during gluing and curing will either be relieved or fade away with proper curing.

Sunken joints are typical problems often found in edge gluing. They are most often the result of surfacing or planing glued panels too soon after gluing. The wood adjacent to the joint absorbs water from the glue and swells the surrounding wood fibres. When the panel is surfaced before this excess moisture is distributed or dried, greater amounts of wood are removed from the glue-line areas than from other areas of the panel.

When the joint moisture diffuses, permanent depressions are created. (See Illus. 112 and 113.)

Steps to minimize sunken joints include conditioning before machining, using less glue to minimize squeeze-out, or applying heat to speed the drying of the wood. Generally speaking, woods of higher density require longer conditioning periods than the lighter, lower-density softwoods.

Creep

Creep occurs when the respective members of a glued assembly shrink or expand at different rates. They, in effect, slide on the glued surfaces, resulting in something similar to the condition shown in Illus. 114. Creep produces surfaces that are not flush, and is essentially caused by changes in temperature and, more importantly, changes in the humidity. Using rigid thermosetting glues rather than the thermoplastic glues such as polyvinyl acetates will minimize such conditions.

Illus. 112. Sunken glue lines. Upper panel: urea resin glued at left and animal hide glued at right. Both were surfaced immediately after clamping. Lower panels were similarly glued, but were allowed to condition seven days before surfacing. Note the differences in panels.

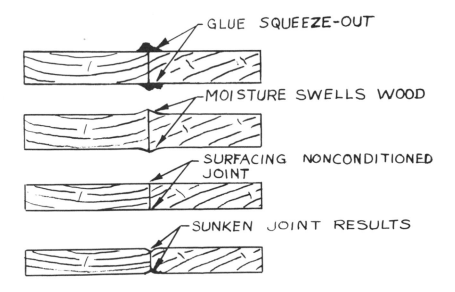

GLUE SQUEEZE-OUT

MOISTURE SWELLS WOOD

SURFACING NONCONDITIONED JOINT

SUNKEN JOINT RESULTS

Illus. 113. How sunken joints develop.

Illus. 114. "Creep" is where glued members expand and contract at different rates.

Chapter 4
Clamps and Gluing Tools

Woodworking clamps and clamping techniques have changed very little in the last 50 years or so. There are some new manufacturers entering the market, but dramatically different or new designs in clamping tools are virtually nonexistent. (Incidentally, English manufacturers refer to clamps and clamping as "cramps" and "cramping." Their products are now reaching Canadian and United States markets. Some of these products are shown and discussed in this chapter.) In this chapter I will take a look at both the clamping tools available on the market and tools and accessories that are helpful during the gluing process.

Clamps

Almost all clamping tools can be lumped into categories familiar to the average woodworker: bar clamps, hand screws, C-clamps, and band clamps. There is also a group of specialty clamps that include devices for clamping picture frames and mitre joints, as well as other work-holding devices.

Builders of wooden musical instruments have different clamping requirements than do furniture makers, whose needs are, in turn, different from the needs of boatbuilders. Some clamps do a broad range of jobs, and others, such as mitre clamps, are special-purpose tools.

Clamps should be selected or purchased according to the kind of clamping and/or gluing jobs you intend to do. The more expensive "heavy-duty" or "industrial" clamps may be cumbersome for light woodworking jobs with soft woods. On the other hand, if you work with heavy hard woods or glue up larger soft wood planks and timbers, the less expensive clamps will not provide the long-term service you need because they are just not built for continuous, rugged work.

Sometimes a job comes along for which you can't find a commercially made clamp or a pressure system. In such cases, you will have to devise your own clamp. At Spielman's Wood Works, we often need a lot of pulling power to bring a large assembly into place or to take the twist out of big timber. We also work a lot of 2-inch material into large panels that are glued edge to edge. Even though most of the work is done with softwood species, we usually have more than double the surface area in our joints than does the average woodworker edge-gluing standard 3/4 inch-thick lumberyard stock.

Clamps are available in a broad range of qualities, types, sizes, and can be purchased at various prices. Think about your clamping requirements. Remember the primary purpose of clamping in gluing—at least in most jobs—is to bring the two wood pieces of a joint into very close contact. Clamps need to be matched to the kind and size of wood being glued, as well as to the particular kind of glue itself. If your materials and workmanship are such that you can always fit parts and pieces together that are near "perfect" without excessive pressure, use medium-duty rather than the heavier, expensive clamping tools. Less expensive tools are generally of poorer quality and do not perform as well.

Projects glued with epoxies require less pressure than jobs assembled with urea and resorcinol resins. The latter requires specific, tight-fitting joints and substantially more pressure to achieve durable bonds. Dense hardwoods like oak or maple withstand and require much more pressure for good joints than softwoods such as pine or cedar. Not enough pressure results in thick glue lines (which are weaker than thin ones), regardless of which type of glue is used.

There are a good number of gluing jobs for which you may not need or be able to use commercially manufactured clamps. In these cases, various weights might provide the right pressure. Some objects that will help obtain the necessary pressure or torque are bricks, sandbags, pails of water, nails, heavy rubber bands, springs, twisted rope, and wire.

The three reasons for applying pressure in gluing are: (1) to smooth the glue spread and drive the air from the joint to form a thin continuous glue film; (2) to bring the wood pieces into close contact; and (3) to hold the pieces securely in position until the glue sets. The exact amount of clamping pressure can vary widely from just using a few pounds of light, finger-tight pressure to turning the handles with all of your strength in an attempt to distribute high pressures of as much as 300 p.s.i. over the entire gluing area.

Bar Clamps

Bar clamps are made in many styles. Some bars are of an I-beam design; these bars are the most durable. (See Illus. 115 and 118.) The T-bar "cramp" (Illus. 116) is also very strong. Two flat bar clamps are shown in Illus. 119. They are used for general assembly work. Deep-throat bar clamps (Illus. 120 and 121) are used for light assembly work; because of their quick adjustment capabilities, they are often preferred over C-clamps and should be used where hand screw clamps cannot be used. Illus. 122 shows a rather novel modification to the bar clamp. It has a swivel plate on the stationary end of the clamp with screw holes for optional permanent mounting, such as under a workbench or any other convenient place. This swivel "foot" also fits into an optional accessory track. Therefore, it has the potential to swing up and slide laterally to any spot where clamping is required.

When not needed, it conveniently swings out of the way. Any number of clamps can be used with the swivel "foot." (See Illus. 123.)

Another bar-clamp design is simply a set of cast fixtures that are threaded and fitted to standard black pipe. (See Illus. 124 and 125.) This system allows you to make clamps of any length you desire.

Illus. 115. A heavy-duty "I"-beam bar clamp.

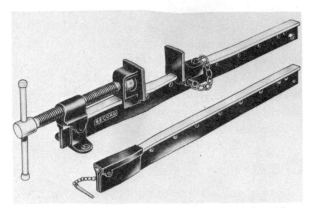

Illus. 116. The "T"-bar "cramp" designed with a lengthening bar offers a potential clamping length up to 126 inches.

Illus. 117. A good bar clamp has the jaws square to the bar.

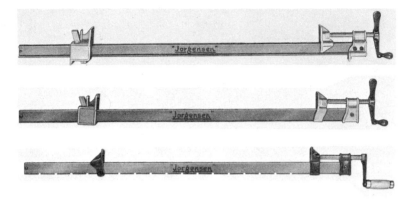

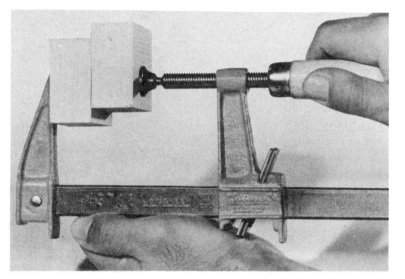

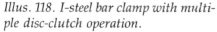

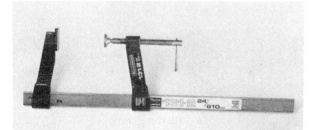

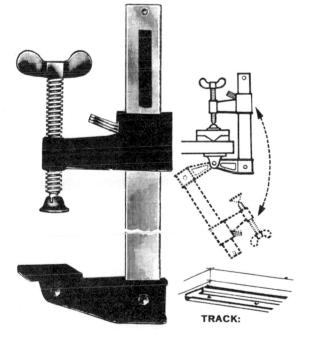

Illus. 118. I-steel bar clamp with multiple disc-clutch operation.

Illus. 119. Left, top: a joiner's bar clamp for edge-gluing and light assemblies where great pressure is not required. Below: "notched bar" is another design for easy-opening adjustment.

Illus. 120. Steel bar clamp with a jaw reach of 2½ inches from the edge of the bar to the middle of the screw. Some refer to this as an "F" clamp.

Illus. 121. Another quick-acting bar "cramp" design with more jaw reach.

Illus. 122. (right). A hinged swivel on the head of this clamp is designed to mount permanently under a bench or it will slide laterally in the accessory track. In either application, it swings out of the way when not in use.

TRACK:

Illus. 123. These hinged clamps are screwed to the underside of a saw horse.

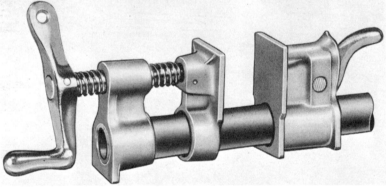

Illus. 124. Typical pipe clamp fixture.

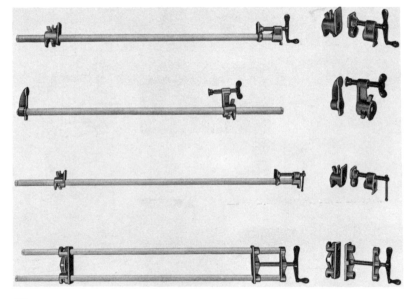

Illus. 125. Other pipe clamp fixtures. The double-bar design gives pressure to both sides of the work. This clamp is good for edge-to-edge gluing as it prevents any tendency for the pieces to buckle under pressure.

A double-bar pipe-clamp design, as shown in Illus. 125, exerts pressure on both sides of the work. This prevents the work from buckling. The double-bar design is advantageous in edge-to-edge gluing—especially when the work is not thick.

Piling clamps (Illus. 126) are ideal for those who do a lot of edge-to-edge gluing. These clamps save space and time. They consist of two independently operated screw clamps within a single steel frame. One side clamps the work below the frame, and the other clamps the work above. The handle is removable, so the screw-jaws can be operated individually. The piling clamps available can edge-glue panels 6 feet in width, and of any thickness.

Illus. 126. Jorgensen's piling clamps are production, space-saving devices for edge-to-edge gluing. Essentially, they are two clamps within a single steel frame.

Wood bar-clamp fixtures (Illus. 127 and 128) are available in several designs. With a piece of lumber, they can be made to whatever lengths you require. Although these are good clamps, they cannot be adjusted as conveniently as metal bar clamps. Precautions must also be taken so that glue squeeze-out does not glue the workpieces directly to the wooden bar of the clamp.

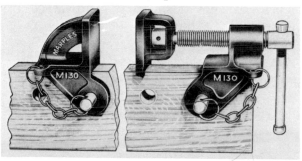

Illus. 127. Wood-bar clamp fixture.

Illus. 128. Another style of wood-bar clamp fixture.

Aluminum channel bar clamps (Illus. 129) are strong, yet lightweight. The manufacturer of these clamps claims that because of their aircraft alloy construction, these clamps are stronger than pipe clamps. They also have another advantage. Some glues react to the steel in steel clamps; this reaction causes dreadful stains on the work where the clamps touch the wood and glue squeeze-out. (See Illus. 110 on page 62.) Aluminum bar clamps do not stain the wood. Aluminum bar clamps are available from Shopsmith Inc., and Universal Clamp Company.

Illus. 129. Aircraft aluminum alloy bar clamps are light in weight; their manufacturer claims they are stronger than pipe clamps.

The Universal Clamp Company of Van Nuys, California, also manufactures what it refers to as "face frame clamps." (See Illus. 130.) This invention is a short clamp that replaces conventional long-bar clamps for gluing the cabinet-facing framework. Another fairly new clamp design is offered by Griset Industries of Santa Ana, California. This is a combination clamp and straightedge. (See Illus. 131.)

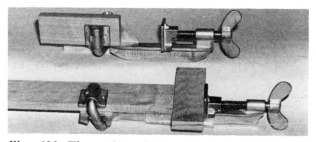

Illus. 130. These cabinet-facing clamps made by Universal have pieces of wood to demonstrate how they grip the work and do the jobs of conventional clamps of longer length.

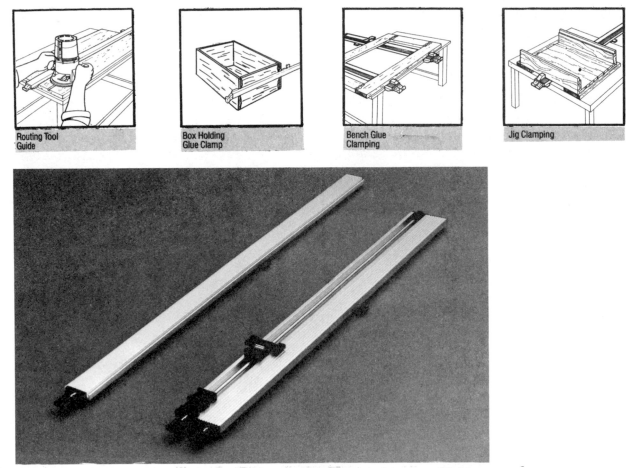

| Routing Tool Guide | Box Holding Glue Clamp | Bench Glue Clamping | Jig Clamping |

Illus. 131. Left : "Clamp'n Tool Guide" is a bar clamp inside a straightedge. Right: a "back-to-back bench clamp." This has bottom jaws that clamp to the bench while the top jaws hold the workpiece. Grip sizes range from 18 to 50 inches. Illustrations show jobs they can be used for.

Edge Fixtures Edge or cross-clamp fixtures for bar clamps are available. They apply pressure at right angles to the regular clamping pressure. They may be of the single-screw type, as shown in Illus. 132, or the double-screw type, shown in Illus. 133.

C-Clamps

C-clamps (referred to by English manufacturers as "G" cramps) are practical clamps for a good number of woodworking jobs. (See Illus. 134 and 135.) These clamps are all similar in design and operation. The essential differences come from the materials they are made of, how they are formed (cast- or drop-forged), and their size.

C-clamps are either drop-forged steel, cast iron, cast aluminum, or pressed steel. They vary in size from 3/4-inch to 12-inch opening capacities. They also vary in distance of throat depth, which may be as much as 6 inches or more.

One disadvantage in using C-clamps for a glue-up where several must be used is that one is forever threading out or threading in the screws. However, some new clamps in the typical "C" design have a quick-action thread.

One wonderful adaptation to the "C" design is the 3-way edging clamp. (See Illus. 136.) This clamp has 3 screws, which expand its versatility. It can be used as a conventional C-clamp.

70

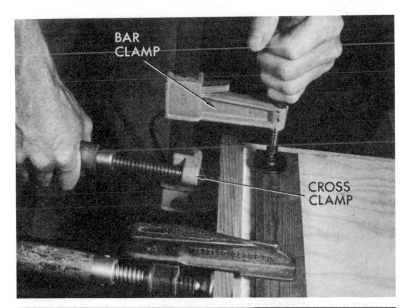

Illus. 132. A combination of a bar clamp and a single cross clamp fixture directs pressures in two directions.

Illus. 133. A double-screw cross clamp used with bar clamps to give pressure to the edge of a panel.

Illus. 134. C-clamps used for face-to-face gluing. Note the scrap pieces of wood under the "foot," and the swivel tips of the clamps to protect the work surfaces and to help distribute the pressure.

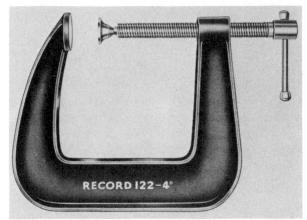

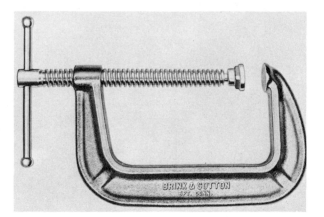

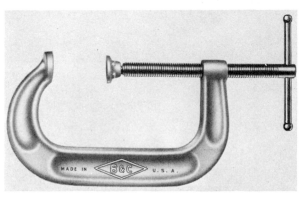

Illus. 135. (above, left and right, and right). Three standard C-clamps. They are available in various sizes and various distances of throat openings.

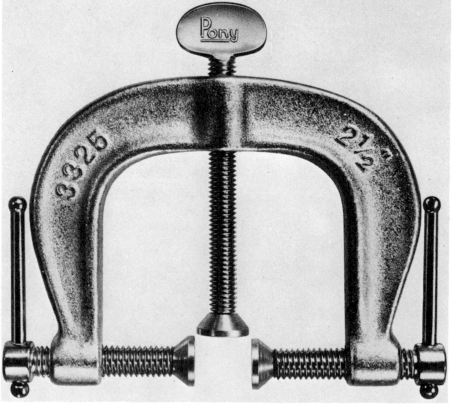

May Be Applied
To Clamp Around "Returns"

May Be Applied With Right
Angle Screw "Centered"

May Be Applied With Right
Angle Screw "Off Center"

May Be Used As A
Conventional "C" Clamp

Illus. 136. Three-way edging clamp and some of its applications.

Hand Screw Clamps

Hand screw clamps are very versatile clamps that can be used by woodworkers. (See Illus. 137.) They are made with jaws from 4 to 24 inches in length, with corresponding opening sizes from 2 to 17 inches. I would almost always select a wooden hand screw clamp over a C-clamp or deep-throat bar clamp for jobs where any of these clamps could be used. The maple-wood jaws do not mar the work surfaces as readily.

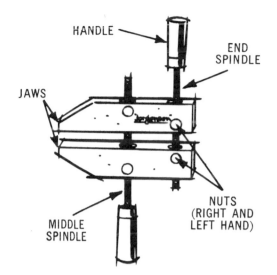

Illus. 138. Basic parts of the hand screw.

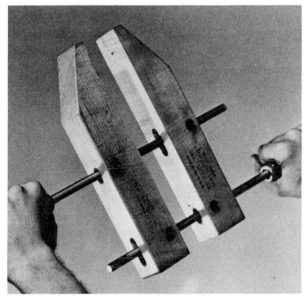

Illus. 137. Hand screw clamp.

Hand screws can be easily adjusted to clamp nonparallel surfaces with ease, and do not "crawl," as some other clamps do. Jaw-opening adjustments are quickly made by swinging or rotating the jaws end for end while holding the handles. (See Illus. 137.) To use, place the clamp to the work with the jaws gripping the work; apply initial pressure with the middle spindle. (See Illus. 138.) Firmly secure the end spindle so the jaws can be closed tightly against the work. Using the end spindle for the final "surge" of pressure creates a fulcrum-like action created by the middle spindle. (See Illus. 139 and 140.) The jaws can also be used in a nonparallel position for clamping odd-shaped objects, as shown in Illus. 141.

Illus. 139. Securing a hand screw clamp. Initial pressure is made by tightening the middle spindle (user's left hand), and then final pressure is obtained with the end spindle (user's right hand).

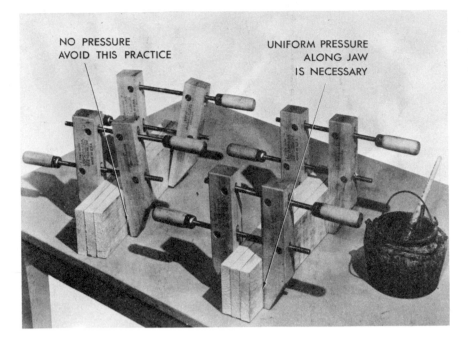

NO PRESSURE
AVOID THIS PRACTICE

UNIFORM PRESSURE
ALONG JAW
IS NECESSARY

Illus. 140. This shows the "rights and wrongs" of using hand screws in face-to-face gluing.

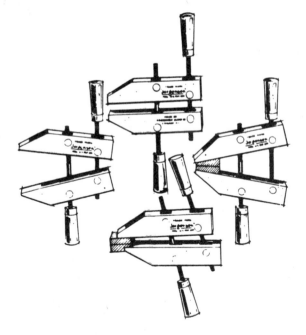

Illus. 141. Hand screws will hold parallel or angular shapes.

Make sure the jaws are kept clean and smooth. Glue drippings from squeeze-out that adhere to the jaws can leave nasty marks on work surfaces. One company manufactures hand screws with protective soft-metal shields that fit over the jaws. However, should you anticipate such problems, simply tape small patches of polyethylene film to the jaws, as shown in Illus. 142. This will assure that the surfaces of the jaws will always be clean and true. (See Illus. 143.)

If you want to make your own hand screw clamps, kits are available that provide all of the necessary parts except the jaws. (See Illus. 144.)

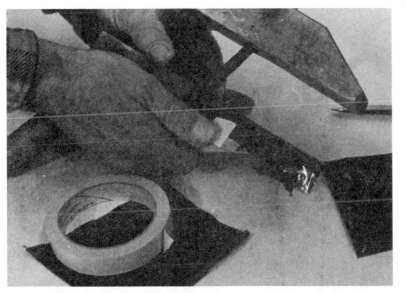

Illus. 142. Tape pieces of a plastic garbage bag to the jaws to protect them.

Illus. 143. If not protected, this messy gluing job would result with cured glue adhering to the jaw.

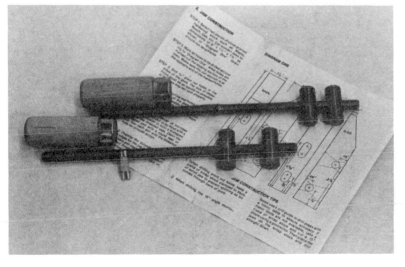
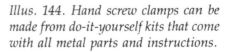

Illus. 144. Hand screw clamps can be made from do-it-yourself kits that come with all metal parts and instructions.

Cam Clamps

Cam clamps (Illus. 145) can be used for light clamping jobs. They are popular with wooden-instrument makers and other craftsmen who do light wood clamping. They do not have screws to turn to gain pressure. Instead, an unusual lever-design cam provides the pressure. (See Illus. 146.) Most cam clamps have cork linings covering the jaws to protect delicate or finished wood surfaces. (See Illus. 147.) Available sizes vary from 8- to 32-inch jaw openings that can be obtained in standard or deep-throat versions. Illus.148 shows how to clamp a workpiece to the bench so it can be used for routing or hand carving. Clamping the workpiece in this manner provides an unobstructed working surface and facilitates carving, routing, etc. (See Illus. 148.)

Mitre and Corner Clamps

Mitre and corner clamps are available in a wide selection. (See Illus. 149–154.) Some, such as those used in the assembly of picture frames, are intended only for clamping. Others also hold the workpieces during sawing; once the workpieces are cut, clamps can be used to hold the parts in assembly. (See pages 215 and 218 for some other homemade devices for clamping picture-frame assemblies.)

Hold-Down Clamps

Hold-down clamps are mounted to your workbench with bolts. (See Illus. 156–158.) These devices can be used in many ways to hold work, and are used on some gluing jobs too. Some can swivel. Hold-downs have many uses in jig and tool design. Use them for special work-holding jobs on drill presses, saws, for shaper work, etc.

Band Clamps

Band clamps are used to draw together assemblies of irregular shapes such as furniture frames, or components of columns. (See Illus. 159–162.) Band clamps consist of canvas or steel that encircle the work; the canvas or steel is drawn tight by means such as a screw or self-locking cam mechanism. The heavy-duty types (Illus. 160 and 161) have large screws and iron castings that can crank up pressures having 2,800 pounds of force. The steel-band version of the heavy-duty variety should be used only to clamp round shapes so the steel doesn't "kink." Hose clamps make a very small version of steel-band clamps. An inexpensive steel-band kit, available by mail order from Craft Supply Co., consists of 10 feet of stainless banding and extra pairs of housing screws so that you can make clamps for your own special-size requirements. (See Illus. 162.)

Illus. 145. Quick-action hardwood cam clamp has a fixed jaw (left); the jaw with the cam adjusts to the work thickness.

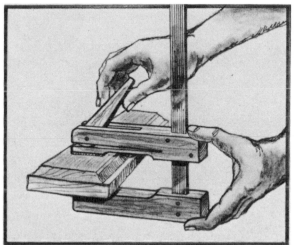

Illus. 146. Working the cam to apply pressure.

Illus. 147. Cork-lined jaws protect the surfaces of this soft pine frame.

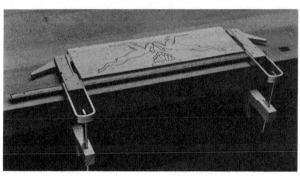

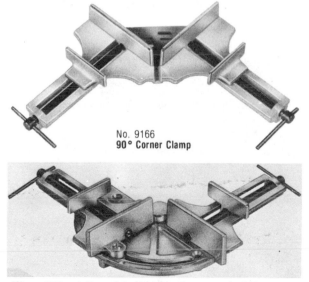

Illus. 148. Clamping a workpiece held in a clamp to the workbench as shown provides an unobstructed working surface.

Illus. 149. One of several picture frame clamps available from Shopsmith.

No. 9166
90° Corner Clamp

Illus. 150. Adjustable Clamp Company's 90° corner clamp (above) and their adjustable version (below).

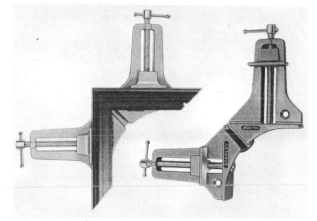

Illus. 151. Light-duty mitre corner clamps made by Stanley.

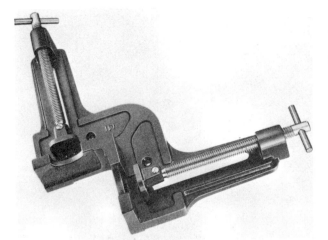

Illus. 152. Marple's corner "cramp."

Illus. 153. Stanley's heavy-duty mitre frame clamp is called a "mitre vise."

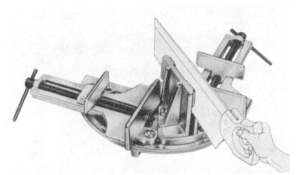

Illus. 154. The "adjustable" mitre box and corner clamp manufactured by the Adjustable Clamp Co.

Illus. 155. A 5-piece clamp kit offered by Shopsmith will clamp butt and mitre joints, as shown.

Illus. 156. Some "hold-fast" clamping devices from Lee Valley Tools.

Illus. 157. A lever-type hold-down clamp.

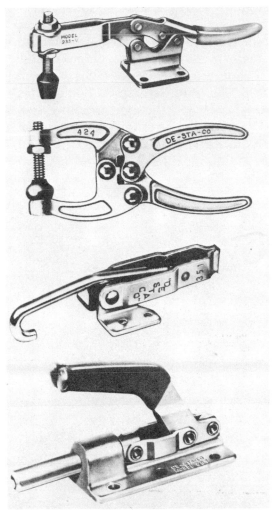

Illus. 158. A variety of other work-holding devices that are used to do special gluing jobs and jig and fixture work of all kinds.

Illus. 159. Light-duty band clamp consists of a 1-inch nylon band with a self-locking cam that's tightened with a screwdriver.

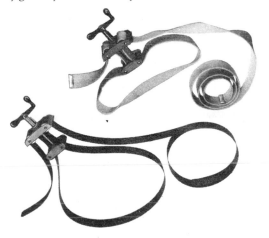

Illus. 160. Above: canvas-band clamp. Below: the steel band clamp, which should only be used for perfectly round objects.

Illus. 161. The heavy-duty canvas-band clamp in use.

Illus. 162. The "Flexiband" Kit from Craft Supplies of Provo, Utah, pulls together segmented and coopered work.

Stretchable Banding

Stretchable banding materials have many applications in wood gluing and clamping techniques. Small assemblies can often be clamped with standard rubber bands, as shown in Illus. 163. Larger, "heavier" clamping jobs can be handled with continuous strips 1 to 1½ inches in width that have been scissor-cut from auto or truck inner tire tubes. (Pages 198 and 203 show how to apply these inner-tube bandings. This technique can be applied to many unusual clamping and repair jobs.)

Illus. 163. Standard rubber bands are perfect for many small jobs.

If you're able to obtain surgical tubing, you'll find it is great for many jobs where high pressure is required. (See Illus. 164.)

Surgical tubing is available in various diameters, with several choices in wall thickness. With a stretch and wrap effect, it builds up surprisingly great pressure. (Incidentally, electrical tape also can be used for "stretch and wrap" clamping pressure. I keep this tape, along with masking tape and fibreglass filament, on hand. Use it for those jobs that do not require the amount of pressure that is given by inner-tube bands or surgical tubing.)

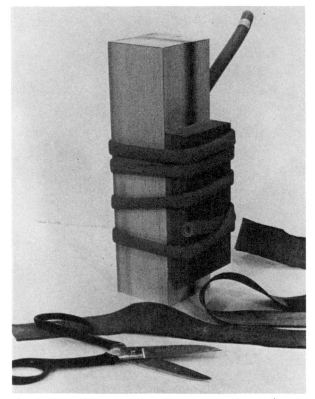

Illus. 164. Neoprene surgical tubing is very elastic, is available in various sizes, and provides excellent pressure when stretch-wrapped. Below are large rubber band strips cut from an automotive inner tube; these are equally effective.

Multipurpose Clamping System

Multipurpose clamping systems, such as the Maxi-Clamp® system sold by Shopsmith, are incredibly versatile and can be used for many clamping jobs. Such systems consist of a series of many individual components that are assembled Tinkertoy (building block) fashion to use for whatever clamping job they are needed for. The components of a "system" consist of threaded rods, a number of interchangeable jaws that will push, pull, or pry in any or all of the three directions, and holding blocks. The Maxi-Clamp® system is, in fact, so sophisticated it comes with a 16-page instruction manual. The system has over 70 components that can be arranged in a multitude of ways to create the setup that satisfies the most general or particular need. Illus. 166–171 show just a few of the many jobs handled by multipurpose clamping systems. (Pages 214 and 220 give some plans and illustrations for a homemade multipurpose clamping system.)

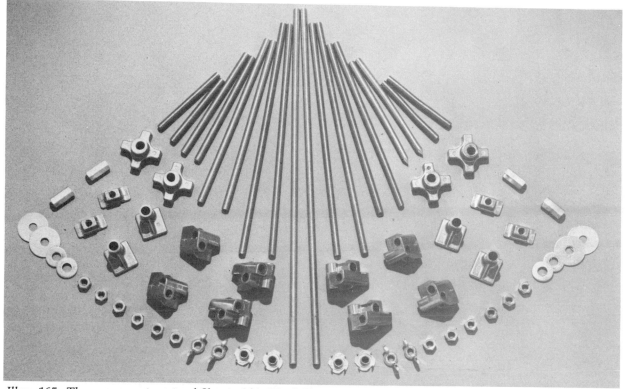

Illus. 165. The component parts of Shopsmith's Maxi-Clamp System.

Illus. 166. Typical frame clamping with the Shopsmith Maxi-Clamp.

Illus. 167. Clamping a center-lap joint with the Maxi-Clamp components.

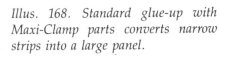

Illus. 168. Standard glue-up with Maxi-Clamp parts converts narrow strips into a large panel.

Illus. 169. Special jigs and fixturing become commonplace when the standard components from the Maxi-Clamp system are used as shown here.

Illus. 170. Shopsmith's multipurpose clamping system is put to good use even when making the most sophisticated projects, such as this challenging grandfather clock.

Illus. 171. You can use the Maxi-Clamp components with other self-made parts to invent your own clamping system for special jobs like this mini-press.

Presses

Presses are extremely useful for the serious amateur and professional woodworker. Presses simplify and facilitate many panel-clamping jobs, such as those involved in veneering and laminating. You can make your own veneer press (Illus. 172) using press screws (Illus. 173) manufactured by the Adjustable Clamp Co. of Chicago. (Page 216 shows you how.)

A larger factory-made press is shown in

Illus. 174. This press has two heavy, screw-adjustable platens, and a very large work capacity. Also shown in Illus. 174 is a removable filler box. A few singular or multiple panel lay-ups can be done on top of the filler box.

Presses can also be made for various wood-laminating jobs. Homemade presses are easily made for those projects that involve gluing thin, parallel grain laminations together over a curved form.

Illus. 172. A little veneer press such as this is easy to make. (See page 216 for details.)

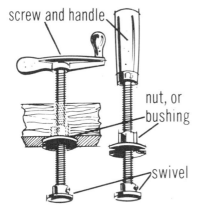

screw and handle

nut, or bushing

swivel

Illus. 173. Typical press screws for making presses or jigs and fixtures.

Illus. 174. A laminating press has a 2 × 4 foot capacity.

The Fire-Hose Laminating Press

This is used to laminate smaller members with curved shapes. (See Illus. 175.) Regular fire hoses are plugged at the ends and inflated with air. (See Illus. 176–178.) With this system, pressure can be distributed evenly over the entire surface area of the joint. (More information on curved wood laminating, presses, and form construction is discussed in Chapter 12.) The pneumatic fire hoses can be used to make veneering or flat-panel presses, as shown in Illus. 178.

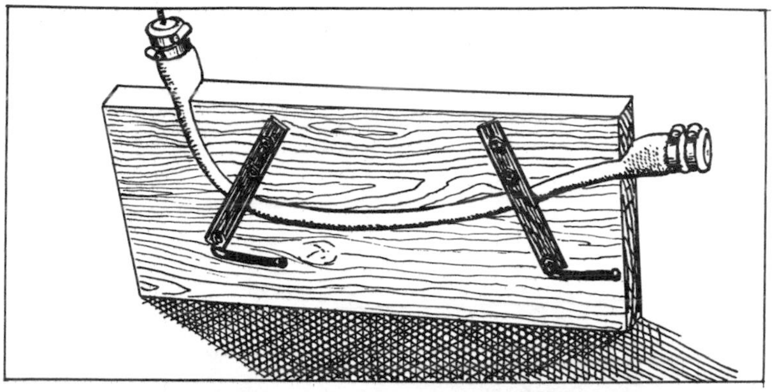

Illus. 175. A fire-hose press for glue-laminating a curved bow limb.

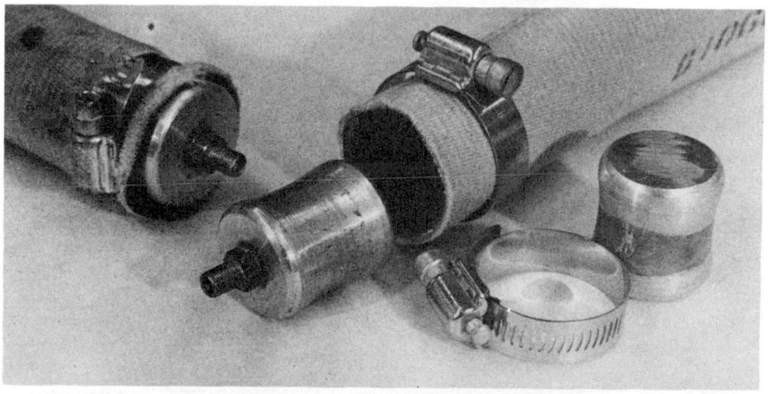

Illus. 176. The components of a fire-hose set-up used for laminating work are comprised of turned, solid hose plugs (one with an air valve) and hose clamps.

Illus. 177. Standard air valves with ⅜-inch standard pipe thread are available from auto-parts and hardware stores. They may also be sold as "snifter" valves.

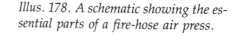

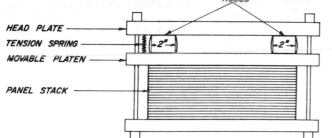

HOSES

HEAD PLATE

TENSION SPRING

MOVABLE PLATEN

PANEL STACK

2"   2"

Illus. 178. A schematic showing the essential parts of a fire-hose air press.

Miscellaneous Tools and Accessories

Now that we've had a thorough look at clamps, let's look at some accessories that are not only practical, but interesting.

Spring Clamps

Spring clamps (Illus. 179) are like spring-loaded clothespins. They are useful for a variety of jobs that require pressure about as great as hand pressure. The spring clamp shown in Illus. 179 has vinyl handles and tips that prevent it from marring the work.

Bench-Top Clamping Vise

A bench-top clamping vise consists of some unusual clamping cams secured directly to a bench top. (See Illus. 180.) This system, offered by Shopsmith, is best set up by drilling a series of 3/8-inch holes, 2 inches on center in a grid pattern.

Clamp Hangers

These simple, heavy-gauge steel brackets screwed to a wall make storage of almost all clamps easy (See Illus. 181 and 182.)

Illus. 179. Spring clamp.

Illus. 180. Bench-top clamping cams from Shopsmith can convert a workbench into a "clamping bed" when holes are bored in a grid-like pattern.

Illus. 181. Hang-up brackets for wall clamp storage are available from the Adjustable Clamp Co.

184.) The bar-clamp cradle pieces are made of ¼-inch tempered hardboard, with "notches" cut to fit your clamps. These in turn are set into grooves cut into bases of straight 2 × 4's or similar stock.

Illus. 183. A clamp rack-table supports bar clamps for edge-to-edge gluing jobs. The shelf below, covered with polyethylene, catches glue drippings.

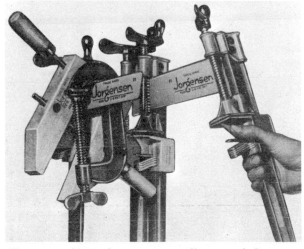

Illus. 182. Clamp hangers store all types of clamps.

Clamp Table

A clamp table is a very convenient thing if you can afford the space. (See Illus. 183.) These can be self-made to any size desired. Notice that they have cradles, which keep the clamps upright and level with each other. A plastic-covered shelf catches glue drippings so they don't hit the floor. Workbench clamp cradles (supports) can be made. (See Illus.

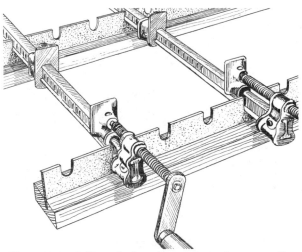

Illus. 184. Self-made bench-top bar clamp cradles make edge gluing jobs a lot easier.

Clamp Pads

Clamp pads are commercially available. They provide a protective cushion between the work and the clamp jaws. (See Illus. 185.)

Illus. 185. Slip-on pad cushions pressure and protect the wood.

Glue Injectors

Glue injectors get glue into those hard-to-reach areas. Injectors are available in various sizes and of plastic or aluminum construction. They are best used with water soluble glues; however, other solvent-based glues can also be used. The better injectors come with protective tips that prevent the contents from drying out. (See Illus. 186 and 187.)

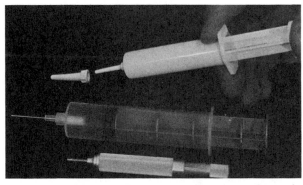

Illus. 186. Glue injectors come in various styles and sizes.

Illus. 187. Glue injectors are ideal for hard-to-reach areas.

Pinch Dogs

Pinch dogs are used to align joints and to put some pressure on joints for edge-to-edge gluing jobs. (See Illus. 188.) Once the joints are aligned, clamps can be applied as usual if so desired. Pinch dogs are especially useful when gluing up large panels in which some of the boards may be bowed. These useful devices are available by mail order from several wood-craft mail-order suppliers. Alternative pinch dogs that can pretty much do the same thing are ordinary fence-post staples and corrugated fasteners. (See Illus. 189 and 190.)

Illus. 188. Pinch dogs are used to align edges and to bring some pressure to the joint.

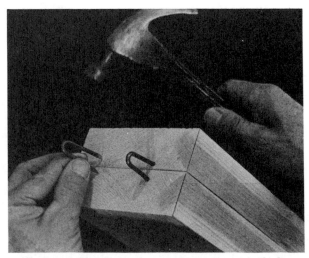

Illus. 189. Fence staples can be used as pinch dogs.

Illus. 190. Regular corrugated fasteners, when driven part-way into the ends, align glue-ups just like pinch dogs; remove them with pliers after glue sets.

Other innovative ideas and some noteworthy gluing and clamping tips are shown in Illus. 191–197. Most of these ideas are reprinted from the manual on using Aerolite glues supplied by Ciba-Geigy (UK) Ltd., of England. Note how they incorporate the use of threaded rods, various weights and wedges, twisted cord, strings, etc.

More gluing and clamping techniques are depicted in other chapters, particularly in Chapter 12. Clamping devices are also illustrated in Chapter 11, Veneering. Plans for some homemade clamping tools and systems are shown on pages 214–219.

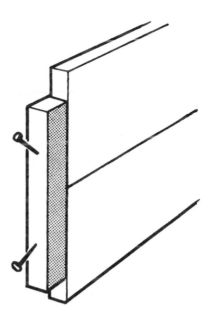

Illus. 192. A piece of wood with two nails slant-driven will work for some jobs.

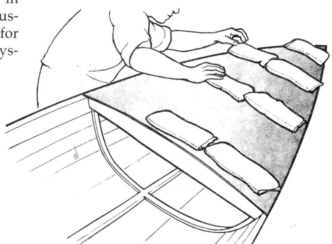

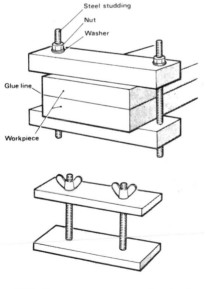

Illus. 191. Screw pressure customized for the job at hand using continuously threaded rod with nuts and washers.

Illus. 193. Using weights for pressure.

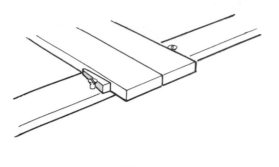

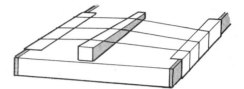

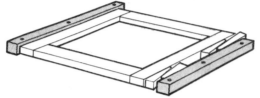

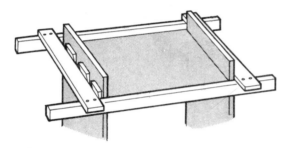

Illus. 195. Strings to hold and pressure edging strips.

Illus. 194. Some methods of wedging for clamping pressure.

Illus. 196. Jig-sawn or band-sawn C's and wedges for clamping technique.

Illus. 197. Twisting cord loops create clamping pressure and are effective in chair repair.

Electronic Gluing Equipment

Electronic gluing equipment is used in industry to reduce curing time of glued-up components. (See Illus. 198–200.) Heat is generated within the glue line without appreciable heating of the surrounding area. This equipment can be very sophisticated, and is best suited for industrial work.

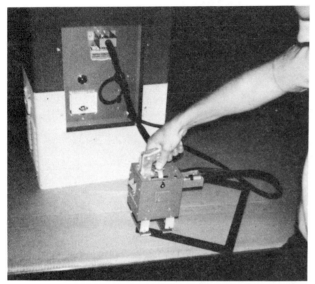

Illus. 198. The Workrite Electronic wood welder cures picture-frame joints in 3 to 5 seconds using the standard hand gun and flat electrodes.

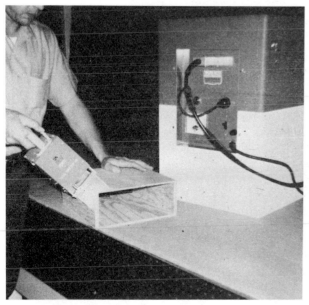

Illus. 199. Outside mitre electrodes are used for square or mitre corners.

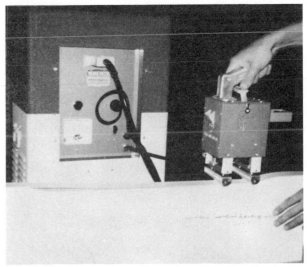

Illus. 200. Roller electrodes are used to bond panelling, banding, and self edges of plastic laminate work.

However, one company, Workrite Products Co., of Burbank, California, manufactures the "Electronic Wood Welder," which is useful for cabinet shops and professional custom woodworkers. This equipment consists of a high-frequency (millions of cycles per second) electric generator and an electronic hand gun. Interchangeable electrodes in various styles (shapes) attach to the hand gun. Workrite offers two models, with the least expensive being approximately $2,000. According to the manufacturer's instruction manual: "The units work on the theory of dielectric heating, which is based on the fact that disturbed molecules create heat. The disturbance is created by a very high-frequency cycle change, which moves the molecules of glue at such a tempo that the friction creates heat, and the glue bond is completed."

Workrite Products Co. also claims that resorcinol and phenol-formaldehyde resins are easily cured with dielectric heating, as are urea resins. Bonds in wet or dry woods can be completed in a matter of seconds. Workrite's largest units will handle wood up to 2 inches thick; their smaller units will handle wood up to 1½ inches thick. Electrodes vary in shapes; shapes range from rollers to a variety of electrodes for inside and outside corner joints and mitres.

Glue Spreaders

Glue spreaders provide a quick and consistently accurate glue application. (See Illus. 201 and 202.) These tools reduce glue waste and handle most of the standard adhesives. They are also great time-savers for small-production requirements. The hand spreader shown in Illus. 201 comes in either 3- or 6-inch roller widths, and various types of interchangeable rollers of foam, rubber and carpet (for contact cements) are available from the manufacturer, The Adwood Corp. of High Point, North Carolina.

The motor-driven tabletop version shown in Illus. 202 has a grooved aluminum roller that is 5 inches in diameter and 10 inches long; it rotates at 67.5 rpm. The manufacturer is Rosenquist, Inc., of North Wilkesboro, North Carolina.

Illus. 201. Hand glue spreader has flow-control lever for correct adhesive spread. It's ideal for PVA and contacts. Storage container (center) eliminates daily cleanup.

Illus. 202. Motor-driven table top spreader.

Chapter 5
Safety

The containers of many modern adhesives mention the following words of caution: toxicity, sensitizers, irritants, dermatitis, infections, flammable, etc. Pay attention to these words of warning and be careful with adhesives of all kinds. Remember, however, that there is no reason to be afraid of modern glues if you know what they can do, understand that these side effects can be dangerous, and take steps to prevent any mishap from occurring.

It is a good idea to familiarize yourself with the adhesive or gluing product before using it. Know the possible hazards before opening or mixing the glue; also be aware of the possible effects of working the cured glue (sanding and so on). Read all instructions and data sheets provided by the manufacturer very carefully. (See Illus. 203.) There are different "do's" and "don'ts" for different gluing systems.

Proper ventilation is extremely important in small, confined, home workshops. Also, approved masks or respirators must be used in the presence of hazardous vapors. Powdered resins, hardeners, solvents, special additives such as formaldehyde, and sanding dust from working resins can cause skin rashes, dizziness, unconsciousness, poisoning, eye damage, sickness, fires, or explosions.

Obviously, smoking in solvent- or vapor-filled rooms or work areas that are poorly ventilated is very dangerous. Also, remember that chemicals are dangerous to your eyes when you are working either with the chemicals themselves or their vapor. Wear goggles or safety glasses with side shields at the appropriate times, and be certain that contact lenses are not worn when working around chemicals. Don't expose yourself to the possibility of any dusts or sprays getting into your eyes. When gluing, use disposable gloves (Illus. 204), stirrers, bench covers, and mixing containers. You can dispose of these materials, which will ensure cleanliness and safety. Also, wear barrier-forming skin creams to protect the skin.

When some people are slightly exposed to chemicals, they have the following reactions:

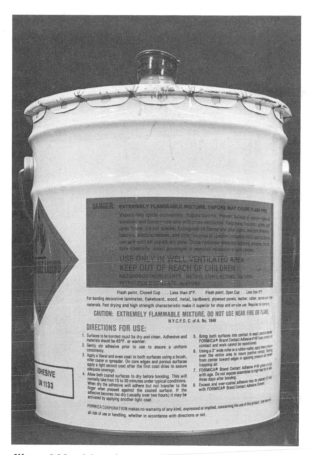

Illus. 203. Manufacturers' labels and instructions warn users of dangerous ingredients and unsafe practices regarding their products.

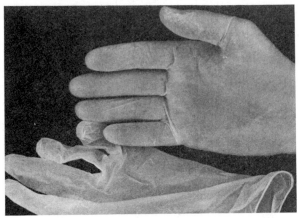

Illus. 204. Disposable gloves and barrier skin creams help to protect skin against harmful reactions.

rashes much like poison ivy, swelling of the eyes, nose, throat, and limbs, and nausea. Other people, with the same exposure, might not experience any reaction. (Some authorities claim that certain types of people with fair skin are more susceptible to irritants from certain resin adhesives.) This, however, does not mean that they should ignore the safety measures. Those who take appropriate safety measures and still experience such reactions should discontinue the use of that particular adhesive.

Do not use solvents for removing adhesives from the skin, as they themselves are skin sensitizers. Solvents dissolve and remove natural protective skin oils and contribute to the intensity of skin irritation. Therefore, using any solvent in direct contact with the skin should only come *as the last possible resort* for removing adhesive components from the skin. Soap and water are the best flushing and cleansing agents short of qualified medical attention.

Glue Hazards

The danger of using formaldehyde has been publicized lately. Formaldehyde is a widely used powdered component of several glues. It is more dangerous in its fresh powdered state than as the dust that results when cured formaldehyde is sanded. The fresh powder is worse because it is "free" formaldehyde; that is, it has not yet chemically reacted with water. Sanding dust in general is often more dangerous as simple dust particles than as expelled fumes or vapors.

Some adhesives like liquid animal glue, white glue, and yellow glues are relatively safe for everyone and can even be used on toys and woodenwares. Some companies exploit their nontoxic qualities and market such glues as toy or toymaker's glues.

Epoxies are only dangerous when in their uncured states. Most cured epoxies are nothing more than plastics, and are usually safe for use on projects such as cutting boards, salad bowls, etc.

A word of warning is again in order when using the "super" or "krazy" glues; they do have a reputation for gluing human skin together (i.e., fingers). If this occurs, the proper corrective measures as prescribed by the manufacturer should be put into effect.

Finally, remember that some water-based glues or cements, even though nonflammable, may still give off toxic gases or fumes. Pay attention to the manufacturer's safety measures (such as the proper ventilation), regardless of the purity of the adhesive ingredients.

Incidentally, it should be stressed that manufacturers do everything within their power to minimize the dangerous elements of their products. They provide appropriate safety warnings and are always trying to improve their products. For example, cements for models now contain ingredients that "discourage" the customer from sniffing and inhaling the product.

Chapter 6
Gluing Edge to Edge

Sooner or later every wood craftsman needs to make wide boards or panels by gluing two or more narrower pieces together at their edges. (See Illus. 205.) Edge-gluing success hinges on some very important procedures and considerations that are essential to accomplish this seemingly simple task. For example, if the job at hand is to glue up some solid hardwood boards to make a beautiful tabletop (Illus. 206) that process is obviously more involved and complex than "sticking" some 1×4's together for a closet shelf.

Edge-gluing is done for several reasons: 1) to make wider panels or boards than are otherwise available, 2) to remove defects such as knots, splits, checks, and warpage by ripping and regluing; 3) to help stabilize a panel or board by ripping to relieve stresses and, thus, minimize future warpage; 4) to decorate by gluing together boards of different species or color into various patterns and designs, such as in a checkerboard or pinstripe water ski; 5) to conserve and utilize waste material by gluing narrow strips and scraps into wider, useful boards; and 6) to form some shapes as in strip-canoe building. The following step-by-step procedures will show you how to edge-glue successfully.

Illus. 206. This table top of plain-sawed walnut stays flat throughout all seasons because it consists of a number of narrower edge-glued boards. Note how the pieces were selected and matched for uniformity of color and figure.

Selecting and Preparing the Material

If you have a power jointer and a surfacer or thickness planing machine, the procedures are somewhat different than if you have to prepare the material by hand. If the necessary equipment is available, it's best to start with your stock totally in the rough, that is, in the largest possible nominal thickness and width dimensions. (See Illus. 207.) If the stock is cupped (warped), it is best to rip it before doing anything else. If you are selecting or buying stock that has already been surfaced, insist on flat, cup-free material.

Illus. 205. Individual boards are ready to be glued together at their edges to make a wide panel.

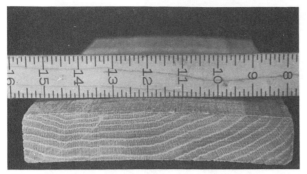

Illus. 207. Plain-sawed oak 1 × 7 inches that's "cupped."

Illus. 208. The same piece ripped, with trued surfaces and the pieces positioned for gluing (with one piece upside down). Observe the direction of the end-grain growth rings (indicators of the pith and bark sides of the boards).

Rip boards into narrower widths if they have any cup at all, whether they are in the rough (Illus. 207) or already surfaced (Illus. 208). Also, rip wide boards (greater than 6 inches) that are flat, especially those that have been plain-sawed, as they tend to cup with any change in humidity. By ripping and regluing, much of the internal stresses will be relieved and future warping tendencies will be dramatically reduced.

Most craftsmen observe the generally accepted rule: "Do not use a board with a width more than 8 times its thickness without ripping it to minimize cupping." I like to rip boards (1- and 2-inch stock alike) that are wider than 6 inches. The best approach is that whenever in doubt, rip it down and reglue it. In two similar panels of equal width,

the one with more edge-to-edge glue joints is likely to stay flatter.

Sawing Pieces to Rough Size

Usually it's best to saw your pieces an inch or so longer than the desired finished dimension, then either rip them to remove defects or divide up the wider boards as necessary. A glued-up panel can be made of boards that are of random widths, unless you want to use their uniformity in width to achieve a special effect.

To true up the surfaces of your boards (Illus. 208), begin by face jointing on a jointer (Illus. 209) or with a hand plane. Make the surface flat and true, then work the stock on the opposite face until a uniform thickness is achieved. This is done by hand or with a thickness planer. Leave your stock as thick as possible. Final thickness is best obtained after all the pieces have been glued together.

Next, true the edges; make them straight and perfectly square to the faces of the board. (See Illus. 210.) If you're using stock that was purchased surfaced or if you planed it yourself, getting the edges true and square is a very critical step. Carefully use a long hand plane (Illus. 211) or a jointer (Illus. 212). If using a jointer, be sure the fence is set square and that the faces of the boards are kept tightly against the fence throughout the cut. Always check your work with the square, as shown in Illus. 210.

Illus. 209. Truing the best face on the jointer or with a hand plane is the first step. (Guard removed for photo clarity.)

Illus. 210. Board edges must be worked straight and perfectly square to the board faces. This is done after the board is made flat, true, and uniformly thick throughout.

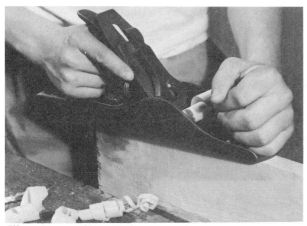

Illus. 211. A sharp hand plane skillfully used makes a good gluing edge.

Illus. 212. Edge preparation is easily and accurately accomplished on the jointer. (Guard removed for photo clarity.)

Arranging the Panel

Now take the time to study and analyze the pieces for their best qualities. Lay them in the most desirable order so grain direction and color-grain pattern meet your satisfaction. If it's to be a tabletop, then all the best faces should be placed up. Run a tape across all pieces to make sure there is sufficient stock to satisfy the total width-dimension requirement of the final panel. It's a good idea to have an inch extra in width for softwood panels, and about ½ inch or so extra width for hardwood glue-ups.

Clamping pressure may crush and damage the outer edges unless other protective measures are taken. Place narrower pieces nearer the middle of the panel when possible. If they are placed at the outer edges, the clamping pressure will not be as uniform along the joint. There will be more pressure at the jaws than along the other areas of the joint.

Once you have shifted the pieces around and have gotten the panel to look the way you want it to, face mark it. Face marking is simply drawing a large triangle over the entire panel arrangement. (See Illus. 213.) This step will guarantee that the planned placement order or arrangement of the pieces within the panel will not get mixed up. (See Illus. 214.) If there is to be a top or bottom edge of the glued-up panel, draw the triangle on the work so the base of the triangle identifies the lower edge, and the point is the top edge.

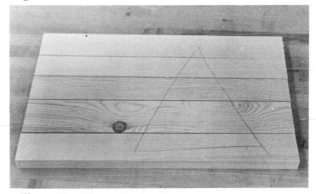

Illus. 213. A large triangle (face mark) drawn over the surface records the arrangement of the individual pieces.

97

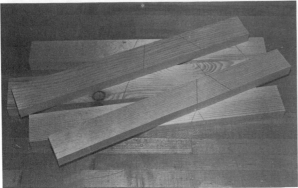

Illus. 214. Mixed pieces. Simple rearrangement (so the triangle is complete) returns them to their original order.

Now is the time to visually check the assembly. This can be done in a couple of ways. You can "eyeball" along the length of each piece and look for distorted pieces. Another method is to stack the boards edge upon edge vertically. (See Illus. 215.) This allows you to eyeball down across the width of the unglued panel as the panel is supported by finger pressure or just gravity.

Illus. 215. Visually check narrower panels. Stacked, unglued pieces should be "eyeballed" to detect problems before gluing.

Dowels and Splines

While visually checking the assembly, you may notice that the panel is exceptionally long or that some pieces are warped and distorted along their length. In such cases, the actual gluing process could prove to be very difficult. Dowels, splines, and other joint forms can be used in these cases to hold the

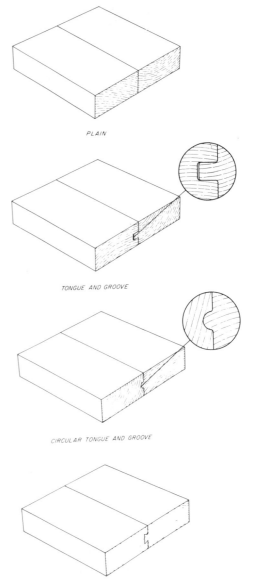

PLAIN

TONGUE AND GROOVE

CIRCULAR TONGUE AND GROOVE

DOVETAIL

Illus. 216. Various types of edge-to-edge glue joints. When properly done, the plain-butt edge joint above is sufficiently strong and easiest for the craftsman to accomplish.

assembly together more easily. They are used to guide the pieces together at the time of clamping so all the surfaces are flush. It is my opinion that these joints of dowels or splines do not appreciably add strength to the joint, and should only be used where necessary and only if you have difficulty in bringing all the faces flat and flush to each other in the clamps. Also, if you prepare the stock properly and get a clean, tight, plain butt joint with a strong, thin, glue line, the joint should be stronger than the surrounding wood anyway.

A tongue-and-groove joint is considered stronger than other joints because there is more gluing surface on the joint. This is true, but it is extremely difficult to get the correct fit and pressure over all the 10 surfaces that comprise the tongue-and-groove joint. (See Illus. 216.) Should dowels or splines be necessary for your job, see Chapter 9 for more information.

The Dry Run

It is important to make a dry run of the assembly before the actual glue-up. The dry run is a complete "dress rehearsal" of the clamping process, but it's done without glue. (See Illus. 217–219.) It should be done for all types of assemblies, not just when edge-gluing.

Illus. 218. A quick look should spot problem-producing gaps.

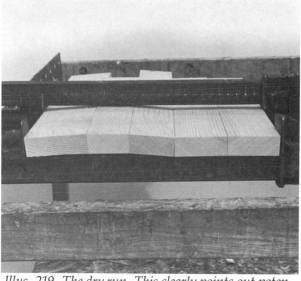

Illus. 219. The dry run. This clearly points out potential problems. Here you can see (as in Illus. 215) some edges that were not worked square.

Illus. 217. Top view of pieces arranged in order on the clamps, ready for a "dry run."

When making a dry run, make sure the clamps are in line and are parallel to each other. Illus. 220 shows how misaligned clamps can cause a twisted panel.

Illus. 221 shows some of the procedures to follow in the dry run when edge-gluing. By following these procedures, you will have the opportunity to correct any problems you may find.

Illus. 220. Clamps must be supported level and parallel to each other to ensure that a twist (as shown) is not unintentionally built into the panel.

CLAMPS ABOVE & BELOW
PREVENT BUCKLING

ALTERNATE
END GRAIN

TRIANGULAR MARK
ASSURES CORRECT
ARRANGEMENT OF
PIECES

Illus. 221. A completed dry run.

The Glue-up

Have everything you need on hand. If you use the liquid white or liquid yellow glues, you will have to move more quickly because these glues set rather quickly. If working with a very large panel or a complicated one with dowels or splines to insert, consider using urea or liquid animal glue. Space the underside clamps in their appropriate places and place the boards in order and on edge on the clamps, as shown in Illus. 222. Spread the glue by laying on a uniform bead, as shown in Illus. 223. Make sure the glue completely covers the edges of each board as uniformly as possible. Use your fingers (Illus. 224) or a stick to get a smooth uniform spread. When the right amount is spread,

the glue will appear glossy. Dullness indicates glue penetration into the wood and a need for more glue.

With most glues, the glue need only be applied to one edge of each board. Turn the boards so they lay flat onto the clamps, and hand-press them closely to each other as you go along. This allows the glue-applied edge to adequately "wet"-out the nonspread, adjacent edge before clamping pressure is applied.

If you don't want to damage the edges under the clamp jaws, place a couple of scraps between the jaws and the panel. These should also have square edges. (See Illus. 225 and 226.)

Illus. 222. Pieces arranged in order with one edge up ready to receive glue.

Illus. 223. Run a uniform-size bead of glue onto all of the up edges.

Illus. 224. Spread the glue uniformly, completely covering the one edge of each board. Here the fingers are used to quickly even out a spread of liquid yellow glue.

Illus. 225. A good glue-up. Note: 1, the wood scrap under the clamp jaws to protect the panel's edges; 2, the clamp arrangement is alternating top and bottom; and 3, the amount of squeeze-out is just right.

Illus. 226. Gluing narrow strips into a panel takes a slightly different approach. The wide boards (cauls) between the clamps jaws and the strips shown here are not part of the glued panel. They serve as cauls to distribute the pressure.

Applying Pressure

Pipe or medium-duty clamps should be spaced about 8 to 10 inches apart. If in doubt, use more rather than fewer clamps. Heavy-duty I-bar clamps can be spaced further apart; always space them proportionately closer to each other when gluing thicker stock. I like to snug-up (fit the pieces together without applying pressure) the top-center clamp first and gradually work each way towards the end of the panel, keeping the upper faces aligned as close as possible as I go from clamp to clamp. Don't be afraid to put some muscle into the pressure, but not too quickly after spreading.

Illus. 227. Using a putty knife to take up the partially cured glue.

Dealing with Squeeze-Out

Dealing with the squeeze-out is a subject of much debate among woodworkers. A commonsense approach should be taken based on the kind of wood and what happens to the panel later. If the panel is of porous or absorbent wood and is now fairly close to the final thickness, be extremely careful not to force glue from the squeeze-out into the face of the wood. It is usually best to allow the glue to set to a point where it isn't too runny, and carefully lift and "sweep" the excess off with a putty knife, as shown in Illus. 227. It is okay to allow the glue to completely cure. In such a case, the best approach would be to use a sandable glue (urea or liquid hide). A power sander will clean the panel up nicely. However, if the panel is glued with the liquid white or yellow glues, a paint scraper can do the job on cured glue, but use it carefully so as not to pull slivers of raw wood up with the globs of cured glue. (See Illus. 228.)

Illus. 228. Carefully using a paint scraper removes cured glue.

If the panel is still too thick, and will be cut down to finished size on a thickness planer, wipe up the squeeze-out with a damp (not wet) rag as quickly as possible. (See Illus. 229.) If the panel is to be painted rather than stained or finished, use the damp-rag cleanup. Whenever possible, let the glued panel sit in the clamps overnight. (See Illus. 230.)

Illus. 229. A damp-rag cleanup can be done if the panel will later be reduced in thickness.

Illus. 230. Sometimes it is necessary to clamp straight-edges to the panel to ensure that all surfaces will be aligned. Remove before the glue sets.

Edge gluing is a lot of work, but it's certainly worth the effort to do it correctly. Avoid wide glue lines, as shown in Illus. 231. Warped wide boards that have been previously surfaced to their thicknesses are simply impossible to work into flat panels suitable for tabletops and good-quality furniture. Illus. 231–233 are vivid examples of shoddy preparation and poor workmanship. Illus. 234 shows large sign panels approximately 8 feet × 11 inches in size glued with pipe clamps in our shop. Pipe clamps provided the pressure.

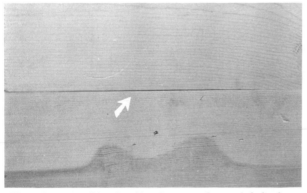

Illus. 231. A wide glue line is not only unsightly, but terribly weak. Wide glue lines can occur when wide twisted boards are glued, as shown in Illus. 232.

Illus. 232. Two 1 × 12's were cupped and twisted before gluing, resulting in a warped and twisted panel.

103

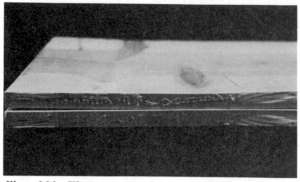

Illus. 233. The same panel stressed at the glue line reveals very low wood failure—a very weak joint.

Illus. 234. Large sign panels, 8 × 11 feet, are edge-glued. They have 2-foot dowel spacing to aid in assembly alignment. Urea resin was used with pipe clamps.

Special Edge-Gluing Applications

Gluing Panels with Rough Faces

In our business, large panels with rough faces are often required for both wood signs and our line of "Country-Rustic" furniture. Two types of panels we do are shown in Illus. 235 and 236.

The problems associated with glue squeeze-out are more easily handled in the type of panel with "V" grooves at the joint. Panels of this type are made by gluing together boards that have been previously chamfered at their face edges. (See Illus. 237

and 238.) In panels of nonchamfered pieces, the cleanup of squeeze-out is done the same way—using a putty knife, followed by scrubbing with a damp rag. Panels are left clamped overnight. We have almost no failures and minimal warpage even though all pieces are glued with their bark sides up, as shown in Illus. 239. For more information about our construction techniques using rough-sawn softwoods, see my book *Making Country-Rustic Furniture* (Sterling Publishing Co., Inc., 1985).

Illus. 235. A panel comprised of edge-glued rough-sawn boards. The rough surfaces were lightly touch-sanded before and after gluing.

Illus. 236. A panel similar to that shown in Illus. 235, but here the joints are accentuated with a "V," resulting from gluing together boards with previously chamfered face edges.

Illus. 237. Controlling the amount of squeeze-out makes putty knife cleanup in the smooth "V" fairly easy.

Illus. 238. Final cleanup is achieved with a damp rag.

Illus. 239. A close look at the end grain shows that adjoining pieces have the bark side up.

Panels with Curved Glue Joints

Panels with curved glue joints are for some projects more interesting than panels made of boards with parallel edges. (See Illus. 240 and 241.) However, there is also more waste. The panels are made by making one saw cut per joint, as shown in Illus. 242. The pieces are stacked together one on top of another, and held in place for sawing with double-face tape or a couple of spots of hot-melt glue. For the best results, the curves must be gradual; epoxy or other good gap-filling glues with minimal pressure must be used. Conventional glues are not recommended because of the poor-quality gluing surfaces produced by the band saw cut.

Another problem encountered when making panels with curved glue lines is clamping. The pieces will slide laterally unless a jig is prepared to limit this movement as clamping pressure is applied.

Gluing Difficult Woods

Sometimes chemicals and oils in the pores of exotic, oily or other wood (Illus. 243) will cause gluing problems. For example, the dark resin streaks found in teakwood prevent the glue from wetting the surfaces completely. The surfaces of teak will not be able to hold the glue less than an hour after machining.

However, there are certain techniques that will make the gluing process more effective and strengthen the joints. Cutting the surfaces with a jointer or plane right before gluing will help the surfaces hold the glue. Another method is to wipe the gluing surfaces with solvent. Lacquer thinner is good for most woods, and trichlorethane is best for teak.

Use double-adhesive spreads so the glue is on both surfaces being bonded. Teak and almost all other exotic wood can be successfully glued with liquid white, urea, and animal glues. Do not rush the open assembly times because that can lead to excessive squeeze-out, which will result in a starved joint.

The oils and extractives in some rare woods will inhibit the normal curing rate for some glues. Consequently, it's best to increase the clamping time to the maximum to make sure that the adhesive has ample curing time before releasing the pressure. It's always best to make a test sample before proceeding with a large, expensive project.

Illus. 240. This panel, comprised of curved glue lines, was made by Riverside Woodworks.

Illus. 241 (right). Riverside Woodworks makes boxes and cutting boards featuring decorative panels.

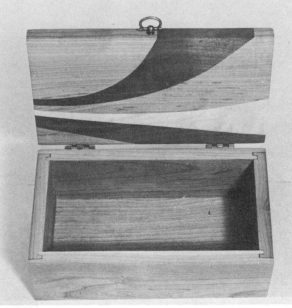

Illus. 242. Stack-cutting gradual curves makes the pieces for edge-glued panels with irregular curved glue lines.

Illus. 243. A cutting board fabricated by Riverside Woodworks consists of various species of wood, including some exotic woods.

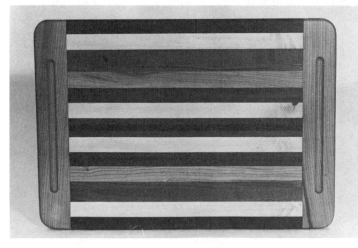

Strip-Canoe Building

Strip-canoe building is another application of the edge-gluing process. (See Illus. 244 and 245.) Surprisingly, edge-to-edge clamping is not a serious problem in this work. The objective is only to hold the pieces together so they form the basic shape. The strips, usually ¼ inch × 1 inch cedar, are bent very easily over a mould and held in place with ordinary ⁹⁄₁₆-inch construction staples. They are glued to each other along their edges as the pieces take form over a premade mould.

Any number of different glues can be used. A good gap-filling slow-set glue is very suitable. The strips are glued to each other and held with staples. One leg of the staple goes into each strip while it's held in place with hand pressure only. The glue need not be waterproof because it is used only to hold the pieces together long enough for the surfaces to be sanded smooth and covered with an epoxy saturation coating, followed with matrix of epoxy resin and fibreglass inside and out. This gives the necessary waterproofing.

Illus. 244. A canoe made of ¼ × 1-inch cedar strips is built upside down over a mould. The strips are temporarily held to the mould and to each other with staples.

Illus. 245. A sheath of fabric, impregnated with epoxy inside and out, provides strength and the necessary waterproofing. Strip canoes are exceptionally light in weight and unbelievably strong—a tribute to modern glues and techniques.

Chapter 7
Gluing Face to Face

Gluing two or more pieces together face to face to increase the thickness of stock is a common practice in many areas of wood-crafting. (See Illus. 246.) Woodturners, wood carvers, furniture makers, model builders, and other craftsmen need heavier, thicker stock than is normally available in one piece. Wood members that have been built up from thinner and/or narrower pieces, and have their grain run parallel to their length are called "laminated stock." Laminated stock can be glued-up wood that is of a straight form, as shown in Illus. 247, or of a curved form, such as in an archery bow or water ski. Here I will deal with face-to-face gluing of straight forms. (See Chapter 12 for information about laminating curved forms.)

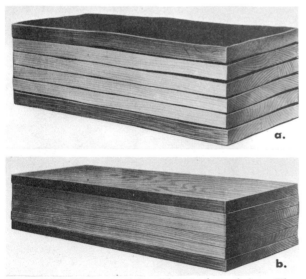

Illus. 246. The essentials of face-to-face gluing. The boards at A must be trued and smoothed to make a stack of tight-fitting joints, shown in B.

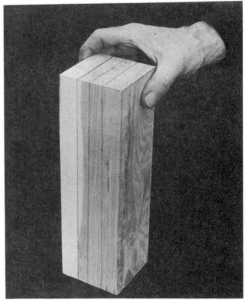

Illus. 247. A face-to-face laminated member. Note how the pieces are arranged by color.

Preparing Stock

Depending upon the project involved, all laminations are pretty much prepared in the same way. If knots, splits, or checks are objectionable, they can sometimes be "buried" inside the glue-up by a simple arrangement of the individual pieces. If this isn't possible, the pieces with those defects should not be used. The two major concerns regarding face-to-face gluing are: (1) preparing good, smooth, flat surfaces; and (2) achieving ample pressure over the total gluing surface to get tight joints. Using a jointer (Illus. 248) or a hand plane skillfully are two ways of truing the surfaces. As a rule, power sanders should not be used. They do not leave a good gluing surface and it's difficult to get a true, flat surface by sanding. A surface (thickness) planer is very useful for this class of work. It can level and work stock to smooth, flat faces that are true and parallel in thickness. "Knife"-cut surfaces are best for gluing. (See Illus. 249.)

If you purchase material that has already been prepared with trued surfaces on two sides (S2S), it's likely that no other preparation is necessary. Slightly cupped pieces can often be flattened in the gluing process. As in edge-gluing, face-marking (Illus. 250) and a "dry run" are essential. See Illus. 251–254 for some turning projects that have all been derived from blanks assembled by gluing face to face.

Illus. 248. Truing a face on the jointer.

Illus. 249. A thickness planer makes pieces smooth and perfectly uniform in thickness.

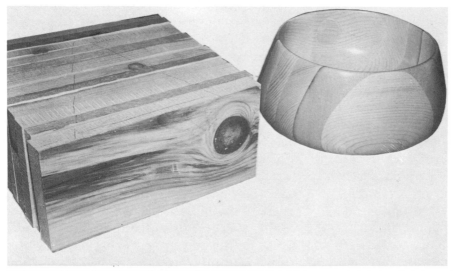

Illus. 250. Face-to-face laminations in bowl turnings. Note the face marking and location of the piece with the large knot that will be removed when the bowl blank is cut to its initial round shape.

Illus. 252. Randomly cut pieces of the same species give an interesting look too.

Illus. 251. Interesting grain patterns result, even when the individual pieces are much alike.

Illus. 253. Here's an idea: stack-laminated particle-board bowl turning!

Illus. 254. A turned stack of glued plywood scraps make a good lamp base.

same size. Objects that take much impact, such as bowling pins (Illus. 255), baseball bats (Illus. 256), and workbenches, have a far greater service life glue-laminated than the same objects made from one piece of wood.

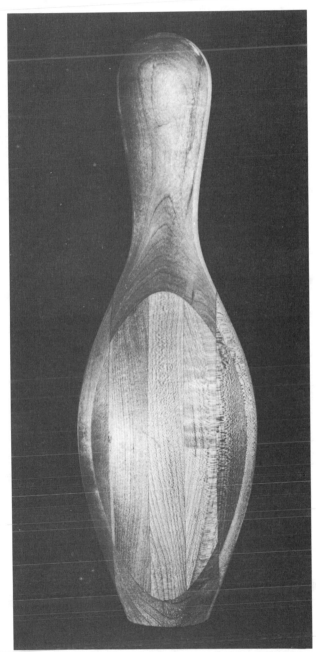

Illus. 255. A laminated member consisting of individual layers that were edge-glued for width and then glued face to face.

Sometimes the individual laminates are first edge-glued to achieve the necessary width of the individual laminate members then face-glued. It's almost impossible to do a glue-up where, in one single operation, members are edge-glued and face-glued simultaneously. In such work, it's best to prepare the edge-glued members individually first, letting them cure. Then true the faces, and, in another separate step, make the face-to-face glue-up. (See Illus. 255.)

Glue-laminated parts have less tendency to crack and split than solid members of the

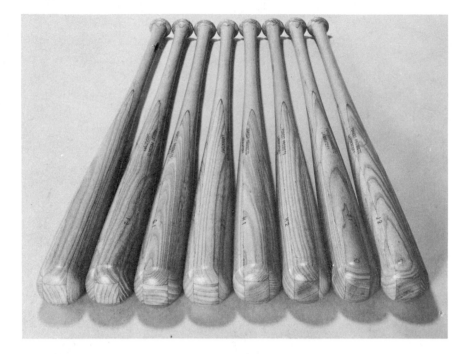

Illus. 256. Laminated base-ball bats are stronger and last longer than the solid, one-piece versions.

Applying Pressure

The major problem with face-to-face gluing is distributing adequate pressure over the total area of the joint. Smaller-sized laminations, such as those needed for small spindle turnings (Illus. 257), and somewhat larger laminations (Illus. 258) are not serious problems as long as there are enough clamps. Increasing the glue line area proportionally increases the amount of pressure required and the number of clamps that must be used. Don't worry about exerting too much pressure or using too many clamps. If in doubt, use more clamps.

If, for example, you are gluing a piece of hard cherry 4 inches square by 30 inches long for a spindle turning, it will involve 120 square inches of glue line. Cherry, being a dense hardwood, requires nearly 200 p.s.i., or 24,000 pounds of total pressure. That's a lot of pressure for a relatively small job. It's best to start with good-fitting joints and use lots of clamps.

Illus. 259 shows three hand screw clamps used for a glue-up of cedar with approximately 5 inches × 12 inches of glue line.

Cedar, a softwood, requires up to 150 p.s.i. or a total force of 9,000 pounds. Thus, each clamp must deliver 3,000 p.s.i. Pressure should also reach and be uniformly applied to the center of the work rather than just around the edges.

Heavy duty C-clamps (Illus. 260) can exert good pressure. Deep-throat bar clamps (Illus. 261) are good for smaller assemblies. Excessive hand torque can cause these clamps to bend. (Illus. 262 and 263 show a large table-base spindle turning made from a 9 inch × 9 inch square lamination.)

Often, in completed works of laminated carvings and wood turnings some glue lines may appear thicker than they actually are. This is because the contour of the surface of the turning or carving is such that it runs almost parallel to the glue line. (See Illus. 263.) Another reason is that because glue lines do not take stains or finishes like raw wood, they appear magnified. There isn't a great deal one can do about this situation. Changing the stock thickness or revising the profile shape of the object are the only alternatives.

Illus. 257. Solids and veneers glued face to face and then sawn obliquely create this unusual turning.

Illus. 258. Applying pressure on a laminated structural beam. Lots of clamps are required to ensure that sufficient pressure is distributed over the entire surface area.

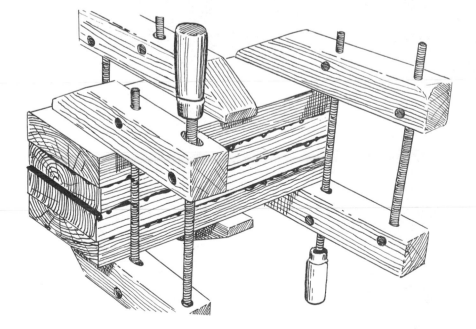

Illus. 259. This unassuming glue-up requires about 9,000 lbs. of total pressure.

Illus. 261. Deep-throat bar clamps are good for smaller glue-ups.

Illus. 262. This 9-inch diameter turning by Lance Nelson required careful gluing techniques.

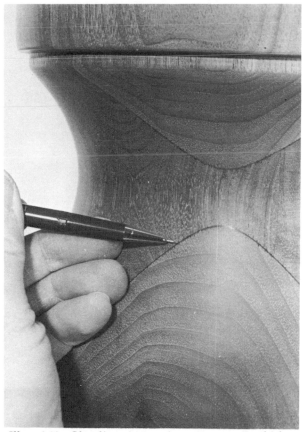

Illus. 263. Glue lines in turnings may appear thicker or wider than they actually are, because some surfaces run almost parallel to the glue line.

Face-to-Face Gluing Projects

Illus. 264 and 265 show two built-up lamp projects that require face-to-face laminating. Illus. 266 shows the end of a glue-up for another turned lamp. Note the plugs glued into premachined slots for the lamp cord. Laminations for turnings and carvings can often be precut to rough shapes to conserve wood and reduce the amount of glue and pressure required. A typical example of such a technique for carvings is shown in Illus. 267. Illus. 268 shows some ways to glue up stock for various wood turnings.

The use of veneers combined and glued together with solid boards makes for some interesting design options. Illus. 270 shows a basic glue-up used to prepare a blank for the wood candle design shown in Illus. 271. Illus. 272 and 273 show more ways to use glued veneers.

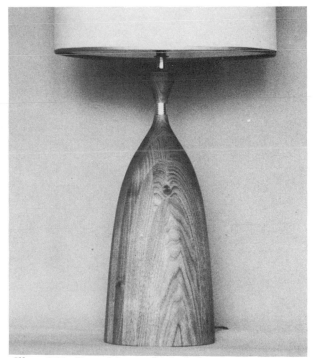

Illus. 264. Turned lamp of 1-inch face-laminated butternut.

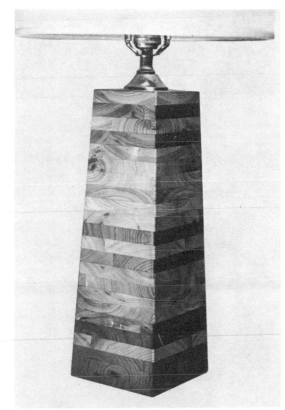

Illus. 265. Another lamp of 1-inch face-glued butternut.

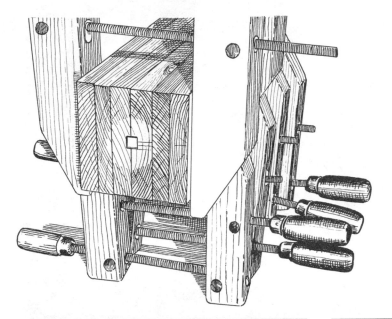

Illus. 266. A lamp glue-up. Precut and plugged groove for lamp cord is prepared before gluing.

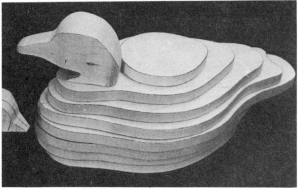

Illus. 267. Example of stacked laminations precut to rough shape prior to gluing. This technique saves stock, reduces glue area, and reduces the amount of glue and total clamping pressure required.

Illus. 268. Some ways to glue up wood for specific turning shapes.

Illus. 269. The results turned from the blanks shown in Illus. 268.

Illus. 270. Veneers and scrap glued together make a turning blank.

Illus. 271. A "quickie" candle turning. It's designed to hold changeable candles for food warmers.

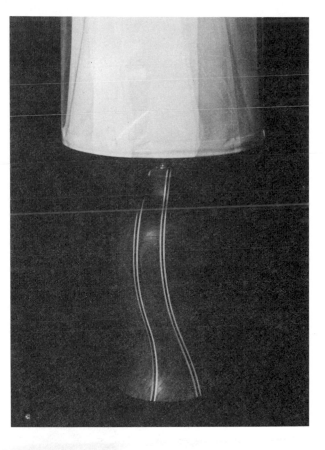

Illus. 272. (right). Veneers glued to gradual curves band-sawed through a typical turning blank.

Illus. 273. Projects of glued veneers.

Illus. 274 shows an ambitious gluing project made with all of the parts built up face to face. This authentic maple butcher's table was fabricated by Lars Johnson. Urea and epoxy resins were used. The top is solid and a full 8 inches thick. All of the grain runs vertically, so the entire table surface is all end grain. The assembly has two continuously threaded rods running horizontally across and through the solid top. These were used to draw the assembly together along with bar clamps used above and below. The steel rods are also insurance if a glue line lets go or if the tabletop cracks or separates. Remember, the top is one big mass of wood!

The legs are 3¼ inch square and 28 inches long. They are glued and lag-bolted to the "notched" corners of the top. The leg lags and two through rods were set into countersunk holes and concealed with wood plugs of contrasting color.

Illus. 275 and 276 show some other table designs. Illus. 277 shows the bottom end of a laminated Douglas fir sailing mast that is 100 feet long and hollow except at the top and bottom. The center is solid, as are the areas where mast fittings will be installed.

Illus. 278–280 show a large gluing project made in our shop. We had to glue large sign panels 8 feet × 11 feet face to face. A slower-setting urea resin was spread in the central areas and epoxy was used around the perimeter (Illus. 278). We had to have enough manpower to help spread and "fix" the clamps in time before the resins set (Illus. 279). The outer edges of the panels extended over our workbench. The perimeter was clamped all around with hand screw clamps. To apply pressure to the central areas of the large panels, we wedge-forced long timbers between the work and against the ceiling trusses. Illus. 280 shows the overall view of the clamping involved.

Illus. 274. Lars Johnson's butcher's table measures 20 inches square with an 8 inch-thick top; 3¼-inch square legs are 28 inches long.

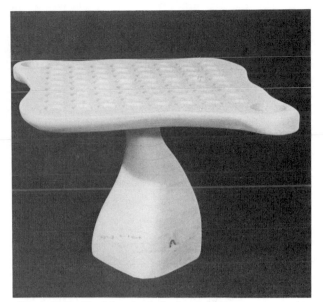

Illus. 276. Stack-laminated pine table.

Illus. 275. Another butcher's table design built by Kevin Mueller.

Illus. 277. Lamination gives great strength. This shows the bottom end of a glue-laminated Douglas fir mast 100' long.

119

Illus. 278. Spreading epoxy around the perimeter of a large sign panel.

Illus. 279. Since epoxy does not require excessive pressure, fewer clamps than normally required give sufficient pressure to the outside edges.

Illus. 280. A total view of the clamping involved. Timbers were wedged between the ceiling and panels lying on the workbench.

Chapter 8
Gluing End To End

To date, there has not been a viable glue system invented that makes end-grain butt joints strong enough for common use. Consequently, joining wood members end to end is not a very common practice among wood-crafters.

The gluing of end grains poses some serious problems. However, with sharp cutting tools, careful sawing, tightly fitting joints, the right choices of glue, and employing all preventional measures possible to guard against "starved joints," one can create some joints such as mitres that are stronger than expected. Avoid, when possible, end-grain joints made of porous woods, and the use of thin glues that have low solids content. Also, avoid slow-setting glues, as these continue to soak into end grains before setting, leaving less than the optimum amount of glue on the joint surfaces. These factors prevent glue from soaking into porous end grains to the extent that they cause a starved glue joint.

Scarf and Finger Joints

Wood glue-joined directly end to end to increase the length is best done with two types of joints—the *scarf* and the *finger joints*. (See Illus. 281 and 282). The design of these joints is such that their mating surfaces somewhat approach the side grains common to face-to-face joints.

Boat builders often use the scarf joint to remove knots and other defects from planking strips. When properly made, the glued member is exceptionally strong, and boards can be glued up so they are clear and defect-free in any length desired. Although scarfing is not routinely done, it appears to be the most viable approach for the craftsman who needs to extend the length of certain members.

The longer the "slopes" are cut on each of the members, the stronger the glued joint will be. The basic scarf joint, as prepared in Illus. 282, has a slope ratio of 1 to 8. This means that if the stock is 1 inch thick, the slope length is 8 inches. A 1 to 12 slope is even stronger.

Finger joints (Illus. 281) are also very strong joints. They are used in industrial wood-product manufacturing. They do not involve as much wood waste as scarf joints, and they are easier to machine and bond on a production basis. Finger jointing requires special cutters and large production equipment. Finger joints can be found in mill work, some structural members, and laminated wood products. Finger joints have been in use since the early 1940s.

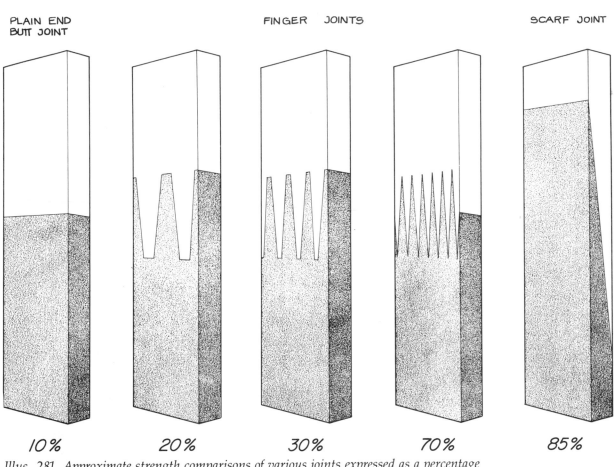

PLAIN END BUTT JOINT	FINGER JOINTS			SCARF JOINT
10%	20%	30%	70%	85%

Illus. 281. Approximate strength comparisons of various joints expressed as a percentage of clear, solid wood of the same size and species.

Illus. 282. The long, taper scarf is the best for end-to-end joints.

Illus. 283. Large and expensive special tooling is required for making finger joints.

Scabbed Butt Joint

One joint entirely different from finger and scarf joints is the *scabbed butt joint*, which can be glued and/or nailed. (See Illus. 284.) This is a quick and easy-to-make joint that is strong but purely functional. Few tools are required.

Illus. 285 depicts end and mitre lap joints—two easy joints that are alternatives to scarf joints for jobs where great strength is not an essential factor.

Segmented Joints

Gluing tapered segments together, as done in some wood turnings (Illus. 286) and other objects, is almost like gluing end grain to end grain. Joints in this category are essentially mitre joints, but they indeed can be glued.

For those types of joints that have a high percentage of end-grain exposure (Illus. 287), some important gluing steps should be followed. First of all, the best approach is to double-coat each surface with glue. Allow it to dry partially in 3 to 7 minutes, and observe the surfaces for excessive penetration. Recoat where necessary and maximize the open assembly time. (See Illus. 288.)

When possible, cut stave-like segments. These are cut from the board differently—so the gluing surfaces are closer to the edge grain rather than the end grain. (Several wood-turning books available can supply you with more information about segmenting and other types of special glue-ups for lathe work.)

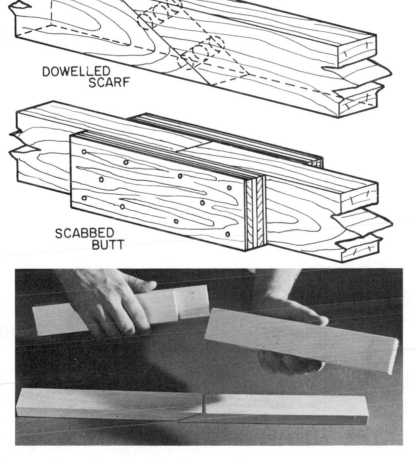

DOWELLED SCARF

SCABBED BUTT

Illus. 284. Two variations of end-to-end joints.

Illus. 285. An end lap or a mitre lap is suitable where strength is not required.

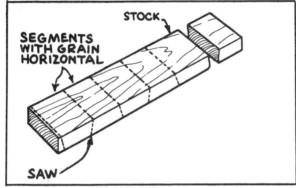

Illus. 287. Segments cut in this fashion must be treated like gluing the end grains of mitre joints.

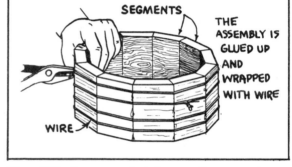

Illus. 288. One way of gluing up the segments.

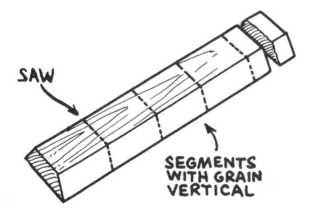

Illus. 289. (left). Stave segments cut in this manner glue better. The joints are more like edge-to-edge joints.

Making Scarf Joints

Preparing the Surface

Because scarf joints are the best joints to use when gluing wood end to end, I will

concentrate exclusively on them. Illus. 290-293 show the essential steps in making scarf joints. As with any glue-up, preparing the gluing surfaces properly is highly important. Surfaces must be smooth and flat, and

124

must fit very closely together with minimal clamping pressure. In order to accomplish this, each member of the joint must have precisely the same slope or angle.

For most work, a 1 to 8 slope is sufficient. If gluing denser woods and/or an exterior application is intended, a slope of not less than 1 to 10 is recommended. The longer the slope, the greater the gluing area, and the stronger the joint; but, also remember that more wood will be wasted to make up the joint.

Begin by marking the bevels on the ends of the stock. Remove most of the excess material by any convenient means; I like to rough-cut them close to the layout line on the band saw. I use the first one that I cut as a pattern, and rough-cut all the scarf slopes on all pieces.

When end-scarfing very narrow strips, as might be done in strip-canoe building, I make a setup on the belt sander. (See Illus. 290.) This is simply a guide block clamped to the sander table at the slope angle of the scarf.

If gluing with epoxy, no further surface preparation is necessary because the joint fit is not as critical as it is with other glues. To prepare stock for any of the other glues, a clean fit can be achieved with a hand plane. The scarf ends are stacked on top of each other, and clamped on top of a flat supporting board. (See Illus. 291.) The arrangement of the scarf pieces and support board should be such that the feathered edge of the bottom member is supported during planing. Plane the surfaces flat and true. Several or more joint members can be planed at one time, depending upon the thickness of the material.

Illus. 291. Scarf hand planing. These four pieces cut simultaneously will all have the exact same slope angles. Note the supporting board extending to the feather edge of the bottom piece.

Gluing the Joint

Gluing the scarf joints should begin with a dry run clamped to a smooth and flat surface. During the gluing operation, some method has to be devised to prevent end slippage. Leave a very slight overlap; in this way a little stock can be removed during the cleanup of the cured joint. (See Illus. 292.) Both pieces must set flat on the surface and be located laterally at such points where the bevels will be tight when pressed.

Remember, this job is more like end-grain gluing than face-to-face gluing. So, take the appropriate steps to minimize excessive glue

Illus. 290. A guide block clamped to the sander table (at the scarf angle) makes machining small scarf joints easy.

penetration. Place plastic or wax paper under the joint area so the drippings don't glue the work to the surface under the joint. (See Illus. 292.) Be sure that the two pieces are also aligned perfectly lengthwise so the glued member will be straight along its edges.

Applying Pressure

Clamps (Illus. 293) or temporary nails can be used to prevent end slippage as the scarf area is pressed together. It's a good idea to put plastic or wax paper under the clamp, giving pressure to the joint. If the scarf area is larger than the clamp jaw, place a caul block under the clamp to distribute pressure over the entire joint. A caul block also prevents clamp marking on softwoods. Use a putty knife and clean up as much of the uncured glue as possible. Once cured, the remaining excess glue is removed with a sharp block plane. Sand the joint if desired.

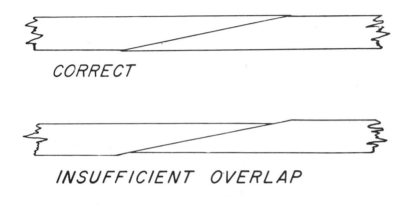

CORRECT

INSUFFICIENT OVERLAP

TOO MUCH OVERLAP

Illus. 292. Correct alignment of the scarf joint is essential. A very slight overlap is actually preferred to allow stock for cleanup of the cured joint.

Illus. 293. Gluing the scarf over plastic film on a flat workbench. Clamps at left and far right prevent lateral end slippage. Middle clamp brings pressure to the joint.

Chapter 9
Gluing Joints and Assemblies

Joints are at the very heart of almost all areas of woodworking. And regardless of the simplicity or complexity of the project, the same basic techniques are used to glue and hold the joints together. (See Illus. 294 and 295.)

Many kinds of joints, their basic construction details, and alterations that will make them stronger are discussed in this chapter. All these joints require special attention during the following steps: designing, machining, fitting clearances, spreading glue, and clamping. The various strengtheners that make joints more durable are also discussed.

Illus. 294. Even small projects often involve a lot of joinery. Here's a face-to-face glued spindle with turned tenons, an edge-glued top, and lap joints at the base.

Illus. 295. This corner cabinet by H. T. Cushman Mfg. Co. involves many different joinery applications.

These strengtheners include nails, feathers, and splines. The box, case, corner, and frame joints that are used in furniture making and cabinetry are dwelled upon, as are the assemblies made with plywood.

Types of Joints

There are hundreds of different types of joints used today. They range from simple butt joints and the common dado or rabbet joints (Illus. 296) to special joints that serve the requirements of a particular product design (Illus. 297.). Often, simple joints can be redesigned to increase the ultimate appearance and the overall value of the product. (See Illus. 298.)

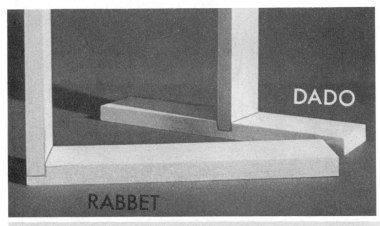

Illus. 296. The dado and rabbet are two of the most basic right-angle joints.

Illus. 297. Chair joinery is a highly technical and sophisticated craft, as typified in this chair by Scan Furniture.

128

Illus. 298. Another chair detail by Scan Furniture. The look of the sculptured exterior form visually overshadows its fundamental, but well-executed, joinery.

Dowel Joint

The dowel joint will be the first joint described because all of the gluing techniques used on this joint can be applied to most other kinds of joints.

Dowels are round pins (usually made of birch) that are easy to use as butt-joint strengtheners. Common sizes range from ⅛ to 1 inch in diameter. Commercially produced glue-joint dowels in the popular sizes of ¼-, ⅜-, and ½-inch diameters (Illus. 299 and 300) will handle most joint dowelling jobs. They come spirally grooved or straight-fluted.

Some woodworkers cut their own dowels from regular, smooth dowel stock. These are adequate, but it's essential that a lengthwise flute or two be cut into the surface of the dowel. This allows air and the extra glue that often runs to the bottom of the hole to escape as pressure is applied. Forcing a dowel pin without some type of groove into a hole full of glue is likely to split the wood.

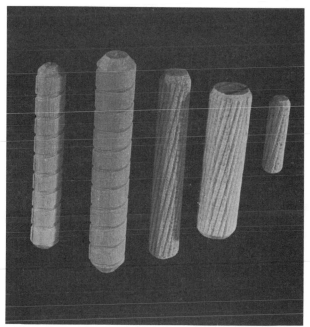

Illus. 299. Commercially produced glue joint dowels come spirally grooved or straight-fluted in a variety of diameters and lengths.

Illus. 300. Dowels strengthen these plain butt joints very effectively.

There is much debate among wood-workers over which is the best dowel—spiral-grooved dowels or straight-fluted dowels. Some contend that spiral-grooved dowels grip like screws; others think that more glue stays on the surfaces of straight-fluted dowels. Although I have used spiral-grooved dowels for many years, I agree with those experts recommending the dowels that have grooves parallel to their length. (See Illus. 301.) It is important for the dowel diameter to equal the hole diameter within a plus or minus 0.005-inch tolerance. (See Illus. 302 and 303.) Roughly cut holes are not conducive to good fits or good dowel gluing. Poor hole-surface quality may be the result of dull bits, but more often wood fibres are torn away from the sides of the hole by feeding the bit into the work faster than it can cut.

The optimum fit is such that the dowel does not have to be driven in with a hammer.

Illus. 301. Dowel holes should be cut cleanly and be as deep as possible for the greatest strength.

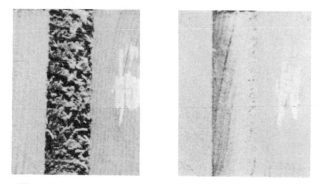

Illus. 302. Holes left and right were drilled in the same material and at the same bit rpm. The hole at left was made with too fast of an entry feed rate, resulting in its rough, poor-quality surface.

Illus. 303. Some dowel "fits." Left: *too loose;* Center: *too tight (requiring driving fit, which will force glue spread in hole to the bottom and scrape excess off the surface of the dowel;* Right: *just right.*

It's impossible to get a ⅜-inch dowel into a ⅜-inch hole without force. To remedy this situation, heat a batch of dowel pins in your household oven until the dowels slip freely into a predrilled hole. Keep them in an airtight plastic bag until needed.

An interesting footnote to this subject of dowel fits is worthy of discussion here. One chair manufacturer makes the dowel ends of stretchers that are ¹⁄₃₂-inch oversize in diameter. These ends are then compressed in a special chuck to fit into the smaller glue-coated hole. The compressed area tries to swell back to its original size as the glue moisture is absorbed. The result is a joint that's so strong it's nearly indestructible.

Various *drill guides* are available that make exact hole locations very easy to execute. (See

Illus. 304 and 305.) Some are self-centering, and locate the hole in the precise middle of a board's edge. The only layout required is a line marked squarely across the edge or end of the members. It's best to mark the mating holes of the joint at the same time. (See Illus. 306.)

Dowel Length Increasing dowel length increases joint strength because the gluing areas of the hole and dowel are increased. According to one authority, the most effective dowel lengths for common dowel diameters are: 2 inches for ¼-inch diameter dowels, 3 inches for ⅜-inch diameter dowels, and 3½-inch lengths for dowels ½ inch in diameter. An 8 to 1 length-to-diameter ratio for dowels is a good guideline.

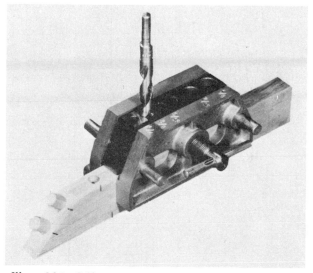

Illus. 304. Self-centering dowel jig guides the drill straight and exactly centered.

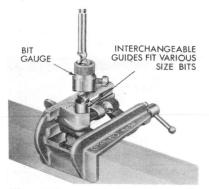

Illus. 305. Another type of guide for boring dowel holes.

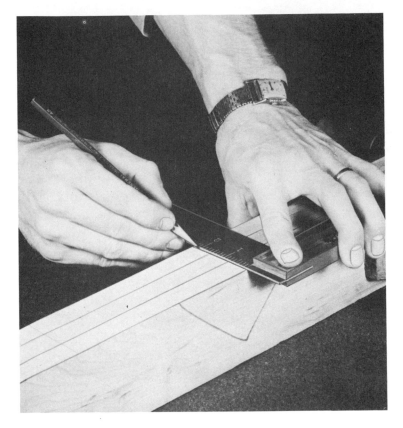

Dowel Spacing Illus. 307 provides a basis for evaluating dowel-joint strengths in stiles and rails or similar dowelled frame assemblies. Greater cleavage strength is obtained when the dowels in the ends of the rails are spaced further apart, as joint A-A in Illus. 307 shows. One must use some common sense here. Do not locate the dowels so close to the outside edges that the rail would crack when the dowels are inserted. Increasing the width of the rail in small amounts, such as from 2 inches to 2½ inches, increases joint-stress resistance by well over one-third.

Spreading Glue on Dowels The preferred practice is to always apply glue to all mating surfaces of a joint. In a dowel joint, spread the glue around the entire surfaces of the dowel holes. (See Illus. 308 and 309.) Also spread glue on the dowels (Illus. 310 and 311), and on the end grain of the rail member. If glue soaks in quickly, reapply glue as needed. Assemble the joint with clamping pressure to bring the mating parts tightly together.

Illus. 307. Joint A-A will be stronger than B-B because of the spacing between the dowels.

132

Illus. 308. *Dispense glue around the top inside of dowel joint holes.*

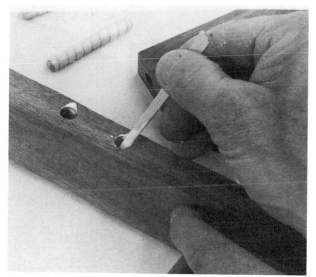

Illus. 309. *With a small stick spreader, work the glue to cover the walls of each hole.*

Illus. 310. *Spread glue on about ½ of the dowels' length and insert to full depth. Then spread glue on the remaining surface area of the dowels.*

Illus. 311. *Spread glue on end grain (once or twice) and spread glue on the inside of the rail holes.*

Right-Angle Joints

Right-angle joints are much different from the plain edge-to-edge, plain face-to-face, or the special end-to-end joints discussed in previous chapters. When wood is edge-glued or built up face-to-face, the grain of all members runs in the same direction.

Joints that involve joining end grain, such as the end-butt joints (Illus. 312), mitres (Illus. 313), or end-to-side grain joints are difficult to make sufficiently strong even when the strongest adhesives are used. This is be-

cause the end grain does not hold the glue well. Therefore, it is necessary to use auxiliary fasteners (nails and screws) in the joint and/or supplementary devices such as glue blocks, dowels, splines, or tenons to reinforce the joint. These devices (see page 135) bring side grain into contact with side grain. Some of these joint strengtheners provide larger gluing surfaces that counteract the shrinkage or expansion that can result when wood members vary in moisture content.

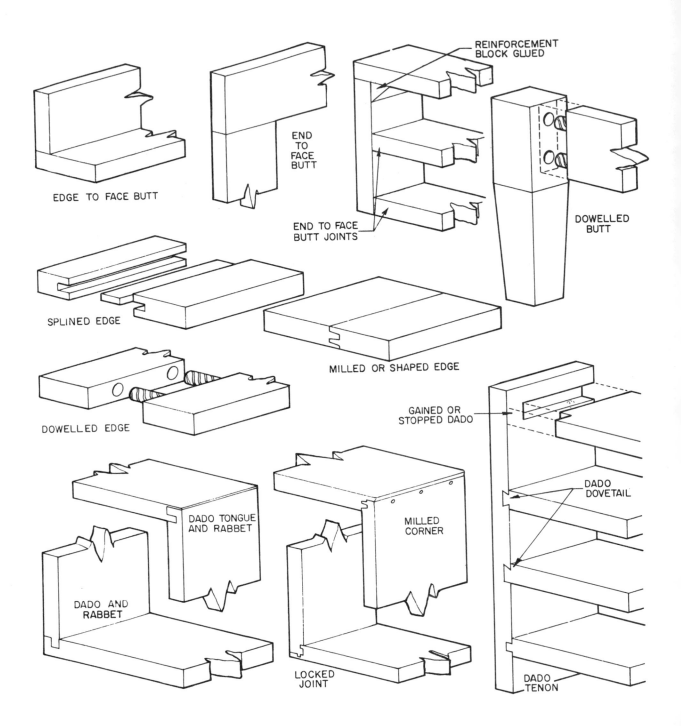

EDGE TO FACE BUTT

END TO FACE BUTT

REINFORCEMENT BLOCK GLUED

END TO FACE BUTT JOINTS

DOWELLED BUTT

SPLINED EDGE

MILLED OR SHAPED EDGE

DOWELLED EDGE

GAINED OR STOPPED DADO

DADO DOVETAIL

DADO TONGUE AND RABBET

DADO AND RABBET

MILLED CORNER

LOCKED JOINT

DADO TENON

Illus. 312. A variety of butt, edge, and right-angle joints.

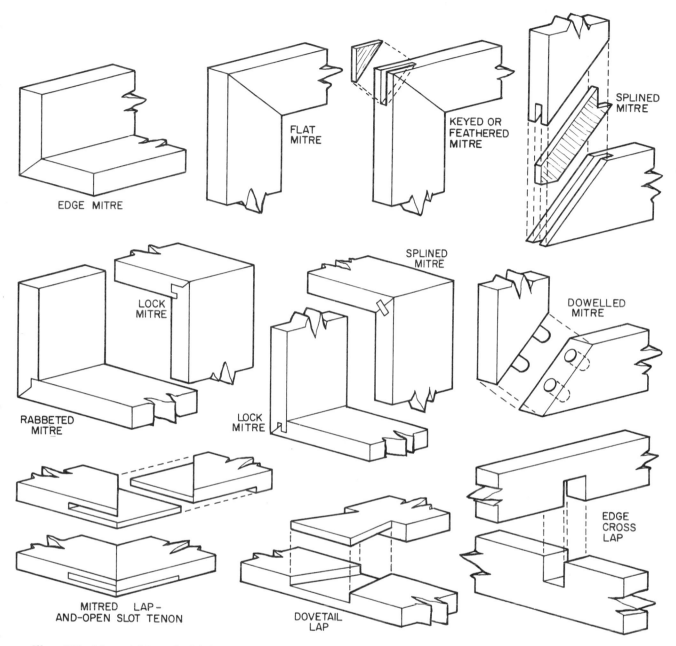

Illus. 313. More right angle joints.

Mortise-and-Tenon Joints

The same general principles of dowel gluing apply when fitting and gluing tenons into mortises. (See Illus. 314–316.) It is vitally important to make sure that the moisture content of the tenon member is at least as low as it will be in the environment where it will be used. If not, the tenon will lose moisture, shrink in size, and weaken the joint. Some basic considerations regarding mortise-and-tenon joints are: 1) Make sure the tenon is about ⅛ inch less than the depth of the mortise; 2) the common thickness of the tenon is approximately ½ the thickness of the stock it's being cut on (it's best to work in even fractions, such as ¼ inch, ⅜ inch or ½ inch); 3) the clearance on each side of a tenon should allow for a 0.002-inch-thick glue line; and 4) round tenons are treated like dowels. (See Illus. 317–321.)

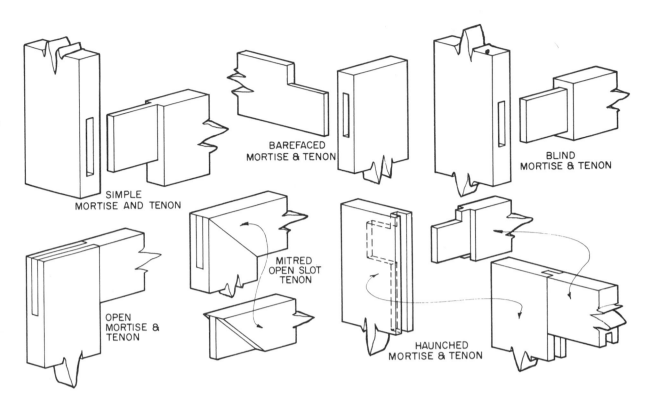

Illus. 314. A variety of tenons. Those with larger joint surface areas are the strongest.

SIMPLE MORTISE AND TENON

BAREFACED MORTISE & TENON

BLIND MORTISE & TENON

OPEN MORTISE & TENON

MITRED OPEN SLOT TENON

HAUNCHED MORTISE & TENON

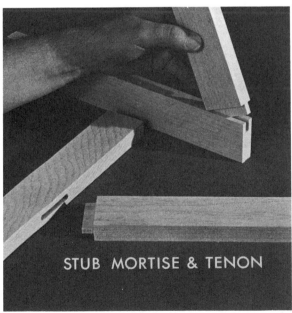

STUB MORTISE & TENON

Illus. 315. Not all tenons are intended for great strength.

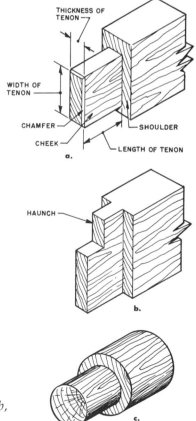

THICKNESS OF TENON

WIDTH OF TENON

CHAMFER

CHEEK

SHOULDER

LENGTH OF TENON

a.

HAUNCH

b.

c.

Illus. 316. (right) Tenons: a, basic terminology; b, haunched tenon; and c, round tenon.

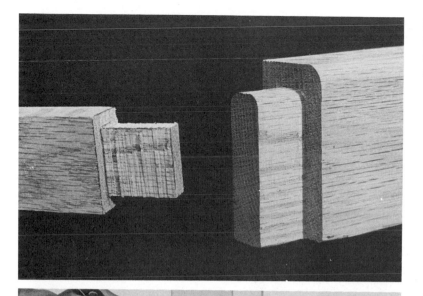

Illus. 317. A poorly machined tenon (left) prevents close contact, giving an erratic, thick glue line and a weak resulting joint.

Illus. 318. Sawing the cheeks of a tenon with a special table saw attachment.

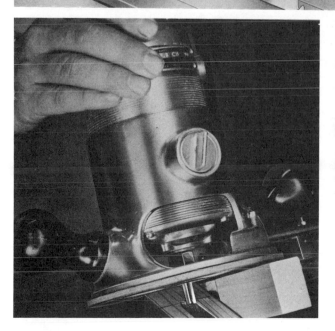

Illus. 320. Making multiple shoulder cuts with the router guided by a straightedge.

Illus. 319. One way of cutting a mortise with a router.

Illus. 321. The component parts of a four-poster bed. Note the regular and blind mortise-and-tenon joints used along with turned round tenons for extending the length of the turnings.

Tongue-and-Groove Joints

Tongue-and-groove joints run with the grain. (See Illus. 322.) Otherwise, they are much like mortise-and-tenon joints. This type of joint is not generally used in furniture work. It can be useful in aligning assemblies and for wood flooring or wall panelling. This joint also requires more material to make it up than does plain, edge-glued butt joints, which are the stronger of the two.

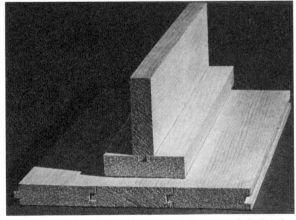

Illus. 322. Tongue-and-groove joints are helpful for alignments.

Compressed Plate or Biscuit Joints

These involve the use of commercially made oval-shaped splines and special electric slot-cutting tools. (See Illus. 323 and 324.)

Many claim that this is an ideal system to replace mortise-and-tenon, tongue-and-groove, and dowel joints. Though that seems unlikely, the system certainly merits some discussion. The biscuits or plates are die-cut from beech. They are compressed in their thickness and have their grain running obliquely to their length. The mating slots or grooves, cut by a special 4-inch saw blade, are slightly larger than the football-shaped splines. (See Illus. 325 and 326.) Moisture from the glue applied to the joint swells the plates tightly in their slots to create very strong joints. The plate system can be ap-

Illus. 323. "Biscuits" are commercially made splines of compressed beech that swell tight in the joint as they absorb moisture from the glue.

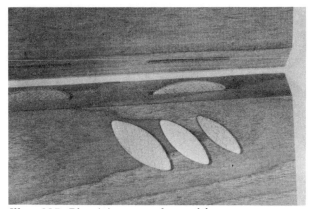

Illus. 325. Plate joinery can be used for many conventional joints, including edge gluing and even edge mitres.

Illus. 324. A Virutex plate (biscuit) joiner. Tools of this type carry a 4-inch diameter saw blade and have a fence or guide that sets the location of the cut.

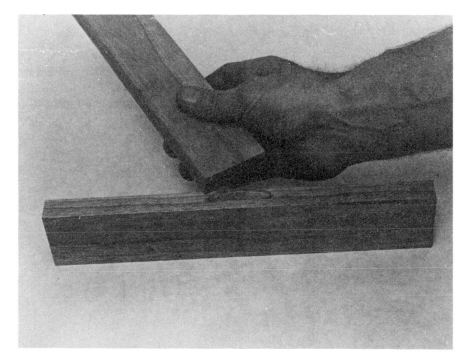

Illus. 326. Right-angle frame and/or cabinet rails 2 inches or wider can be assembled with plate joints.

plied to many of the conventional joint configurations. (See Illus. 327.) One manufacturer makes a special glue-bottle dispenser designed with a nozzle that provides a good glue spread onto both walls of the slots.

Currently, three foreign manufacturers make plate-slotting power tools. From Switzerland comes the Lamello; the Eilu is from Germany; and the Virutex (Illus. 324) is made in Spain. All are marketed in the United States through power-tool retailers and mail-order suppliers.

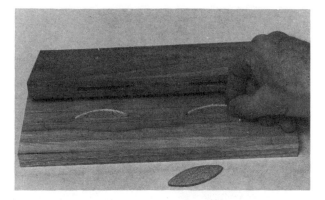

Illus. 327. Some variations of plate joints.

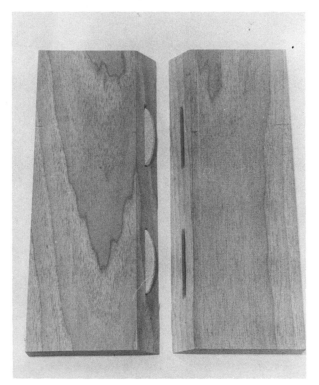

Mitre Joints

All types other than edge mitres are, as discussed previously, difficult to make sufficiently strong with just glue alone. Edge mitres (Illus. 328–334) are, *in theory*, just as easily glued as plain edge to edge butts. The major problem is clamping or holding the pieces tightly together until the glue sets. For this reason clamp nails along with other devices are used to hold the bevelled pieces together until the glue sets.

Clamp nails look like thin metal splines. They are designed to draw and pull the mating pieces together as they are driven into thin, precut saw kerfs. A special saw blade is required for clamp-nailed kerfs. Clamp-nailed joints, unlike wood-splined joints, are less likely to separate as a result of wood expansion and contraction. Two popular types of clamp nails and some applications are shown in Illus. 335.

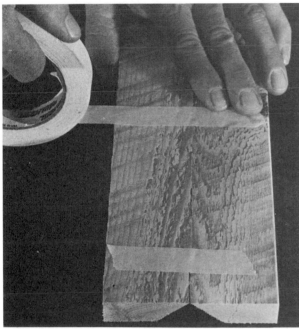

Illus. 328. Taping for a 45° angle mitre joint.

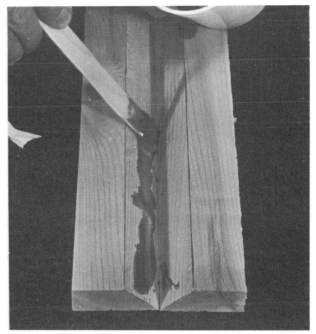

Illus. 329. Spreading glue.

Illus. 330. Closing the joint. Wrap it with more tape to hold the parts together until the glue sets.

Illus. 331. With the wood fibres at the "point" of the joint soft and wet with glue absorption, burnishing with a blunt tool will blend and mesh the fibres together, making the joint nearly invisible.

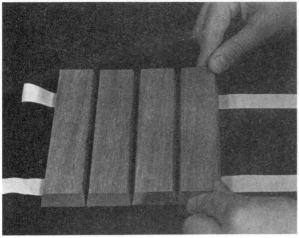

Illus. 332. Mitres comprised of bevelled staves can also be assembled with just tape and glue. Here staves are set onto strips of tape.

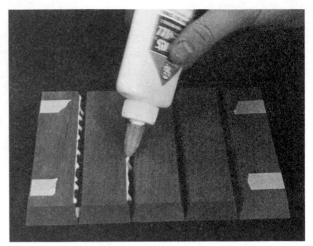

Illus. 333. Spread the glue.

Illus. 334. Tape "hinges" and holds the pieces tightly together. Entire cylinders can be assembled in this manner.

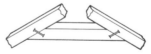

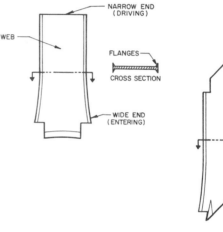

Illus. 336. A close-up look at a clamp nail. Note the entry end at right, which is the widest, and the flanged edges along each side.

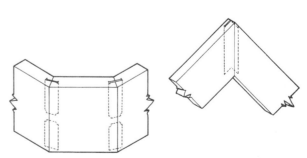

Illus. 335. Clamp nails and some applications. Left: standard clamp nail. Right: special type for flat mitres.

Mitres other than edge-to-edge mitres often have a high percentage of end grain, which makes them difficult to glue. Clamp nails are ideal for strengthening this type of joint. (See Illus. 337 and 338.)

Splines (page 145) strengthen certain mitre joints. One table saw setup for sawing kerfs for splines is shown in Illus. 339.

Clamp nails and splines often are not visible in the finished project. Stopped splines (Illus. 340) are used in situations where the spline or clamp nail must be concealed. Another way of concealing clamp nails and splines is to glue in strips of matching wood to cover them up. (See Illus. 338.)

Illus. 341 shows a router-cut splined mitre joint that has been cut into the face side; it is decorative and helps strengthen the joint.

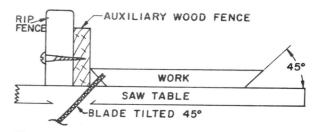

Illus. 339. Setup for sawing the kerfs for clamp nails and splines of 45° mitre joints.

Illus. 340. A hardboard stopped spline strengthens this difficult-to-glue mitred corner.

Illus. 337. As the clamp nail is driven into precut kerfs, the glue-covered surfaces are drawn tightly together.

Illus. 338. With the clamp nail (or spline) "set" about ½" below the surface, a thin strip of wood is glued into the slot to conceal it.

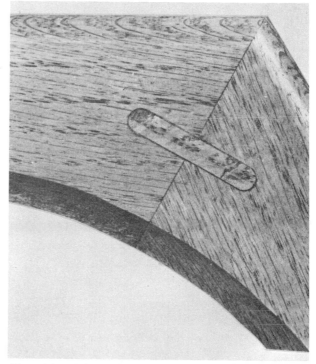

Illus. 341. A face-inlet splined and glued mitre joint.

This joint calls for good workmanship; otherwise, it will be inadequate. If you do not have a router or power tools for machining accurate mitres, a homemade wood mitre box will assist greatly in making consistently accurate cuts. (See Illus. 342.)

Illus. 343 and 344 show some fixturing ideas that are very helpful for gluing and clamping flat mitre joints. Commercial jigs and clamps are available for making mitred frames. One commonly used type is shown in Illus. 345. Flat mitres can also be strengthened with a "feather." The feather is a thin strip of wood with its grain direction perpendicular to the joint line. A table saw setup for cutting feather kerfs is shown in Illus. 346.

Illus. 344. One method of assembling flat mitres uses these easy-to-make clamping blocks.

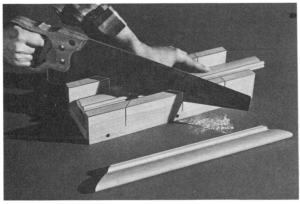

Illus. 342. A homemade wood mitre box.

Illus. 345. A special clamp vise for the assembly of mitre joints.

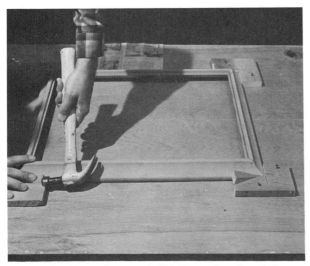

Illus. 343. A simple setup of blocks and wedges brings pressure to this mitred frame.

Illus. 346. Table-sawing a kerf for a "feather"-reinforced flat mitre joint, as shown assembled at right.

Joint Strengtheners

Glue Blocks

Glue blocks (Illus. 347) are small pieces of wood that are used to strengthen joints. They are usually triangular in cross-section with one true right angle. They are glued to inside corners and other inconspicuous spots under shelves, drawer bottoms, tabletops, etc. They can be nailed in place until the glue sets, which gives it greater holding power. Most often, glue blocks are simply glued without nails or clamps. A rubbing motion (back and forth) creates a surface tension on the glue line that holds the glue block in place as the glue sets.

Illus. 347. The glue block strengthens this joint. Nailing only holds it in place until the glue is set.

Splines

Splines (See Illus. 312 and 313) are small, thin pieces of wood, hardboard, or plywood that are glued into a saw kerf or groove in each member of the joint. Kerfs can be machined on a table saw or with a router. As a general rule, avoid when possible the use of splines on edge-to-edge glue-ups. (See Illus. 312.) Splines are not as strong as plain edge joints. It's hard to get a perfect fit, and it's hard to get the glue spread on all surfaces. Also, the area cut away for the spline reduces the area of the best possible gluing surface. Splines are good for flat mitres and edge mitres, because they do effectively strengthen such end-grain gluing.

Keys and Feathers

Keys and feathers (See Illus. 313) are similar to splines, and are most often used to strengthen mitre and other oblique-angle joints. If thin, solid wood strips are used as splines or feathers, they should be positioned so their grain is always at right angles to the joint.

Assemblies

Boxes and Chests

The basic construction details for boxes and chests are shown in Illus. 348. Many dif-

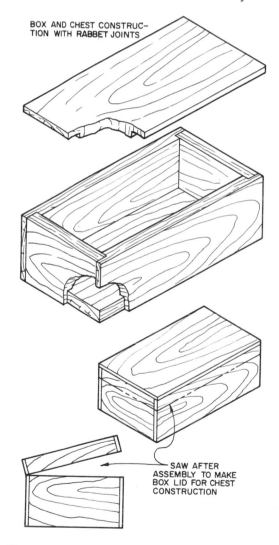

BOX AND CHEST CONSTRUCTION WITH RABBET JOINTS

SAW AFTER ASSEMBLY TO MAKE BOX LID FOR CHEST CONSTRUCTION

Illus. 348. Box and chest details. Though rabbet corner joints are shown, other joints can be used.

ferent kinds of joints can be incorporated into the design or used to match your tooling capabilities. If you do not want to use the end grains of butt joints, use mitre joints. Mitres and *box joints*, as depicted in Illus. 349, are easy to machine with a table saw. Though dovetail joints for boxes, drawers, and chests can now be made with commercially made router fixtures, they can also be made without such fixtures, either by working by hand or by using a router-aided method that is illustrated and discussed step by step in the book, *Router Handbook* (Sterling Publishing Co., Inc., 1983). (See Illus. 350 and 351.) Projects such as boxes, chests, or wall cabinets with box lids are first made up as completely closed boxes. Once the glue has set, the lid is formed by sawing.

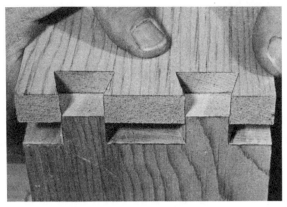

Illus. 351. Router–assisted, handmade dovetail joints are easily cut without commercial fixturing.

Cases

Cases, such as those made for storing books, can be made in a variety of ways. One way that incorporates some simple techniques is shown in Illus. 352. Toeboards or short legs should be designed into the project to support the structure on the floor. They are omitted on wall-hung units. Shelves can be permanently installed in basic joint cuts such as dadoes, or the shelves can be made fully adjustable.

Illus. 349. The "box" joint.

Illus. 350. Through dovetail joints of small boxes routed with a commercial fixture.

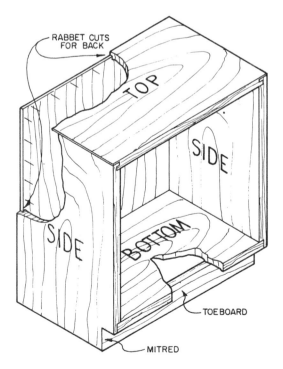

Illus. 352. Basics of case construction.

Cabinet Construction

Cabinet construction involves more joinery. The basics of conventional cabinet making are shown in Illus. 353. The techniques are essentially much like box or case construction. The parts and assembly shown in Illus. 353 are for making up a basic kitchen-cabinet unit. This type of construction has open frames with center guides that support and guide the drawers. The frames fit into dadoes cut into the side panels, which are either made up by edge gluing or made from plywood panels. The forward edges of the skeleton frames and the sides are covered with a framework called the *cabinet facing*. This is glued to the cabinet's front with an occasional finishing nail to maintain alignment until the clamps are secured. The outside vertical members of the facing are called *stiles*. Horizontal framing members are called *rails*. Any vertical divisions of openings are called *muntins*. Study Illus. 353.

Cabinetry often involves much framework for skeleton frames, facings, and door construction. It is important to have a good understanding of how to make and assemble various types of frames for different applications. Lap joints (Illus. 354) are easy to make and, if carefully machined and glued, make strong joints for all frames—even some smaller types of doors. Dowelled frames are not hard to make either, as long as the holes are accurately located with careful layout and drilling. Mortise-and-tenon joints are the best and strongest, but involve more time and fitting. Various *frame assemblies* are shown in Illus. 355–360.

Details for basic drawer construction are shown in Illus. 361. Appropriate clearances in door and drawer openings should be considered because doors and drawers expand in humid weather. A general rule for clearance is to allow ⅛ to ³⁄₁₆-inch all around. However, the type and size of material, how it is sawn, and other conditions may preclude this. The principles of cabinetry just covered can be applied to many areas of furniture making. (See Illus. 362 and 363.)

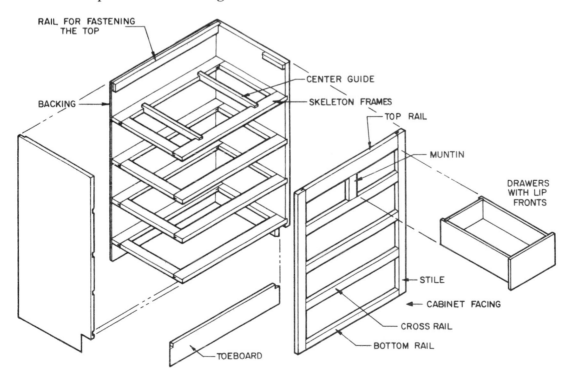

Illus. 353. An exploded view of basic cabinet construction.

147

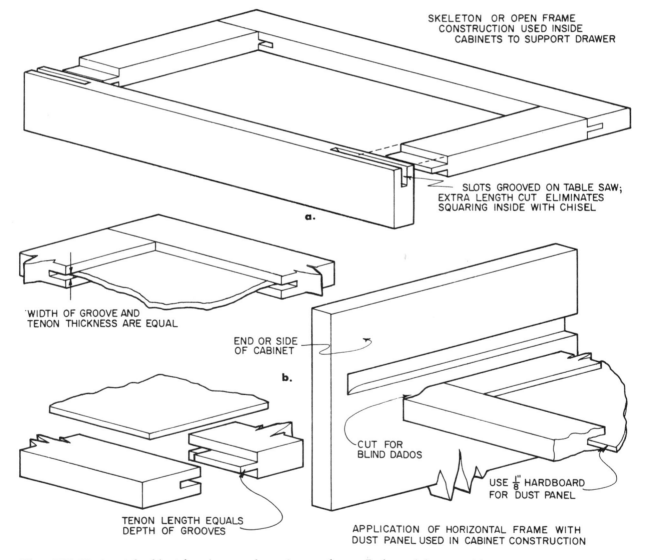

SKELETON OR OPEN FRAME
CONSTRUCTION USED INSIDE
CABINETS TO SUPPORT DRAWER

SLOTS GROOVED ON TABLE SAW;
EXTRA LENGTH CUT ELIMINATES
SQUARING INSIDE WITH CHISEL

a.

WIDTH OF GROOVE AND
TENON THICKNESS ARE EQUAL

b.

END OR SIDE
OF CABINET

CUT FOR
BLIND DADOS

USE $\frac{1}{8}$" HARDBOARD
FOR DUST PANEL

TENON LENGTH EQUALS
DEPTH OF GROOVES

APPLICATION OF HORIZONTAL FRAME WITH
DUST PANEL USED IN CABINET CONSTRUCTION

*Illus. 355. Horizontal cabinet framing members: A, open frame; B, framed dust panel (note
the machining necessary when stopped dadoes are used).*

Illus. 356. Gluing and clamp-ing a frame consisting of a dowelled butt joint.

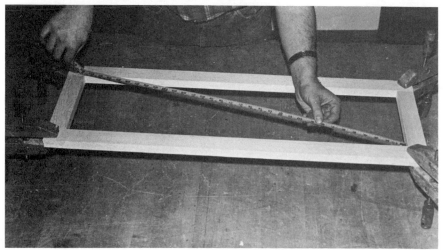

Illus. 357. Checking for square; diagonal distances must be equal.

Illus. 358. Gluing and clamp-ing a cabinet facing frame.

149

Illus. 359. Clamping a frame with a bevelled edge. A special jaw block directs equal pressure to the joint and protects the sharp edge.

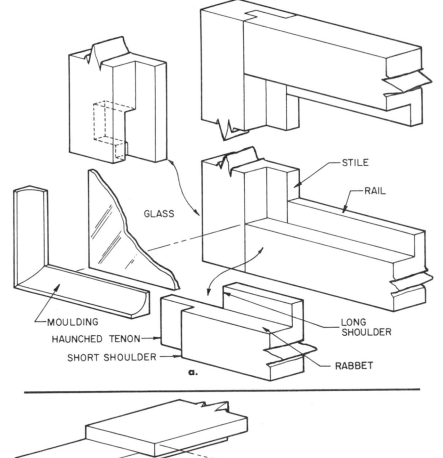

Illus. 360. Details for making glass and/or panel inset doors: A, Typical mortise-and-tenon construction for large doors. B, Simple lap with pre-rabbeted edge suitable for small doors.

STILE

RAIL

GLASS

MOULDING

HAUNCHED TENON

SHORT SHOULDER

LONG SHOULDER

RABBET

a.

b.

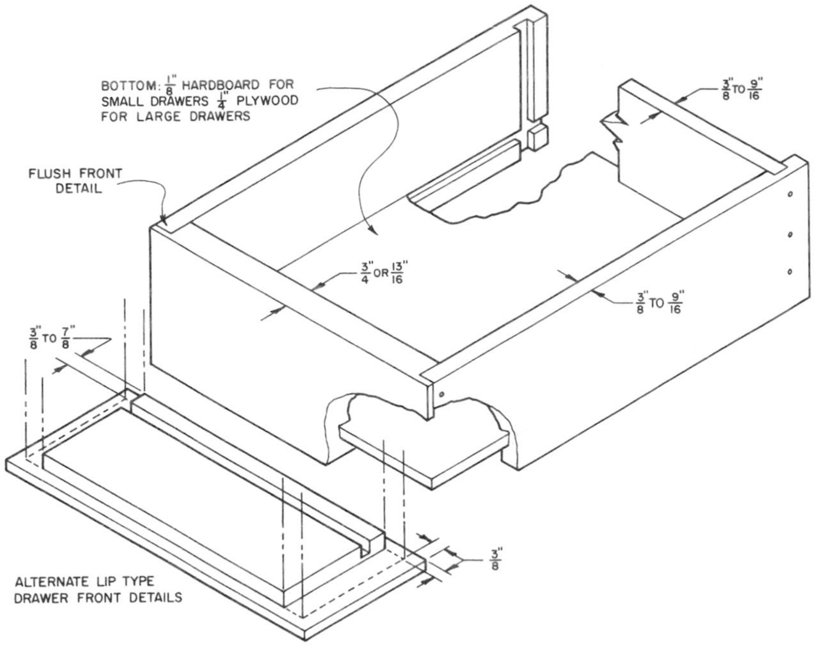

BOTTOM: $\frac{1}{8}$" HARDBOARD FOR
SMALL DRAWERS $\frac{1}{4}$" PLYWOOD
FOR LARGE DRAWERS

$\frac{3}{8}$" TO $\frac{9}{16}$"

FLUSH FRONT
DETAIL

$\frac{3}{4}$" OR $\frac{13}{16}$"

$\frac{3}{8}$" TO $\frac{9}{16}$"

$\frac{3}{8}$" TO $\frac{7}{8}$"

$\frac{3}{8}$"

ALTERNATE LIP TYPE
DRAWER FRONT DETAILS

Illus. 361. The essentials of drawer construction showing both flush and lip-type fronts.

Illus. 362. Pine corner cabinet requires frames for supporting the drawer, the front facings, the framed raised panel, and lip-type doors.

Illus. 363. Rear view of this rustic furniture illustrates some simplified construction methods. Note the glue blocks strengthening the rail to stile facing butt joint. The back is ½ inch above the sides to fit into a rabbeted edge of the top.

Plywood Construction

Plywood construction often requires some modifications in technique that otherwise might not be considered when working with solid boards. Only partially effective glue bonds can be achieved when edge-gluing plywood. Only the edge grain of every other ply bonds to other side grain. Therefore, edge-to-edge glued joints are weak and impractical. Splined or dowelled strengtheners would help some. When used, metal fasteners, such as nails and screws, should be sparingly and cautiously driven into the edges of plywood and other sheet materials. (See Illus. 365–367.) Using nails or screws that are either too large in diameter or spaced too closely together will have a "wedge effect" and split the plywood along the plies.

Joints with short grains that split easily, such as dovetail, some spline mitres, and tongue-and-rabbet joints, are best avoided in plywood construction. When possible, strengthen all plywood corner joints with glue blocks. Another common problem found in plywood projects is dealing with unsightly edges. Some ways of covering the

edges with veneer and solid wood are shown in Illus. 369. Some other ideas for covering ply edges are illustrated in Chapter 11, Veneering.

Illus. 364. End-to-side glued joints of plywood are, in theory, only slightly stronger than the same joint in solid wood, which is very weak.

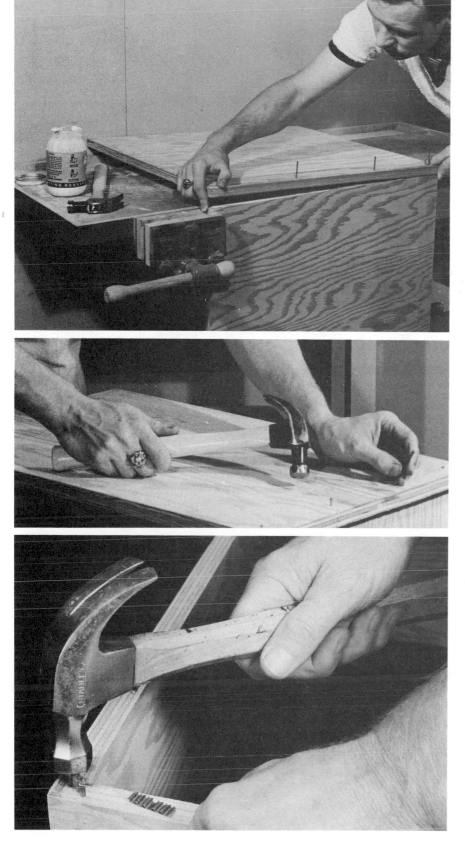

Illus. 365. Gluing and nailing a plywood butt joint.

Illus. 366. Avoid overnailing. Too many nails, too close together can do more harm than good; they tend to split or separate the plies.

Illus. 367. This glued mitre is being secured with a corrugated fastener.

153

Illus. 368. Gluing a cabinet back into rabbet cuts.

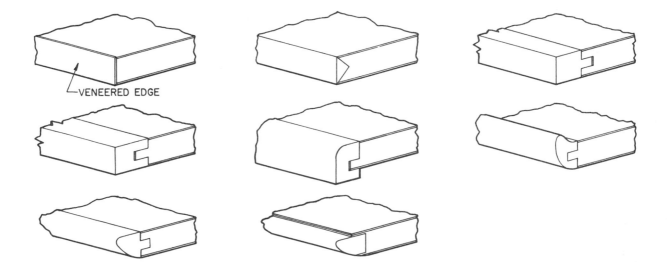

VENEERED EDGE

Illus. 369. Some ways of covering the edges of plywoods and particle board.

Chapter 10
Applying Plastic Laminates

Decorative plastic laminates serve a very wide range of surfacing needs on household and commercial furnishings. The average craftsman can easily learn the techniques and procedures used on this material. And though the professional will use more sophisticated equipment to apply plastic laminates, the home craftsman just needs a few basic tools. (See Illus. 370 and 371.)

Plastic laminates are also fun to work with because all sanding and finishing operations are eliminated. Also, very simple joinery is all that's needed when constructions have to

Illus. 371. Decorative edge treatments in the new solid-color laminates from Formica Corp. Note that the color is through the entire thickness of the laminate, eliminating the usual dark line at joint.

Illus. 370. Wilsonart's decorative laminates. Top to bottom: Leather edge oak with 180° wrap-post formed edge; no drip-post formed edge; self edge; bevelled edge with color insert; bench block with waterfall edge; readymade counter top with covered backsplash.

be overlaid with laminates. (For example, glued and nailed butt joints are all that are needed to strengthen corners, as shown in Illus. 372. And to build up the thickness of counter tops and tabletops, all you have to do is simply glue and nail a narrow strip around the underside edge, as shown in Illus. 373. With a little imagination and the basic skills, you can make many projects from inexpensive materials covered with a variety of decorative laminates. (See Illus. 374 and 375.)

Illus. 372. Simple nailed and glued butt joints are used in the assembly of this counter being covered with a decorative laminate.

Illus. 373. Building up the outer edge of a counter top.

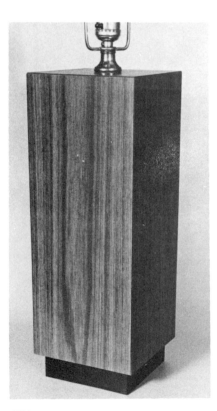

Illus. 375. A game table by Steve Mueller. Scrap—square pieces with grout filler—comprise the game area.

Illus. 374.   (left). A basic laminate practice project is this lamp base, 5 inches square and 15 inches high.

156

Plastic laminates are made from three basic raw materials: paper, resin, and ink. They all are pressed together while heat is applied until they become one sheet. The color or pattern sheet is opaque paper that's ink-printed with wood grains, colors, or other designs. A top transparent sheet is a cellulose paper impregnated with melamine resin.

A wide variety of colors, patterns, and finishes are available for plastic laminates. The number of design choices can reach several hundred, and new designs are introduced regularly. There are four basic kinds of surface finishes available. They are : 1) polished finish, which has a high gloss: 2) satin finish, which has a semi-gloss; 3) suede finish, which is micro-textured to produce a surface that does not reflect much light; and 4) sculptured finish, which is deeply textured for a 3-dimensional effect. Typical examples of sculptured finishes include slate and weathered wood patterns that have the look, dimensional contour, and feel of the real thing.

Types of Plastic Laminates

Plastic laminates are manufactured in five basic types for specific needs: general-purpose laminates, vertical-surface laminates, post-forming laminates, backing or balance sheets, and cabinet liner. General-purpose (also called "standard") laminate is ¹⁄₁₆ inch thick and designed for horizontal applications and for jobs that need more du-rability. It is used for table, desk, and counter tops, interior doors, and similar jobs. It is not recommended for exterior use.

Vertical-surface laminate is ¹⁄₃₂-inch thick. It is usually called "V-32." It's used where severe resistance to stains, heat, and wear is not required. V-32 is suitable for the vertical surfaces of kitchen cabinets, walls, and similar areas. It is not recommended for horizontal surfaces because it will eventually "telegraph," which occurs when the slight irregular surfaces of the core (the area under the laminate) or uneven adhesive spreads show through.

Post-forming laminate is specially manufactured so it will form to a curve with controlled application of heat and pressure. This type of laminate is used vertically or horizontally for curved surfaces. It's heated between 313° and 325 °F, formed, and allowed to cool.

Backing or balancing sheets are laminates about .020 inches thick that do not have decorative surfaces. These laminates are used to prevent panel warpage. Balance sheets are applied to the back or undersides of panels covered with other laminates. (See Illus. 376.) However, if the panel is securely fastened around the edges, such as to a counter base, a backing or balancing sheet may not be necessary.

Cabinet liner is essentially the same as a backing or balance sheet except it usually has a better appearance and is white or buff in color. Cabinet liner is used to cover the insides of cabinets, backs of cabinets, doors, the insides of drawers, partitions, etc.

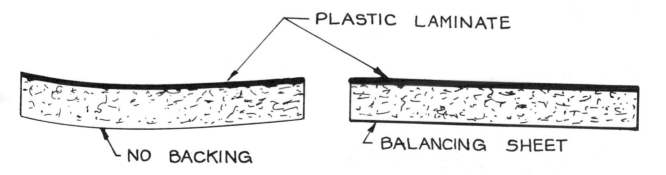

Illus. 376. The backing or balance sheet is required to prevent panels from warping.

Substrates

Substrates (also referred to as cores) are the surfaces under the laminates. The most widely used substrate is particle board (Illus. 377): plywood and hardboard are also popular. The best substrate is hardwood plywood because it has hard, flat surfaces and is highly warp resistant. However, it's expensive. Softwood plywoods (Illus. 378) often telegraph irregular surface defects, especially with thin laminates. High-density particle board is simply the most economical choice. Warpage can occur when balance sheets are not used regardless of the substrate involved. Take the necessary precautions.

Small pieces of solid wood are suitable cores but they should be at least ¾ inch thick, and no wider than 4 inches. Larger pieces are very likely to warp.

Illus. 377. Acceptable substrates (cores).

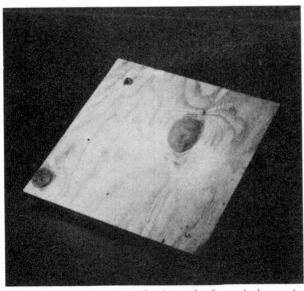

Illus. 378. Surface imperfections of softwood plywood cores will eventually show through.

Selecting the Glues

Adhesives suitable for plastic laminate work include polyvinyl (white liquid) glues, urea resin, resorcinol resin, and contact cement. All the glues except the contact cements require extensive clamping. The adhesive used for a particular job should be selected on its relative properties for end use. For example, polyvinyl glues should not be used in areas where moisture will get to the glue lines.

The most popular type of adhesive for plastic laminate work is contact cement. Contact cements are very helpful to the home craftsman. They are flexible and very easy to use on flat and curved surfaces because no special clamps are needed to obtain suitable pressure, as is required with the semi-rigid adhesives like polyvinyl. Therefore, all the instructions that follow will deal with the application of contact cements specifically.

Preparing Plastic Laminates for Gluing

Make sure the surfaces are flat, true, and free from holes, bumps, dents, or depressions. They must also be clean, and free from dust, dirt, grease, and moisture. Fill all voids and sand or file the surface flat and true. If covering an old laminate, sand the surface with 60-grit abrasive to roughen it. Make sure you have a good bond on the old laminate; if not, remove the laminate. (See page 164 for a thorough discussion of readhering and removing laminates.)

Laminates and substrates should be conditioned for an indoor environment (humidity and temperature) at least 48 hours prior to fabrication. Problems are almost certain to arise when laminates are applied in an environment that is excessively hot, dry, cold, damp, or humid. The best temperature range is between 70° and 75 °F, with a relative humidity of 45 to 55 percent.

Measuring and Marking Plastic Laminates

Use a soft-lead pencil or a grease pencil to make layout marks on the face (decorative) side of the laminate. Always plan to cut oversize. Allow at least a ¼-inch overhang all around. (See Illus. 379.) This allows room for easy positioning, and provides enough material for subsequent trimming or finishing at the edges. Check all dimensions before cutting. Certain designs, such as "wood grains," should be laid out so the pattern runs in the desired direction for end pieces, mitre joints, etc.

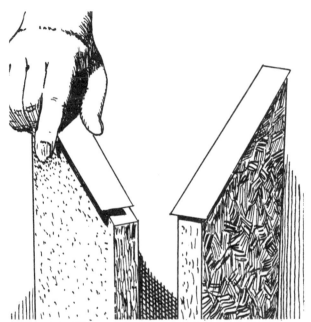

Illus. 379. Plan to allow at least ¼" to overhang.

Cutting Plastic Laminates

Plastic laminates can be cut in a variety of ways. Any fine-tooth hand saw will work, as will routers, band saws, and table saws. Cut with the decorative side up when using hand saws or band saws. Use a fine-tooth crosscut blade to cut rough sizes on the table saw or a 60-tooth, triple-chip grind carbide blade as shown in Illus. 380. Clamp a board to the fence (about ³⁄₁₆ inch above the saw table) to prevent "fluttering" of the laminate while cutting. (See Illus. 381.)

Note: When sawing laminates with portable circular saws or electric sabre saws,

make sure the decorative side is face down and is protected from possible scratching. A plastic laminate *scoring cutter* (Illus. 382) is an effective, inexpensive hand tool. Use it with a straightedge to score the laminate on the face side. The laminate will snap cleanly along the scored line when a folding-like pressure (face towards face) is applied.

Illus. 380. This triple-chip grind, 10-inch 60-tooth carbide tip blade is ideal for sawing laminates.

Illus. 381. Cutting with a fine-tooth blade on the radial arm saw. Wear safety goggles when cutting!

159

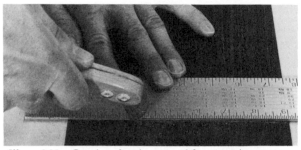

Illus. 382. Cutting laminates with a scoring cutter guided by a straightedge.

Gluing Plastic Laminates

When spreading contact cements, observe manufacturers' directions regarding safety procedures and the specific instructions pertaining to application of the cements. Most bond failures can be traced to improper glue spread, inadequate drying time, or inadequate pressure. For good results, contacts must be spread evenly and quickly. Though thick coatings do not necessarily create better bonds, do not skimp on the glue.

The edges of core materials are, as a rule, more porous than other surfaces. Consequently, they will absorb more adhesive. For this reason it's best to give plywood and particle board edges a second coat (Illus. 383) after the first spread has dried. The first coat acts like a sealer. The second coat provides an adequate base to ensure a good bond.

Spread the back surface of the laminate first, then spread the core surface. This way there's a better chance that both surfaces will be ready for bonding at approximately the same time since the core is usually more porous than the laminate and the cement dries faster on it.

Use a small bristle brush for spreading small areas (Illus. 383) like edge strips. To coat large areas, use a paint roller or notched spreader to control the amount of spread. Avoid the use of paint brushes for large surfaces because it's difficult to maintain a uniform application. Remember, when using contact adhesives it's essential that the spread surfaces are kept apart; if they have contact, they will bond to each other immediately.

Drying Time

The effective tack or bonding time will vary with the type of contact cement and the environmental conditions. High temperatures will shorten drying time, and high humidity will extend the required drying time.

The best or most appropriate drying time can be verified in a couple of ways. First, the adhesive will change from an off-white to a clear amber color when dry. Also, a simple test can be made with smooth kraft paper.

Illus. 383. Double coat plywood and particle board edges with contact adhesive.

Illus. 384. Checking adhesive dryness with kraft paper.

The adhesive will not stick to it when touched lightly if it is dry. (See Illus. 384.) The surface should exhibit a uniformly dull to semi-glossy appearance. Variation in the appearance of the spread surface indicates a poor, nonuniform adhesive spread.

Alignment and Bonding

Do not allow the spread surfaces of the core (substrate) and the laminate to accidentally touch. They will bond and cannot be shifted. Make the alignment (positioning of the laminate) over the core carefully. When doing edge strips, hold the laminate with both hands in such a way that your fingers can sense or feel the correct overlap. (See Illus. 385.) Edge and ends should overlap. Then allow the strip to make contact, and press it firmly in place by hand.

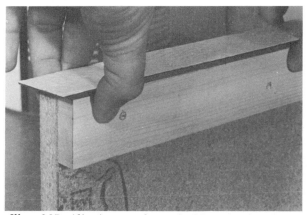
Illus. 385. Aligning an edge strip. Use your fingers to feel for proper overlap before "touching down."

Applying Pressure

Immediately apply pressure with a roller (Illus. 386), followed by a hardwood block and a hammer (Illus. 387). All this pressure is needed to ensure that at least 50 lbs. per square inch of pressure is obtained. It's best to work outward from the center to assure that air bubbles, if any, are removed. Remember as a rule that the greater the pressure, the better the bond.

Avoid using rollers wider than 3 inches. Small rollers enable you to get more pressure

over a given area. Also, do not miss any areas, since inadequate pressure is the major cause of bond failures when using contact adhesives. Contacts do not require curing time, as do other glues, so trimming can begin immediately.

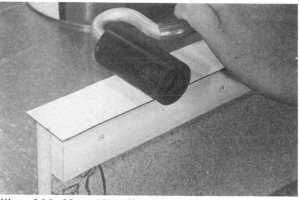
Illus. 386. Use a "J" roller to pressure an edge.

Illus. 387. A hammer on a wood block makes the best contact pressure.

Trimming

Use hand tools or routers to remove the excess overhanging material. A router is easier to use. (See Illus. 388.) Illus. 390 shows some trimming bits. (See *Router Handbook* for information on special bits and tools used in laminate work.) A block plane and file (Illus. 390) can also be used to remove the excess material.

161

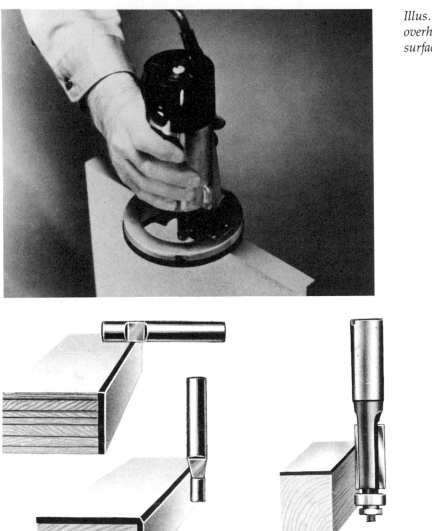

Illus. 388. Trimming to remove the overhang makes the edge flush to the surface.

Illus. 389. Router bits for trimming laminates. The inexpensive bits at left will do the same work as the costly professional bits at right.

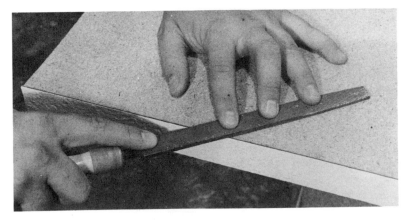

Illus. 390. Always file with the cutting stroke towards the laminate. Here the edge is being "dressed" flush to the surface.

Once the overhang has been removed either by the block plane (or router), a file should be used to dress the edge flush to the surface (Illus. 390). The filing direction should always be against or towards the laminate to prevent chipping and possible delamination. The objective is to make a brisk, sharp corner so when the surface laminate covers the edge a neat, tight seam or joint will result. Use a scrap of laminate and make a visual check as shown in Illus. 391.

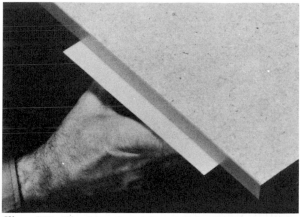

Illus. 391. Checking for a clean, tight surface to edge joint.

Cleanup

Clean up by removing excess glue. This is best accomplished by dissolving the excess cement with the appropriate solvent. Be careful not to get solvent into joints. Do not scrape excess cement off with sharp or metal objects.

Gluing Large Surfaces

Larger surfaces are done in pretty much the same way as doing an edge. Cut to allow for an overhang. Be sure the core and laminate panel surfaces are clean. Apply the contact cement (as usual) to the laminate first, using a brush or a paint roller. Next, apply the contact cement to the substrate (core). Dowel separators prevent premature contact. (See Illus. 392.) Carefully remove the dowels as you press down the laminate with hand pressure and an "ironing-out" motion while

working along. As soon as the laminate is "down," apply extra pressure in the central area of the panel and work the surfaces outward. Use a roller (Illus. 393) and follow with a "pounding" block (Illus. 394.)

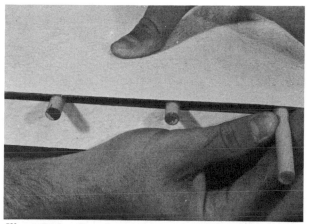

Illus. 392. Dowels separate the adhesive-covered workpieces as the laminate is positioned or aligned for contact.

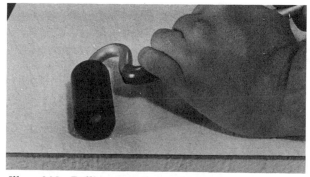

Illus. 393. Rolling over the surface.

Illus. 394. The block and hammer worked over the entire surface provides the needed pressure.

Trimming the Surface

Remove the excess overhang carefully with a block plane or with a router and one of the bits shown in Illus. 395. The job should be completed with a fine mill file held at an angle to the top. Use it to slightly round and soften sharp edges. (See Illus. 396.) Clean up as usual.

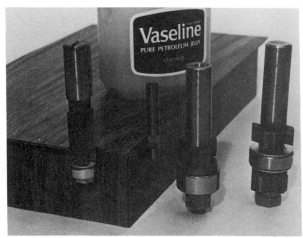

Illus. 395. Bits without roller guides need a lubricant such as petroleum jelly to prevent frictional scarring of the surface.

Illus. 396. A fine-cut file is used to soften all sharp edges.

Troubleshooting

If all steps described so far have been carefully observed, good durable bonds should result. If a problem has occurred, review the following reasons for poor bonds and delamination:

1. Dirty or dusty gluing surfaces. The glue must have full contact with the surface. Make sure no oil or other contaminations exist.
2. Adhesive has not been stirred thoroughly (unless advised otherwise by manufacturer).
3. Insufficient amount of adhesive on one or both surfaces.
4. Bonded below 70 °F. Air and all materials should be 70 °F or above.
5. Bonded in excessive humidities. Moisture may condense on the surface during drying and prevent a good bond. Water-based adhesives are not recommended for use in higher humidities.
6. Bonded when surfaces were overdry or not dry enough.
7. Bonded without adequate pressure. Avoid wide rollers. Use as much pressure as possible without damaging the surface.
8. Water-based adhesives may cause some chipboards to swell, which can result in poor bonds. Test before using water-based adhesives.
9. Panel warpage—use balance or backing sheets.

Readhering and Removing Laminates

It is sometimes necessary to readhere and remove laminates. Occasionally a laminate surface may bubble. This is caused by a delamination of a small area resulting from contact adhesive failure. To readhere, apply heat with a household iron, as shown in Illus. 397.

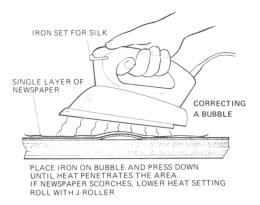

IRON SET FOR SILK

SINGLE LAYER OF NEWSPAPER

CORRECTING A BUBBLE

PLACE IRON ON BUBBLE AND PRESS DOWN UNTIL HEAT PENETRATES THE AREA. IF NEWSPAPER SCORCHES, LOWER HEAT SETTING ROLL WITH J-ROLLER

Illus. 397. Removing a bubble.

Sometimes a laminate may have to be removed entirely from a core surface because of improper alignment or for some other reason. The sooner this is done after initial bonding, the easier the laminate is to remove. Lift one corner and gently squirt contact cement solvent into the glue line. (See Illus. 398.) Slowly peel the laminate away while repeatedly applying solvent. Once removed, it may be necessary to remove the remaining adhesive. However, after the solvent has evaporated or dried completely, apply fresh coats of contact cement to the laminate and core. Then proceed as usual.

Special Techniques

Special techniques with plastic laminates within the capabilities of the wood craftsman include: 1) various edge treatments, including some unusual effects made possible by solid-color laminates; 2) installing a new counter top; and 3) using formed laminate mouldings to make framed panels for doors and drawers.

Edge Treatments

Panel Edges Panel edges can be made up in many different ways. Illus. 399 shows some of the more common applications using the standard laminates. Seldom, if ever, are plastic laminates themselves cut with mitred edges (45°). Such work would be difficult to execute without chipping since the sharp edges would be extremely brittle and fragile. Illus. 400 shows the router cutter used to make the plastic T-edge, which is the easiest edge to make. The plastic T-edge is available from various mail-order sources, including the Woodworkers Store of Rogers, Minnesota.

Illus. 398. Contact cement solvent squirted into a fresh glue line will remove the laminate.

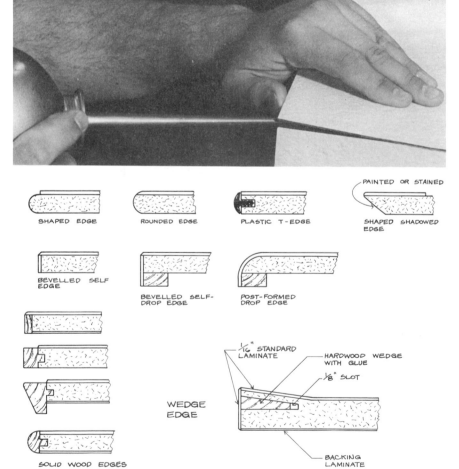

Illus. 399. Common edge treatments for standard laminates.

SHAPED EDGE

ROUNDED EDGE

PLASTIC T-EDGE

PAINTED OR STAINED

SHAPED SHADOWED EDGE

BEVELLED SELF EDGE

BEVELLED SELF-DROP EDGE

POST-FORMED DROP EDGE

WEDGE EDGE

1/16" STANDARD LAMINATE

HARDWOOD WEDGE WITH GLUE

1/8" SLOT

BACKING LAMINATE

SOLID WOOD EDGES

Illus. 400. Router cutter for the plastic T-edge.

Solid-Color Laminates are relatively new sheet materials that eliminate the dark lines evident on joints made with all of the standard or conventional colored laminates. (See Illus. 401 and 402.) These new laminates can be built up, layer upon layer, of different colors for a pinstripe edge or combined with wood to provide some unusual design options. Good, thin glue lines are a must if professional results are desired. Be sure to observe the manufacturer's gluing instruction.

Illus. 402. The through color allows for some new, special designs and surface decorations.

Illus. 401. Formica's new Colorcore®. The color is solid throughout the entire thickness, providing integral color along the edges of laminate-surfaced projects.

The Self Edge is nothing more than a simple 90° angle at the surface and edge. (See Illus. 401 and 403.) Sharpness is removed with a file. Self edges are applied to the vertical surface of a panel. (See Illus. 404.) The vertical surface of a self edge is covered with the laminate first, and then trimmed so the horizontal laminate panel can lap over it. This reduces the possibility of liquids penetrating the glue line.

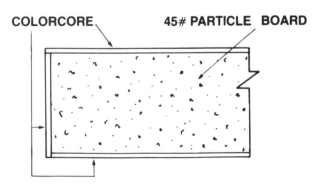

COLORCORE   45# PARTICLE BOARD

Illus. 403. A regular self edge.

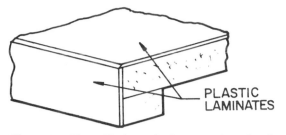

Illus. 404. The self edge. The horizontal surface laminate overlaps the vertical edge laminate.

The Rounded Edge is more durable and safer than other edges. (See Illus. 405.) A ⅛- to ⁵⁄₃₂-inch roundover bit is used with a router to create this edge. The ⁵⁄₃₂-inch roundover bit is the largest radius that can be used with solid-color laminates without exposing the core. Polishing the cut surfaces with lemon oil, Watco® oil, or acrylic car wax will match the original lustre.

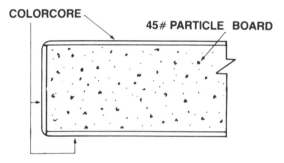

Illus. 405. Detail of the rounded edge has a ⅛ to ⁵⁄₃₂ inch radius.

Pinstripe Edge is achieved by using two or more colors on the edge. (See Illus. 406 and 407.) Various-shaped router bits can be used to expose the multicolored layers. When

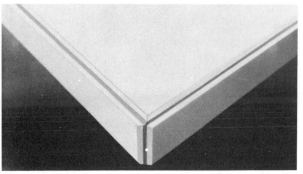

Illus. 406. A pinstripe edge is achieved by "stacking" two or more laminates together on a panel edge and then shaping them with a router.

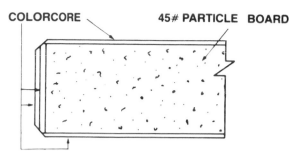

Illus. 407. Basics of the pinstripe edge.

stacking the strips, sand the faces; this permits adhesion to the normally smooth surfaces. (See Illus. 408.) Use a 100-grit abrasive. To glue, use a solvent-based contact adhesive to build up any number of layers. Some clear epoxies work well, but be sure to test the epoxy for suitability before doing a project because epoxy formulations vary greatly. Do not use PVA (liquid white glues). Alternating light and dark colors of laminate makes glue lines less prominent. Trimming with a 45° router bit will expose a pinstripe edge. (See Illus. 406.)

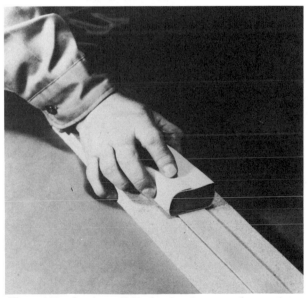

Illus. 408. Sand a solid-color laminate surface to improve adhesion to the same material.

Wood Edges are the easiest to make up and they have very little glue line visibility. (See Illus. 409 and 410.) Two techniques for using decorative strips of wood glued to substrates are shown in the drawings. Using the router with any of a wide variety of profile-cutting shapes will create some unusual, decorative touches. Remember to finish the wood edges accordingly so they will be protected from moisture penetration.

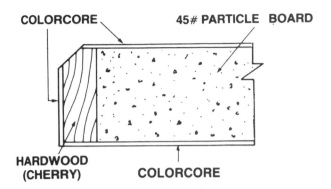

Illus. 409. *This simple chamfer edge exposes a wood insert edge.*

Illus. 410. *A wood corner insert and the joinery involved in this cabinetry form a combination solid-color laminate and wood decorative corner.*

Installing Ready-Made Counters

Sometimes, in the interests of expediency and cost, it is better to buy and install ready-made counter surfacing. Most building-supply centers either have prelaminated, fully formed counter material in stock or they can order it for you. The installation requires a few basic tools (Illus. 411) and some fairly easy techniques. The essential procedures are shown and described in Illus. 412–422.

To prepare for installation, carefully measure for proper size, disconnect the plumbing and—if electrical appliances need moving—shut off the electricity. Plan to use an "end splash" (Illus. 412) where the end of the counter meets a wall. Use "end caps" (Illus. 413) on tops where the counter top has exposed ends.

Cutting the counter to size begins with marking the laminate surface with a soft-lead pencil in the approximate location it will be cut. (Illus. 414). Cover this line with masking tape and lay out another line on the tape that gives the precise location where the counter top is to be cut.

Illus. 415 and 416 show how to saw the counter. The sawn edge should be filed smooth. *Note*: Always file towards the laminate to prevent chipping. Cut out sink and/or range openings. Punch a starting hole at all inside corners. (See Illus. 417.) Boring all the way through (Illus. 418) makes a starting hole for a keyhole saw. Cut with the face upside-down if using a power sabre saw. Remember to apply tape to the decorative side.

Finishing the counter top ends may require installing wood strips to fill in the cut edge. (See Illus. 419.) If the counter's lower edge prevents drawers or under-counter appliances from opening, glue and nail on riser blocks to the underside of the counter top. (See Illus. 420.)

Mitred corners should be cut and prepared by a building-products dealer. Proper equipment for making such cuts is essential to having a strong joint. The joint can be assembled with T-bolt connectors that are easy to use. Apply waterproof or urea resin glue to the mitred edges and draw the joint together firmly. (See Illus. 421.) Install the sink (Illus. 422) or range top. Remember to seal all areas with caulking—especially those areas exposed to excessive moisture, such as those under back splashes that are attached behind sink areas.

Illus. 411. Tools and supplies required for the installation of readymade counter tops.

Illus. 412. Use an end splash where the counter top butts against a side wall.

Illus. 413. An end cap covers the cut on an exposed end.

Illus. 414. Marking the approximate line of cut.

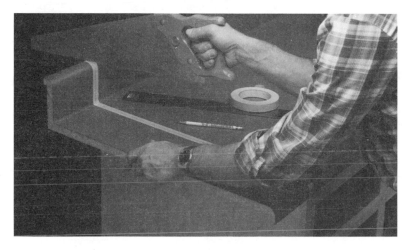

Illus. 415. Hand sawing to length. Note that the face side is up.

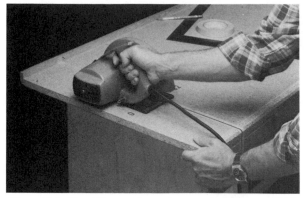

Illus. 416. If cutting with a sabre or circular saw that cuts on the upstroke, mark and cut on the underside. Be sure the opposite (decorative face) side is taped on the cutting line.

Illus. 417. Punch a starting hole for boring at the inside corners.

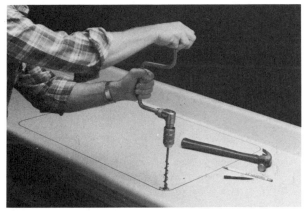

Illus. 418. Boring through holes to make an opening for a keyhole saw.

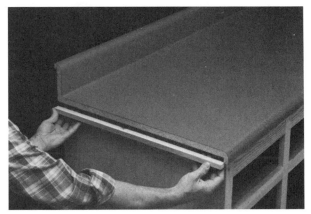

Illus. 419. Fill in the cut edge with a wood strip.

Illus. 420. Blocks glued and nailed to the underside will raise the counter top if necessary.

Illus. 421. Precut mitres are machined on the underside for easy assembly with T-bolt connectors.

Illus. 422. Installing the sink.

Laminate-Surfaced Mouldings

These are available to the do-it-yourselfer from the Le Mica Moulding Products Corp., 19690 Filer Ave., Detroit, Michigan 48234. (See Illus. 423.) They provide many colors and wood-grain patterns that match Formica® Brand laminate sheets and finishes. As you can see in Illus. 423, the laminate is formed around some very sharply curved surfaces of various wood-core moulding profiles. These mouldings, when used in conjunction with flat panel stock, make beau-tiful, matching cabinet doors and drawer fronts. (See Illus. 424 and 425.) Depending upon your style of door, the mouldings are rabbetted for ⅜- or ½-inch panels. The frame moulding is mitre-cut precisely to your dimensions and shipped ready to assemble. (See Illus. 426 and 427.) The advantages of this system include the fact that no cutting, mitring, clamping, or edge-finishing is necessary. Contact Le Mica Moulding Products to check current prices, further instructions, and shipping information.

Illus. 423. Plastic-laminate covered wood mouldings are available in many shapes.

Illus. 424. An exploded view of door fabrication. The flat panels fit into purchased rabbeted frames.

172

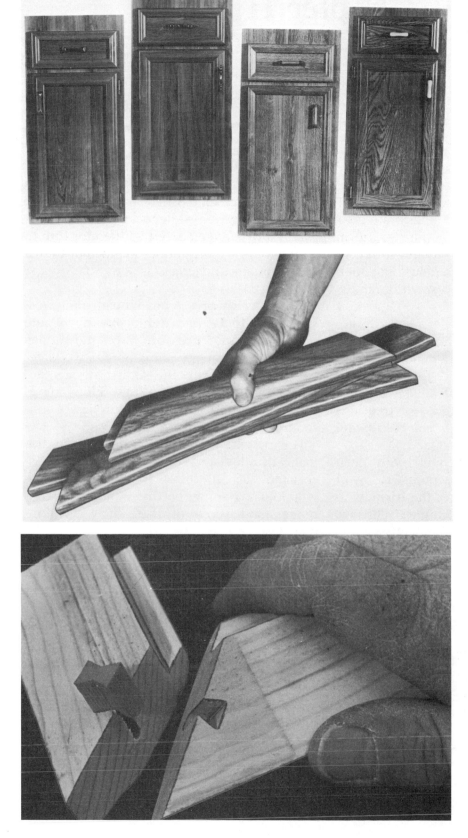

Illus. 425. Some typical "fronts" possible using formed mouldings and your own flat surface work.

Illus. 426. The framing is sold by the linear inch and cut to your exact specifications.

Illus. 427. The premitred joints come with a unique wedged butterfly connector which draws a glue-spread joint tightly together.

Chapter 11

Applying Veneers, Inlays, and Overlays

The art of veneering dates back approximately 3,000 years. Early Egyptian furniture removed from sealed tombs suggests that the first manmade veneers were used for ornamental overlays. The Greeks and Romans used highly figured veneers to decorate their furnishings. Veneering as a pure art form gained momentum in the 17th and 18th centuries with the creations of famous craftsmen like Duncan Phyfe, the Hepplewhite family, and Thomas Chippendale.

Well-crafted veneer work is a sight to behold. It is admired by everyone—especially by the fraternity of experienced woodworkers. (See Illus. 428 and 429.) Veneered work has such high visual appeal because only the finest, highest grades of tree logs are made into face veneers. The results are always spectacular.

Though veneering has traditionally been one of the most artistic and purest forms of woodcrafting, it's also one of the trickiest to master. It's true that only high-grade cuttings are used; however, these cuttings often come with splits, are warped or buckled, or are brittle. Also, the thinness of veneer makes it react drastically to the same conditions that affect drying wood, and to humidity.

Pressing out and bonding the veneer is more complicated than one might think. Flattening the curled veneers may crack them even more. Veneers need a little moisture to soften them—though not too much or they'll shrink again and crack as they dry on the bonded surfaces.

When veneering, glue spread and pressure have to be just right. Too much glue and/or too much pressure forces most glues through the veneers. Some porous wood veneers, like oak, ash, and some burl cuts, are especially susceptible. When glue comes through to the face side, it complicates subsequent finishing procedures.

Fortunately, new developments have dramatically alleviated some of the problems associated with the craft. In this chapter, we will look at some of the traditional techniques and some of these new developments.

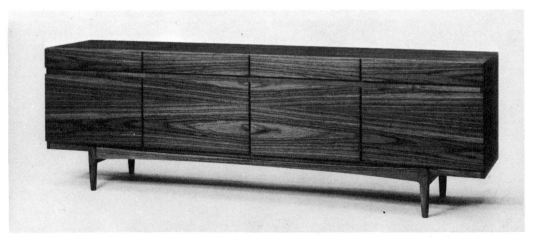

Illus. 428. The high visual appeal of this buffet results from the expertly matched veneer patterns. The buffet was designed by Arne Vodder, of Denmark.

Illus. 429. A parquet veneered tabletop. Projects with tops of this type are veneered on both surfaces to ensure a balanced, warp-free top.

Veneer Manufacturing

Veneers are cut to thicknesses between $\frac{1}{100}$ and ¼ inch. Standard veneers have traditionally been $\frac{1}{28}$ inch thick. The manner in which the veneer is cut determines the visual effect or figure obtained. Illus. 430 compares the three most common methods of veneer cutting.

Also related to the look of the veneer is the portion of the tree from which the veneer is cut. A crotch, for example, will produce a different pattern than a burl or stump cut. (See Illus. 431.)

Matching Veneer

The way in which individual pieces of veneer are joined together is called "matching."

The most popular matching effects are shown in Illus. 432. An example of a diamond match is shown in Illus. 433. The beginner will find the random match a good choice for making wider panels when they are needed. The technique for this match is similar to that used to make boards wider by gluing them edge to edge.

Cutting Veneers

Veneers can be cut in several ways. The most common method is to use a special veneer saw guided along a straightedge, as shown in Illus. 434. Sharp knives (Illus. 435) can also be used, but these tend to follow the grain rather than the intended line of cut. Knives work fine, however, for cutting some of the new, thinner, flexible veneers.

175

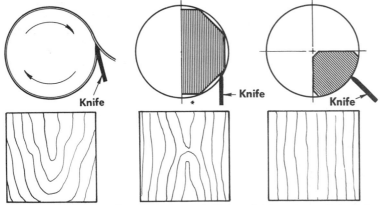

Illus. 430. Types of veneer cuts. Left to right: rotary, flat-slicing, quarter-slicing.

Illus. 431. Burl pattern veneer cut from the stump of the tree.

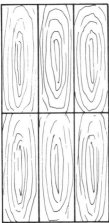

Vertical Butt and Horizontal Bookleaf Match

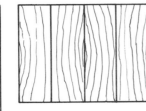

Book Match
All types of veneers are used. In book matching, every other sheet is turned over just as are the leaves of a book. Thus, the back of one veneer meets the front of the adjacent veneer, producing a matching joint design.

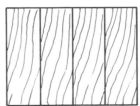

Slip Match
In slip matching, veneer sheets are joined side by side and convey a sense of repeating the flitch figure. All types of veneer may be used, but this type of matching is most common in quarter-sliced veneers.

Random Match
Veneers are joined with the intention of creating a casual unmatched effect. Veneers from several logs may be used in the manufacture of a set of panels.

Special Matching Effects

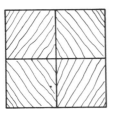

Diamond

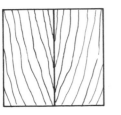

Reverse Diamond

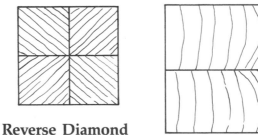

Four-Way Center and Butt
This type of match is ordinarily applied to butt, crotch, or stump veneers, since it is the most effective way of revealing the beauty of their configurations. Occasionally, flat-cut veneers are matched in this manner where panel length requirements exceed the length of available veneers.

Illus. 432. Basic effects achieved by veneer-matching.

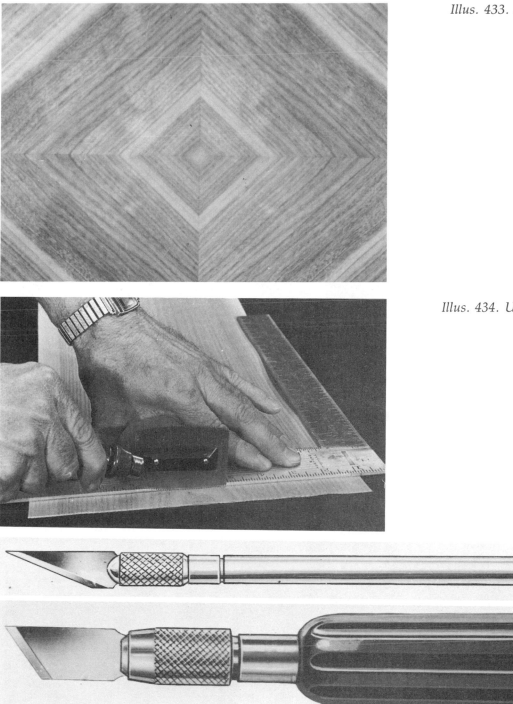

Illus. 433. A diamond match.

Illus. 434. Using a veneer saw.

Illus. 435. Sharp craft knives are useful in veneer work.

Flattening Buckled Veneer

It is often necessary to flatten buckled veneer before it can be matched together or bonded to a substrate. Spray a very light water mist on the veneer with an atomizer sprayer such as a window-cleaner dispenser. Do not overwet it. Place the lightly moistened veneers on a flat surface. There should be a sheet of newspaper between each layer of veneer. Set a flat plywood panel over them and place bricks or concrete blocks on top of the panel. The veneers should be reasonably flat in 24 to 36 hours. Do not moisten veneers just before use. Veneers must be dry when glued or they will shrink on the surface which will most likely result in splits and blisters.

Preparing Standard Veneer

Core materials for all veneering work should be selected and prepared in basically the same way as for plastic laminates (see page 158.) Make sure the surfaces are flat and true. (See Illus. 436.) Cleanliness is important. A speck of sawdust will telegraph through veneer and will be very noticeable.

Illus. 436. Fill and sand voids or dents that would telegraph through the veneer.

Edge-Joining Veneers

The width of the veneer (across the grain) can be increased in either of two ways. One method, using veneer tape (Illus. 437–440), splices the veneers before they are bonded to a substrate surface. The other technique makes the joint at the time the pieces of veneer are bonded to the substrate.

When splicing the veneers, select and match the pieces of veneer that are to be joined at their edges. (See Illus. 437.) The edges must be made straight and true. The easiest way to do this is to clamp them between two pieces of lumber. Depending upon the sizes of the veneer, the lumber pieces and the location of clamps, the planing can be done on a power jointer. If not,

simply use a hand plane, as shown in Illus. 438. This system is probably better.

Next, tape the edges tightly together with special veneer tape or masking tape. (See Illus. 439.) The taping should be done on the face, or up side, of the veneer. Once the joint is taped, check the other side, making sure you have a perfect, tight fit. Fold the joint open to expose the edges for gluing, as shown in Illus. 440. Carefully spread some liquid white glue along the joint. Close the joint, carefully remove the excess glue, and apply some tape to the back side. When the glue has set, remove the tape from the back side only. The tape on the face is left on until bonding to the substrate is completed.

Illus. 437. Arrange the veneer pieces for best appearance and size.

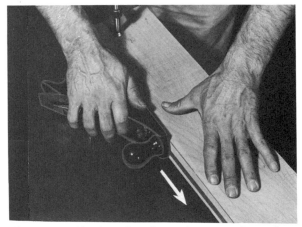

Illus. 438. Planing the edges of veneer clamped between two boards. Here the plane (on its side) rides against the surface of the workbench.

178

Illus. 439. Tape the veneer pieces together on the face side.

Illus. 440. Apply white glue after taping. Fold the joint open, as shown.

Bonding Veneers to Substrates

Laying Veneers

A number of different glues can be used to bond veneers to the substrate. Small areas can be glued with the liquid yellow glues, but the liquid white glues are preferred because they do not set as fast. Urea or plastic resins can be used too. The problem with all of these glues is that they require veneer

presses (Illus. 441) or some system of clamps and cauls or platens. (Refer to page 216 for more information about veneer presses.)

Most experts recommend easier ways for the beginner to bond veneers rather than getting involved with making and/or using veneer presses. Contact cements made especially for veneer bonding (Illus. 442) are ideal. Hot-melt sheets that are applied with a household iron work, too, for some jobs, but they are not, as a rule, recommended for larger areas.

Illus. 441. A self-made veneer press.

Illus. 442. A solvent-base contact cement is recommended for veneer bonding.

Bonding with Contacts

Do *not* use water-based contact cements. They can swell wood fibres quickly, expand and curl the veneer, and can cause splits and cracks when the veneer dries on the bonded surface.

Apply a good solvent-based veneering contact according to the manufacturer's instructions. Use an inexpensive but clean brush for small areas (Illus. 443) or a roller to coat larger surfaces (Illus. 444). Most instructions recommend that a second coat of adhesive be applied to both the veneer and the substrate after the first coats have dried, which takes approximately 30 minutes.

Where there is good glue spread, the surfaces look like they have been varnished. If any dull spots appear, give those areas a third coat; some veneers are often very dry and porous, so they absorb lots of glue It is better to correct these problems now—careful inspection before bonding is time well spent.

Test for dryness by sliding a piece of wrapping paper over the glue-coated surfaces. When you can do this, the glue is ready for contact bonding.

Making the Bond This is fairly easy, but any alignment needs to be done correctly because the contact glue sticks quite easily and any inadvertent contact between the cement-coated base and the veneer can cause a great deal of trouble. If the veneer is prepared with sufficient overhang and the workpieces are not too large, the veneer can be set down carefully. (See Illus. 445 and 446.) In most

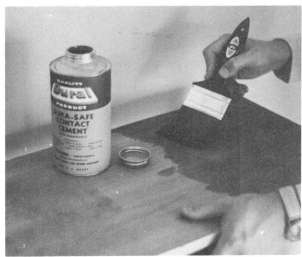

Illus. 443. Apply contact cement with a brush.

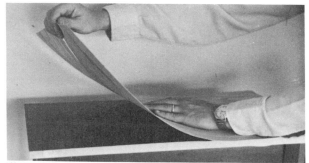

Illus. 445. Laying down the veneer.

Illus. 444. Coat contact cement onto large surfaces with a roller.

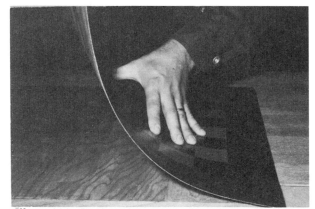

Illus. 446. Laying down a readymade (mail order) veneer chessboard.

cases, it's best to use the "slip-sheet method."
Simply cut a piece of wrapping paper the
size of the surface to be veneered. Place the
paper on the substrate. Place the veneer on
top of it, with the glue-covered side facing
down towards the substrate. Make the alignment and carefully pull the slip sheet out
from under the veneer little by little. Smooth
and press the veneer down as you go. As you
work along, smooth out any blisters or bubbles. Apply pressure with the narrow veneer
roller (Illus. 447). A small block, tapped with
a hammer as it is moved over the surface, can
be used instead of the veneer roller.

Illus. 448. Trimming the overhang.

*Illus. 447. Use a veneer roller to give pressure over
the entire surface.*

*Illus. 449. Overlap method of veneer joining. The
raised lap is sanded flush to get a perfect match.*

If you have used tape, remove it from the
surface. Veneer tape can be removed easily
with *slight* moistening and some heat provided by a household iron. Be careful with
water—try to moisten the tape only, and
have a dry rag ready to blot up the excess. If a
blister or bubble appears, apply heat and im-
mediate hand pressure. If the blister reap-
pears, slit the veneer with a knife and inject
some white glue. (See page 88 .)

Set a weight on the veneer and allow the
glue to dry. Trim the overhanging edge with
the veneer saw or with a knife as shown in
Illus. 448. Place the panel face-down on a
smooth flat surface.

The tapeless, overlap joint is another way of
joining the veneer. (See Illus. 449.) When

making wide panels with this joint, make
sure the joints are made during the application of the veneers. This system only works
for edge joints with parallel grain. It does not
work for end-to-end splices or mitred joints.

About ½ inch of extra veneer width should
be allowed for each joint. One edge should
be reasonably straight. Use contact cement,
and follow the procedures described for laying a single veneer panel. Spread the glue
over all pieces and lay down the first piece.
Lay down the next piece; it should overlap
the first about ¼ to ½ inch. Press as usual,
but add more pressure against the joint.
Force the veneer into the void (cavity) created
by the overlap with the corner of a hardwood
block. Sand off the raised lap to get a perfect
flush joint. This technique works well when
veneering over-curved surfaces, such as the
cylinders shown in Illus. 450.

Illus. 450. These veneered geometric tables or plant stands were made by Helikon Furniture.

Bonding with Hot-Melts

Bonding with hot-melts is neat, odorless, and quick, but some professionals question their suitability when used to veneer large surfaces. The adhesive sheet comes on a paper backing. The glue sheet is first ironed onto the substrate with the paper backing up. (See Illus. 451.) When the glue sheet cools, peel off the paper backing. (See Illus. 452.) Now, place the veneer on the glue surface and heat through the veneer with the iron, as shown in Illus. 453. Immediately follow with a veneer roller to press the veneer down firmly as the glue cools. One supplier of the hot-melt sheet suggests applying a layer of the glue sheet to the back of the veneer and to the substrate. In any case, test these products out yourself before undertaking major projects.

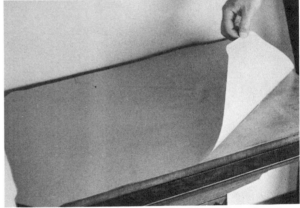

Illus. 452. Peel off the paper backing when the glue sheet has cooled.

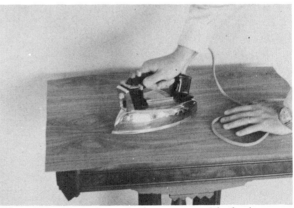

Illus. 453. Heat through the veneer with the iron.

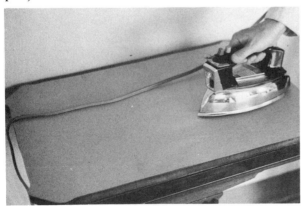

Illus. 451. Use a household iron to iron the hot-melt glue sheet in place.

Newly Developed Veneers

Flexible wood veneers are manufactured improvements over the standard or conventional veneers. These are genuine wood veneers that are cut much thinner—only ¹⁄₆₄ to ¹⁄₇₅ inch thick. They come with a factory-applied paper backing. This is a very tough, impregnated paper that's only about .005 inch thick.

Flexible wood veneers come flat and stay flat. It is not necessary to moisturize or pre-press them. The veneer can be cut with an ordinary pair of scissors (Illus. 454), and is so flexible that it can be folded over fairly sharp corners. (See Illus. 455–457.) Almost any smooth surface like plastic, metal, glass, and even some cardboard materials makes a suitable substrate.

Illus. 456. It's best to soften corners with coarse sandpaper before turning sharply with the flexible veneers.

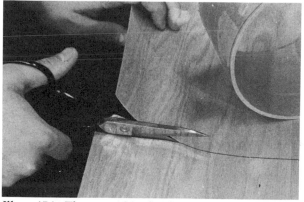

Illus. 454. The new, thin flexible veneers can be cut with scissors.

Illus. 457. Flexible veneers are bonded essentially like standard veneer. Overhangs are trimmed with a sharp knife.

Illus. 455. The flexible veneers will form to various surfaces, even to this router-cut edge.

The usual adhesives can be used to apply these veneers, and the techniques of spreading, applying pressure, etc., are essentially the same as working standard veneers. However, complete glue spread is essential. The material is so thin, it will not bridge uncoated areas. Thus, with a little increase in relative humidity, a blister will appear.

Cleanliness and neatness are also important in the glue spread. Dust particles, minute lumps of glue, and even a hair bristle from a paint brush left trapped in the adhesive is likely to telegraph through.

When working large panels, use the slip-sheet method described on page 181. On larger panels, start in the center and work

183

outward towards the ends. rather than starting and continuing from one end. This will be much easier, and there will be less of a chance for wrinkles or bubbles to occur.

Peel and Stick Veneers

Peel and stick veneers are new developments that take away most of the work in veneering. (See Illus. 458–459.) These veneers are just like flexible wood veneers about ¼₄ inch thick, but with a pressure-sensitive adhesive applied to the back. The adhesive has an aggressive tack, but it should be rolled and hammered with a block to achieve a good bond. (See Illus. 460.)

Illus. 460. Veneer edging is available in rolls of various widths with preapplied adhesive.

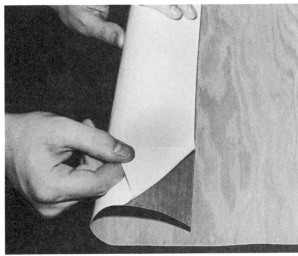

Illus. 458. "Peel and stick" veneer. Removing a backing sheet readies the veneer for bonding.

Iron-on Veneers

Iron-on veneers are available in both sheets and in 1- and 2-inch widths of matching edge trim. (See Illus. 461.) A regular household iron is used to apply the veneer to any flat surface.

The development of new veneers like iron-on veneers has made this craft much less difficult to master. However, the craftsman does

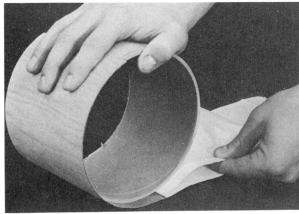

Illus. 459. When a cardboard cylinder is wrapped with peel and stick veneer, a "wood" wastebasket is made.

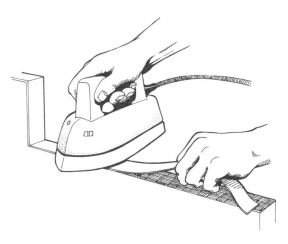

Illus. 461. Iron-on veneer edgings have preapplied thermoplastic adhesives.

pay a price for these modern developments. Just compare the cost of any species of standard veneers to the cost of the new veneers.

Incidentally, one of the new materials that will be available to woodcrafters is a decorative laminate with preapplied thermoplastic. It is a hot-melt glue that can be ironed on just like iron-on veneers.

Veneering "Projects"

Do not make veneers yourself. However, thin edgings can be ripped from solid boards on a table saw (Illus. 462).

Some interesting ideas for panel products are shown in Illus. 463–465. Technically, these are not veneering projects because they are ³⁄₁₆ inch-thick pieces of solid wood overlaid onto thick plywood panels. Checkerboards and chessboards are always popular projects, and an alternative to a conventionally veneered board is shown in Illus. 463. A different look is the knot panel made in essentially the same way. (See Illus. 465.)

As in plastic-laminate work, veneered panels should be balanced to prevent warping. If the panel is "free-floating," such as a chessboard, a box lid, certain table tops, or a cabinet door, both sides should be veneered.

Illus. 462. This homemade veneer edging has been ripped from a solid board.

Illus. 463. Chess-checker board has a solid wood frame around a plywood base "veneered" with solid wood squares ³⁄₁₆ inch thick.

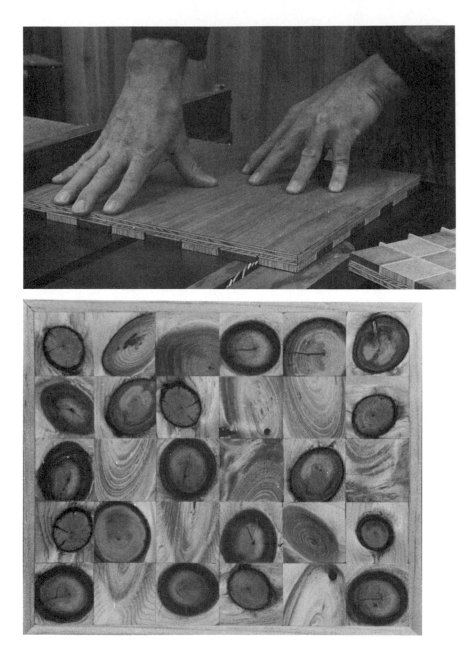

Illus. 464. Right: ³/₁₆ × 1³/₄-inch square veneer blocks glued to plywood. Left: sawing kerfs for inlay divider strips. This will ensure clean, perfect joints throughout.

Illus. 465. Sliced knots "veneered" to a panel with epoxy adhesive.

Inlaid Designs and Borders

Inlaid designs and borders are often combined with veneered projects as final design elements. (See Illus. 466 and 467.) Ready-made inlays are available by mail order in the standard ¹/₂₈ inch thickness. The steps involved to make an inlay are shown and described in Illus. 467–471.

Overlays

Overlays can be regarded as any decorative design, carving embellishment (Illus. 472), molding, or trim glued onto a surface without a prepared recess, which is required for an inlay. Any adhesive and clamping device that gets the job done is appropriate. Epoxy and super glue, of the gel type, can be used where strength is important. Hot-melt is ideally suited for jobs where a great deal of strength or stress resistance is not required.

Illus. 466. Preparing a veneered center inlaid panel with border inlays.

Illus. 467. Inlaying this sunburst design is easy.

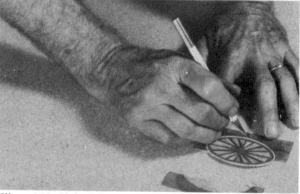

Illus. 468. If the inlay comes with extra material, trim it. Inlays come with tape covering the face side—leave it on.

Illus. 469. With tape-side up, make a reference mark as shown, and cut an incision around the inlay.

Illus. 470. Carefully cut away the veneer. Clean and level the bottom.

187

Illus. 471. Glue the inlay in place with the tape side up and reference mark aligned. Use yellow glue. Allow it to tack. Press in inlay and clamp or weight it until glue sets. Carefully remove squeeze-out with chisel. Moisten tape to remove it. Sand and finish.

Illus. 472. Ornaments, carving, or other embellishments glued to a flat surface are called decorative overlays.

Chapter 12
Gluing Curved Laminations

Huge wooden arches made to support entire buildings (Illus. 473), as well as sports gear (Illus. 474 and 475) and furniture (Illus. 476 and 477),are typical products with curved laminations made by the wood-laminating industries. Curved-wood laminations are dry layers of wood boards, strips, or sheets that are formed or bent permanently to new shapes when they are glued and clamped together over curved forms or pressed together in a die or mould. The resulting glued-up member becomes an exceptionally strong, cohesive unit.

Glued laminated parts have many advantages over parts that are only sawed or steam bent. (See Illus. 478.) First of all, the woodworker has complete design freedom. Prac-

tically any shape can be made. (See Illus. 479–481.) Almost any available material can be used. In fact, low-grade materials, short lengths (see Chapter 8), thin edgings, veneer scraps, etc., can often be used effectively for many projects.

Laminated parts have few cracks or checks and no distortion or warpage. This is not necessarily true of parts made by sawing or by steam bending (Illus. 482).

The laminating process involves four major steps: 1) making the form(s); 2) selecting and preparing laminations; 3) gluing, clamping, and curing (if necessary); and 4) trimming or sizing the glued assembly.

Illus. 473. This "glue-lam" factory produces large laminated timbers. A glued member is on the jig table.

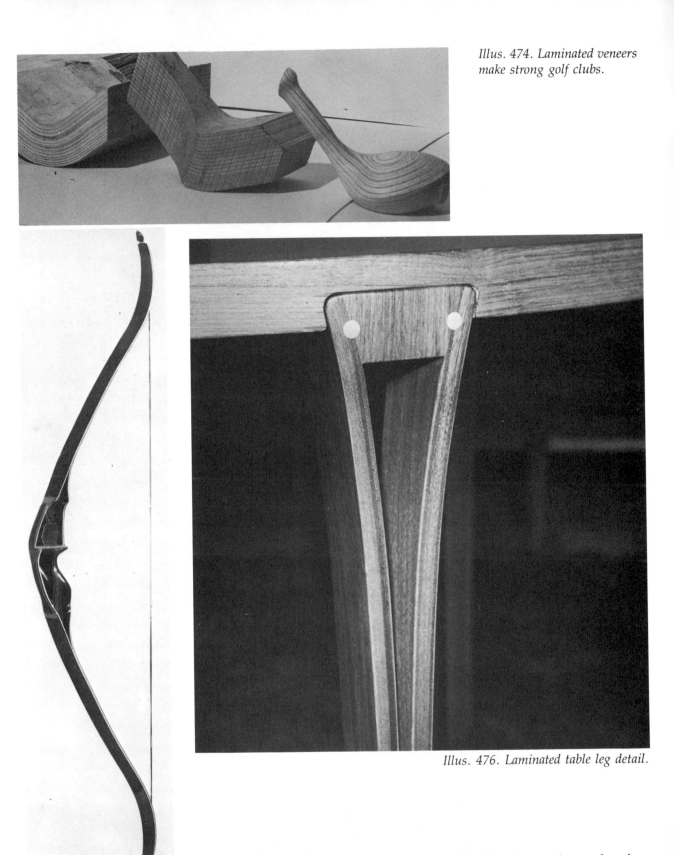

Illus. 474. Laminated veneers make strong golf clubs.

Illus. 476. Laminated table leg detail.

Illus. 475 (left). The laminated bow of wood and fiberglass construction can be a do-it-yourself project.

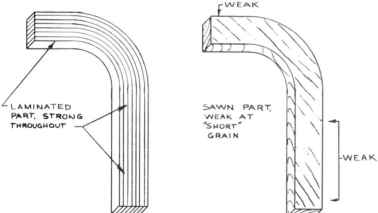

WEAK

LAMINATED
PART, STRONG
THROUGHOUT

SAWN PART,
WEAK AT
"SHORT"
GRAIN

WEAK

Illus. 478. Comparing strength qualities of laminated wood to a sawn part of the same shape.

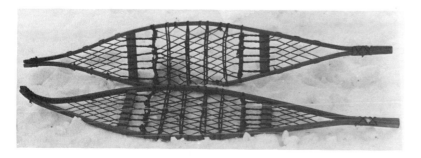

Illus. 479. Snow shoes with laminated frames crafted by Dan Jischke.

191

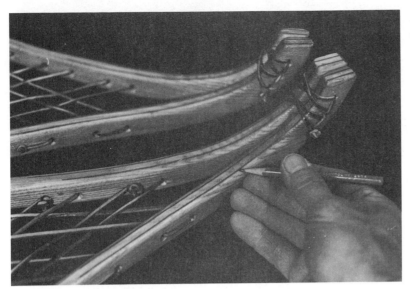

Illus. 480. The tips of Jischke's snow shoes have grain directions that alternate to strengthen short grain.

Illus. 481. Coffee table designed and fabricated by Perry Peterson.

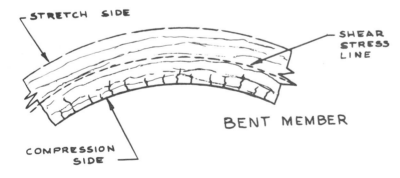

STRETCH SIDE

SHEAR STRESS LINE

COMPRESSION SIDE

BENT MEMBER

Illus. 482. Above: forces and stress in a single bent member. Below: in a laminated member, the shear is distributed throughout the thickness.

SHEAR STRESS IS DISTRIBUTED

LAMINATED MEMBER

Selecting and Preparing Laminations

Selecting and preparing the laminations is pretty much dictated by the design of the project or member to be made. The radius of the bend determines how thick the laminations must be. Make some test pieces from the wood species that will be used to make up the laminations. Flex them over the sharpest curve on the form. As a general rule, the minimum radius to which dry, straight hardwood can be bent without breaking is about 40 to 60 times its thickness. Veneer 1⁄28 inch thick will bend to a radius between 1½ and 2 inches. Veneer ¼ inch thick will bend to approximately a 10-inch radius. In general, hardwoods bend to a somewhat sharper radius than softwoods of the same thickness. Each laminate should bend over the mould fairly easy without breaking. It's usually best to use more thinner pieces than fewer thick ones.

In projects such as an archery bow or tennis racket, select laminations very carefully. Avoid stock that has diagonal or swirly grain or knots. Very critical laminations (laminations that need a precise bend), such as those used in making some musical instruments, will require stock that is all of uniform moisture content. Laminates should either be all flat-sawed or all quarter-sawed—whichever is most appropriate—but they should not be mixed within the same member.

The number of laminations is also an important consideration where strength is concerned. The greater the number of layers in a laminated part, the stronger and more rigid it will be. Have at least three (preferably four) layers for any glue-up.

When only two layers are laminated together, "springback" will occur. Springback is when the curved pieces straighten out. Also, when only two layers are laminated together, the laminated member will only have minimal strength and stiffness.

Adhesives

Liquid white and liquid yellow glues are not used very much for this type of work. They can only be used on jobs that are assembled very quickly, on bends that have minimal stress, and where the project is not subjected to heat and moisture.

Other kinds of glues make much better choices. Resorcinol glues are highly recommended by many of the older professional craftsmen. However, when resorcinols are used, all conditions—temperature, mixture, glue spread, surface preparation, open assembly time, pressure, humidity, moisture content, etc.—must be perfect.

Two-part epoxies are as a rule pretty easy to use. Their major drawbacks are their higher cost and the "mess" they make. Some epoxy glues require heat-curing chambers. If the assembly is to be cured in a heated chamber, the form must be prepared accordingly, since it, too, is subjected to heat. Epoxies are ideal to use on sports equipment, boat ribs, archery bows, etc. Use epoxies where dissimilar materials of fibreglass and wood must be bonded together. Plastic or urea resins work well on indoor projects, and are less expensive than resorcinols or epoxies.

The glue selected must permit sufficient assembly time. This is especially important when many pieces or a lot of layers of laminates must all be spread with glue. This takes time because in most cases the glue spread should be on both surfaces of the joint.

Making the Form

Most projects require the fabrication of a custom-made laminating form or mould. Some jobs require more time to make up the form than to actually laminate the project. Forms that have convex surfaces are easier to make and work with than those with concave ones. (See Illus. 483.)

Illus. 483. Form design: Bending and clamping laminates over a convex form is the easiest.

Preparing and Protecting Forms

If you want a final project without humps or dips, make sure the contact surfaces of the forms you are making have smooth, flowing curves. Cut the surfaces with a band saw, then smooth them out with a hand plane or file to cut down slight bumps or pockets. Higher-quality forms can be made by gluing a hard material over the curved, sawn surface. Tempered hardboard, thin hardwood plastic, plastic laminates, and sheet metal can be bonded to the working surface of the form. Such surfacing materials will help bridge small gaps and• smooth out irregularities that sometimes occur during bandsawing.

Take protective measures to make sure that the glue-up project is not inadvertently glued to the mould. A good mould should be varnished at least once; twice is ideal. Spread several coats of paste wax over all surfaces; this way, when the glue gets on the surface of the form, it will not stick to it. Another recommended measure is to place a thin, plastic film of something like foodwrap between the form and laminations.

One-Piece Forms

One-piece forms (Illus. 484 and 485) are simply curved blocks or cutouts made to produce the shape desired. Clamps hold the work (laminates) directly against the surface of the form.

One-piece forms can be made up with integral clamping systems. For example, the form shown in Illus. 488 is used to make the curved, laminated tips for water skis (Illus.

489). Illus. 490 depicts the resawing setup involved in preparing the laminations for the ski project. Illus. 491 gives the specific details for making the ski laminating form, and the pattern layout for a typical water ski. The same techniques can be used to make chair backs, rockers, and similar projects.

Often, pressure pads or cauls that bend with the work are placed between the clamps and the laminations to distribute the pressure to areas that are not directly under the clamps. (See Illus. 484.) Pressure pads are an important element in many gluing jobs. (See Illus. 492.) Thick pressure pads are better than thin ones, but they must be able to conform easily to the curvature of the form without kinking, buckling, or fracturing. Two layers of a thinner pressure pad are better than just one layer. Illus. 493 shows the role pressure pads play when clamping with the rubber inner-tube clamping method that is discussed on page 198.

Illus. 484. One-piece form of gradual curvature. Clamps provide the pressure; a piece of plywood placed between the clamps and the laminates distributes the pressure.

Illus. 485. Another one-piece form prepared with a true radius.

Illus. 486. Note the thick center laminate saw-kerfed to facilitate the bend. This project, a round table apron, does not require great strength.

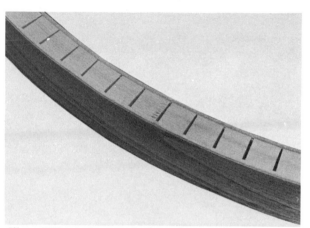

Illus. 487. A close-up look at the completed lamination.

Illus. 488 (left). A one-piece water-ski laminating form, with integral metal clamps made up especially for this form. Hand screw clamps apply pressure to the flat areas.

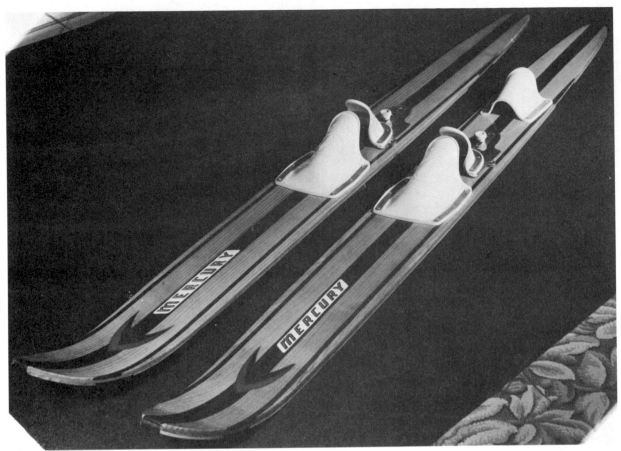

Illus. 489. Fully laminated water skis.

Illus. 490. Resawing to make the water-ski laminations.

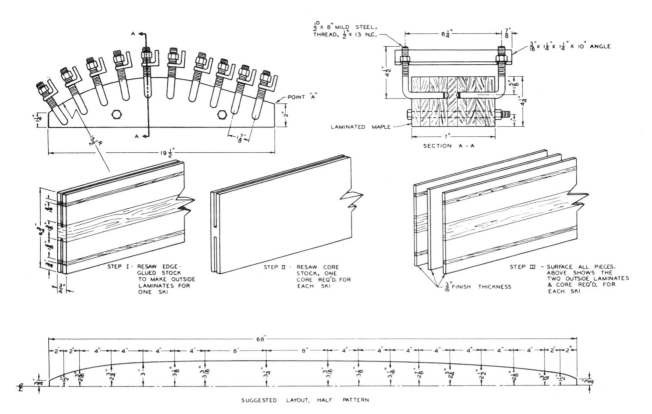

Illus. 491. *Detail of water ski and the laminating form.*

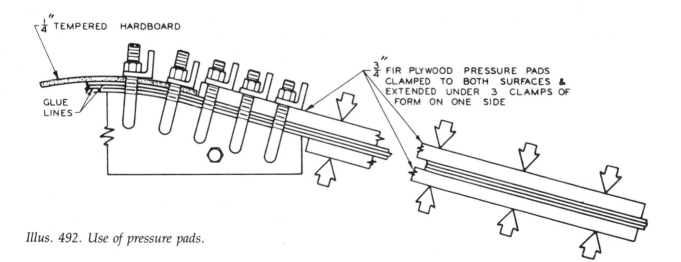

Illus. 492. *Use of pressure pads.*

197

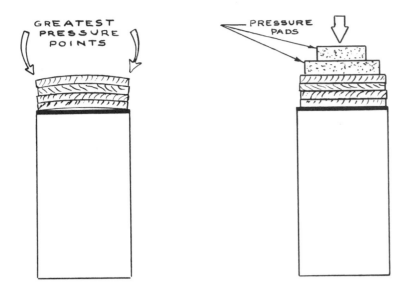

GREATEST
PRESSURE
POINTS

PRESSURE
PADS

Illus. 493. Importance of pressure pads with the rubber-band laminating techniques.

Applying Pressure to Forms

Rubber-Band Clamping

Rubber-band clamping (Illus. 494) in glue laminating of curved wood is exceptionally versatile and effective, and very simple. Lots of pressure can be generated with the pulling and wrapping technique. (See Illus. 495.) Double and triple wrap over the same area increases pressure. One important advantage of this technique is that the pressure is fairly uniform and continuous all along the full curvature of the glue-up. However, still use pressure pads because the wrapping effect produces more pressure at the outside edges than at the central area across the laminates. (See Illus. 498.) If the pressure pads are not used, many clamps must be used closely together.

The rubber band system works very well on both convex and concave laminating directions. The inner tubes are cut 1 to 1½ inches and to any length preferred with heavy-duty scissors or a tin snips. I prefer 4 to 5 foot lengths; when ending one length and starting another during the glue-up, I give the length I just finished a "back-up"

overlap wrap. Very long lengths are somewhat cumbersome when laminating a project such as a fishing net. (See Illus. 496–498.) You always have to take the full length of the rubber band around with each wrap.

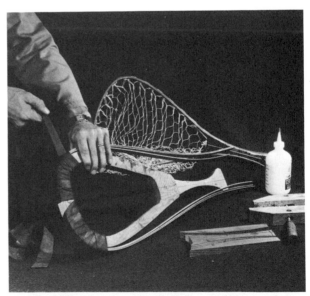

Illus. 494. A laminated landing net glue-up. Large rubber bands cut from inner tubes are stretched and wrapped to provide pressure continually along the glue line.

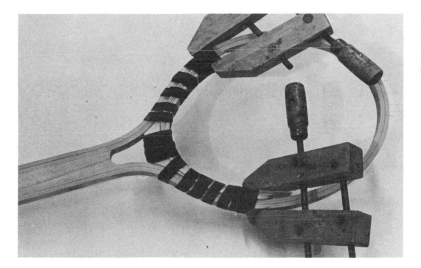

Illus. 495. Experimental tennis racket of laminated veneers (in progress) by Patrick Murray demonstrates the versatility of this technique.

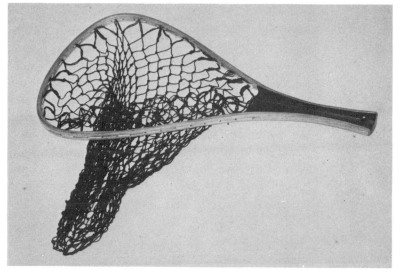

Illus. 496. A laminated fisherman's landing net is a good starting project.

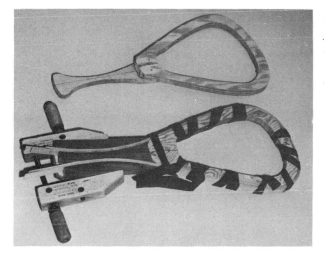

Illus. 497. Landing net laminating forms. Lower form: three water-soaked strips of ash 3/32 inch thick by 61 inches long are first bent over the form and air-dried. Or use 8 plies of dry maple veneers.

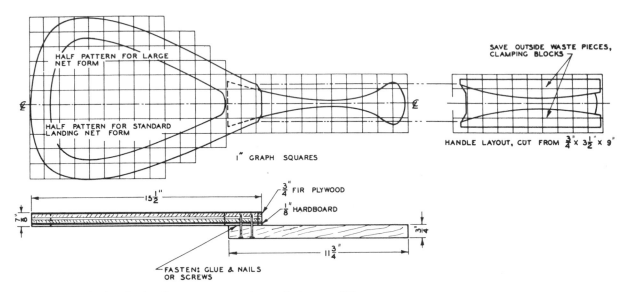

HALF PATTERN FOR LARGE NET FORM

HALF PATTERN FOR STANDARD LANDING NET FORM

1" GRAPH SQUARES

SAVE OUTSIDE WASTE PIECES, CLAMPING BLOCKS

HANDLE LAYOUT, CUT FROM 3/4" X 3 1/2" X 9"

15 1/2"

3/4" FIR PLYWOOD

1/8" HARDBOARD

7/8"

11 3/4"

3/4"

FASTEN: GLUE & NAILS OR SCREWS

Illus. 498. Details for the landing net. It can be made in two different sizes.

The rubber bands can sometimes be re-used. It all depends upon the kind of glue and the amount of squeeze-out one gets. *Caution:* When the rubber bands are undone after the glue has cured, dangerous razor-like slivers of glue may flake off of the rubber or from the plastic film used between the laminations and the form. Illus. 499–512 show how to use rubber bands to make several different laminated projects with a one-piece form. The projects have a simple 90-degree band. The form (Illus. 499) can be utilized to make various table or stool legs (Illus. 500 and 501), shelf brackets and hanging plant-wall support (Illus. 502–504). The system may look crude, but it works very well.

Illus. 499. This 90° laminated member can be used to make several projects, all from this basic form.

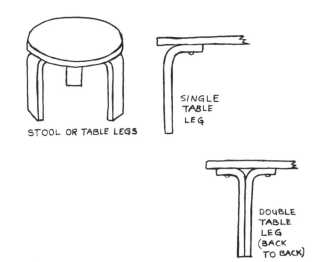

STOOL OR TABLE LEGS

SINGLE TABLE LEG

DOUBLE TABLE LEG (BACK TO BACK)

Illus. 500. A basic table leg design and some applications.

200

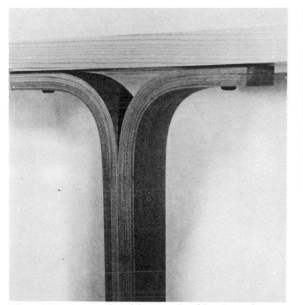

Illus. 501. A completed leg made of laminated veneer.

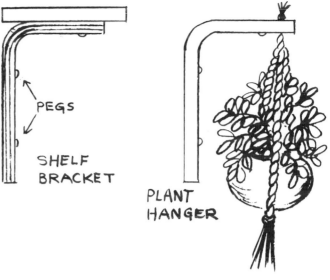

PEGS

SHELF BRACKET

PLANT HANGER

Illus. 502. A basic project that can be used for a shelf bracket (left) or as a plant hanger (right).

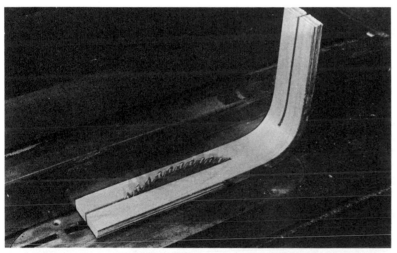

Illus. 503. A wide laminated part is ripped to make two identical pieces.

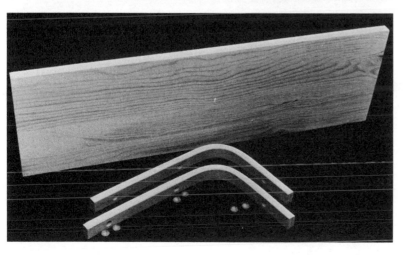

Illus. 504. A board shelf with a pair of laminated shelf brackets.

Illus. 505. Waxing the form. The form is 2¼ inches thick and approximately 3½ inches wide by whatever vertical and horizontal distances are desired. The corner has a 2-inch radius.

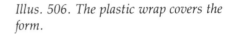

Illus. 506. The plastic wrap covers the form.

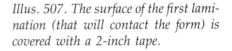
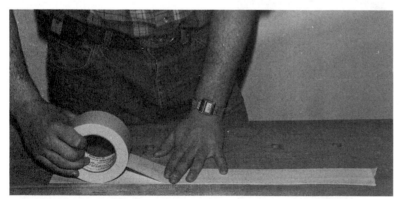

Illus. 507. The surface of the first lamination (that will contact the form) is covered with a 2-inch tape.

Illus. 508. Fourteen layers of veneer result in approximately ½ inch thickness. Using a roller speeds up spreading.

Illus. 509. Laminates are spread on both surfaces.

Illus. 510. Clamp to start at the short, flat end. The small plywood piece (under clamp) is a pressure pad.

Illus. 511. The inner tube is stretch-wrapped progressively around the bend area.

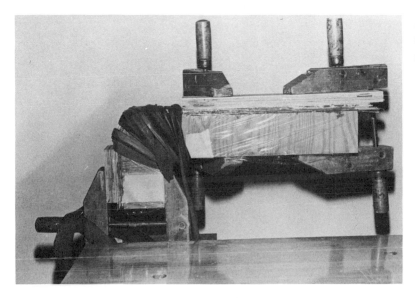

Illus. 512. The inner tube is tied off. Clamps with plywood pressure pads complete the clamping.

Jig Table Laminating

Jig table laminating involves the development and layout of guide blocks or stops on a flat surface so they make up a predetermined curve. The table surface must be protected with some sort of release agent (wax or plastic film) so the squeeze-out does not glue the workpiece to the table. Using the clamps or cam wedges shown in Illus. 513 and 514 is not as effective as the inner-tube wrap because the areas of the greatest pressure are *at* the clamping points, and the areas of less pressure are *between* clamping points. This method is satisfactory if gap-filling adhesives like epoxy resins are used.

Another application of the jig table method is depicted in Illus. 515. This heavy-duty do-it-yourself laminating is done with the aid of the steel-strapping tools that are used in industrial shipping departments. This is the same banding that is used to bundle lumber and steel piping, to secure crating for shipping, etc. Steel (and also plastic strapping), the necessary tools for tensioning, and crimping are available from industrial-supply firms.

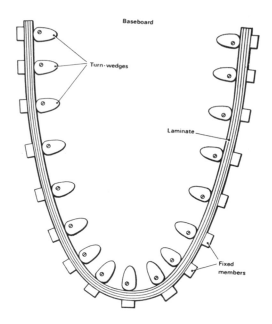

Illus. 514. The same idea, but pressure is applied with cam-type wedges.

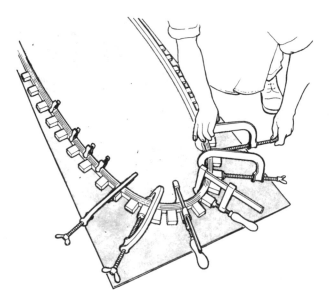

Illus. 513. The jig table method has stop blocks along the curvature for clamping.

Illus. 515. Heavier laminating work is handled with stop blocks, wedges and steel banding tools.

Fire-hose Compressed Air Press

The fire-hose compressed air press is an economically practical approach to quality laminating for the woodcrafter. (See Illus. 516 and 517.) This system has many advantages over other laminating systems. Although this requires a two-piece form, only one of the two must have a true, positive surface. Usually it's the lower half of the form that is worked smooth, accurately conforming to the desired or predetermined curve. The rubber-lined fire hose is available in these common diameters: 1½, 1¾, 2½, and 3 inches. The two smallest diameters are the most widely used. Fire-hose kits (Illus. 518) that can be used for laminating projects such as archery bows, water skis, and furniture are available from Bingham Projects, Inc., 3400 S. 1350 W., Ogden, Utah 84409. This company also sells supplies, epoxy, project kits, and component parts (Illus. 519) for making various laminated sports gear projects. Fire hose in bulk can be obtained from W.S. Darley & Co., 2000 Anson Drive, Melrose Park, Illinois 60160. (See page 85 for more information concerning air valves or making a fire-hose press.)

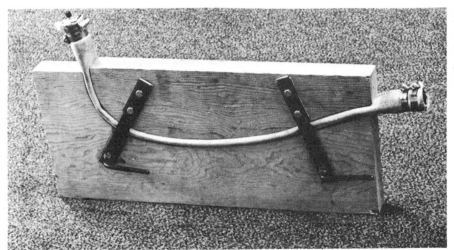

Illus. 516. A fire-hose laminating press. The opening between the two forms is not critical, but it must not be too large.

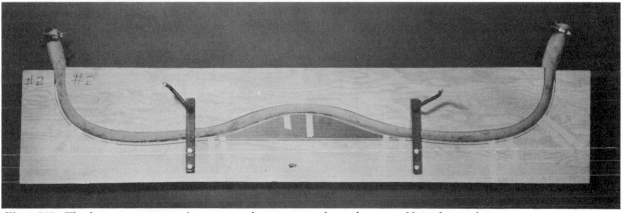

Illus. 517. The bow components in press under pressure, for a dry run. Note the steel connecting straps that prevent forms from separating under pressure.

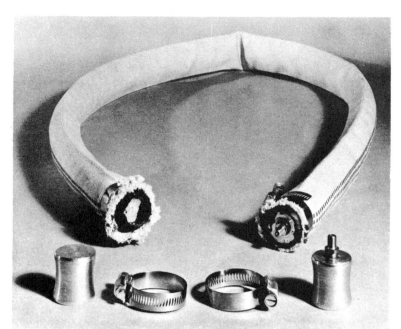

Illus. 518. The essentials of the fire-hose compressed air press.

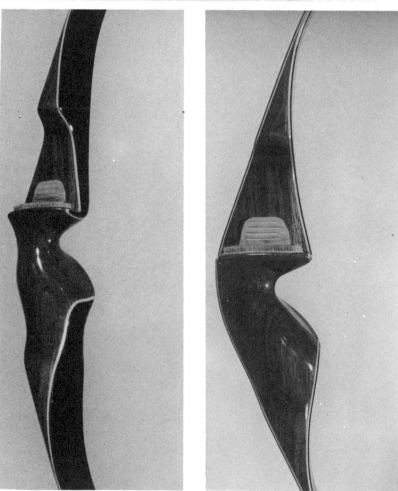

Illus. 519. Closeups of handle inserts of author's bow made with components supplied by Bingham Projects, Inc.

The advantage of the fire-hose press is the fast and uniform pressure it applies to the entire work surface. A hand pump or air compressor provides the air supply. The hose is very strong. It is factory-tested to withstand pressures up to 600 to 800 p.s.i. Usually the hose is inflated to only 60 p.s.i. when epoxies are used; 100 to 150 p.s.i. can be used with other glue-ups. One limitation of this system is that curves cannot be extremely sharp. The system can be used to apply pressure to glue-ups of any width by using two or more hoses side by side. (See Illus. 520.)

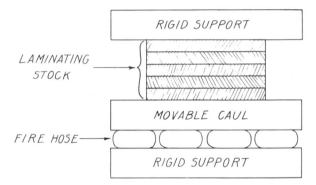

Illus. 520. Detail of press with multiple fire hose.

When making a fire-hose laminating press, be sure to design it with sufficient bulk. This bulk ensures that the whole thing does not burst when pressurized. Plywood laminated to plywood makes very strong and dimensionally stable laminating forms. The working surfaces must be smooth and true. It's best to cover the working (positive) surface with a piece of plastic laminate or tempered hardboard to eliminate minor surface irregularities.

The opening for the fire hose should be of such size that it allows for the thickness of the laminates, the pressure pad(s) if used, and the deflated hose. Remember, the casing of the fire hose does not allow it to increase in diameter as it is pressurized. The casing is simply a retaining jacket for the interior rubber, which is the air bladder. The ends of the hose must be pinched off airtight. It's always a good idea to test the hose. Pump it up and leave it for 24 hours to see if any air escapes.

Check valves with some soapy water for leakage. The surface of the form and the hose itself should be protected from glue. Cover the surfaces of the form with wax and sheet plastic. It's a good idea to wrap the entire surface of the hose with plastic food wrap and tape it securely in place.

Laminating Veneer and Plywood Over a Form

Laminating veneer and plywood over a form can also be done to some extent in the home shop. Two major problems for such work is making (or finding) a suitable form and getting full, uniform pressure distributed over a large area. A basic project involving laminated veneer to make curved plywood is shown in Illus. 521. The form is a 5-gallon can (Illus. 522). The project consists of 5 layers of veneer. The grain runs with the longest dimension (length) in 4 pieces. The center veneer lamination is cut so that the grain runs across the width to give it a plywood effect, but this is not an essential requirement.

Double-coat each joint with glue (Illus. 523). Plastic is used to cover the can and to protect the top surface. A piece of ¹⁄₁₆-inch standard laminate serves as a flexible pressure pad. (See Illus. 524.) Pressure is supplied by cut inner-tube rubber bands. (See

Illus. 521. A formed fruit tray made by laminating veneers together over a form.

207

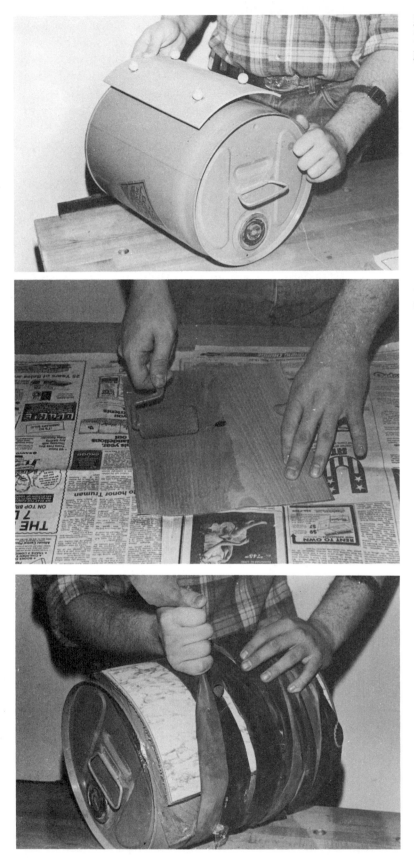

Illus. 522. The form is a 5-gallon can. The tray feet are wood balls epoxied in place.

Illus. 523. Glue is spread onto both surfaces of each piece.

Illus. 524. Inner-tube rubber bands provide pressure. A piece of standard ¹⁄₁₆-inch plastic laminate serves as a pressure pad.

Illus. 525. Clamped and ready to cure—not an exceptionally pretty piece, but it works.

Illus. 525.) Use your imagination—veneer can be laminated over forms like metal pipe, cans, pails, and special wood-turned forms of any circular or curved shapes.

Illus. 526 shows how to glue-laminate 3 pieces of ¼-inch plywood over a block. The finished product obviously has some limitations in the uniformity of the curve and the consistency of pressure along the joint. How-

Illus. 526. Glue-laminating layers of ¼-inch plywood into a moderate curve is suitable for some jobs.

ever, for some jobs this work may be satisfactory and strong enough—if a good gap-filling adhesive is used.

Illus. 527 shows how to form wood shapes by laminating pieces of thin plywood over a custom-made form.

Illus. 527. A more sophisticated mould and clamping technique for curve-laminating plywood.

Curing and Trimming Laminated Members

Make sure you fully understand the curing characteristics of the glue you are using. Some glues reach 75 percent of their strength in a fairly short period, but do not reach full cure until 24 to 48 hours after pressing. Since most gluing of curved laminations does involve some degree of stress on the joints, it is imperative that you allow sufficient time for the glue to fully cure. Removing the clamps too soon may cause problems if the glue is not cured or the assembly is still "green" and some areas of the laminated member are fairly well-stressed.

Some epoxies formulated for handling high-stress joints of laminated projects require a special heat cure. In such cases an enclosed chamber or heat box is recommended. (See page 37 for information concerning heat glue-curing boxes.) Several light bulbs (250 watt) in a plywood box can get the air temperature up to 140 to 175 °F. The heat is slowly transferred by conduction to the center of the glue lines from the outer edges. Sometimes this may take several hours before the glue line at the center of the assembly reaches the temperature specified to cure the glue. Naturally, larger assemblies require longer heating periods than do small assemblies. On the other hand, do not allow the work to remain unnecessarily exposed to heat for extended periods. Excessive heat will draw the moisture from the wood, causing shrinkage and generating internal stresses.

If the project is such that it is impractical to build a plywood-enclosed chamber, consider using canvas or a plastic tarp. Make a temporary canopy over the work and provide the heat electrically with a portable heater or light bulb. *Be certain the heat source is located well away from flammable materials.*

Trimming the laminated member involves removing the glue squeeze-out, sizing it, and smoothing the edges. You will soon learn to remove as much glue as possible earlier in the glue-up before it sets. However, the nature of glue-laminating jobs often makes removing all squeeze-out impossible. You will have lots of cured glue to contend with. Fine-edge tools, such as the hand plane, will dull quickly. Use a power sander with coarse abrasive when possible. The Stanley surform or other files and rasps cut fast, but be careful not to chip or sliver off more material than desired.

Chapter 13

Repairs, Projects, and Other Gluing Jobs

By now, you should have a pretty good idea as to what gluing and clamping techniques work best in most situations. Also, you probably realize at this point there is no "miracle" glue that meets all of the following requirements: very low in cost; will bond all materials (whether they are wet or dry); will fit tight joints as well as those with big gaps; has long, open times for spreading and assembly, but cures instantly; doesn't require pressure; can be used for indoor and outdoor jobs; is nontoxic; can be used at any temperature; and is easy to clean up. Such a product simply does not exist. Therefore, it is important that you make the correct decisions and use the most appropriate methods to handle your particular job. The following look at different repair jobs will show you how to handle common woodworking problems. Another section will show you how to build jigs and clamps in the workshop that will prove helpful to you during certain jobs. Finally, other projects are depicted for which you can apply the techniques you have acquired.

Repairs

Repairing Corner or Edge Splinters

Woodworkers are frequently making repairs with glue. One of the most common problems is repairing an edge or corner splinter. Illus. 528–530 show how a typical job can be handled without using cumbersome clamps. Small or large splinters should be repaired in basically the same way. Usually it's best to avoid the use of clamps because it's difficult to get uniform pressure in two directions. Also, when large splinters

are repaired do not use nails and/or screws. Gluing and clamping with tape is usually the best approach.

Illus. 528. A small splinter that needs glue repair.

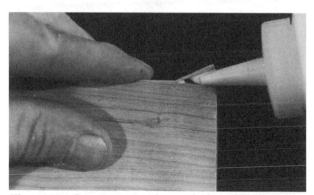

Illus. 529. Get glue onto the cracked surfaces.

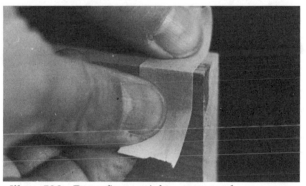

Illus. 530. Press finger tight, remove glue squeeze-out, and tape tight.

211

Repairing Broken Handles

The broken handles of such tools as an ax, broom or shovel can be repaired with glue and the rubber-band clamping techniques. Illus. 531–533 show how to repair such a break to a good-as-new working condition. The key to this sort of repair is to be sure that all surfaces of the crack or fracture will return to their natural fit with pressure. If dust particles or minute nonfitting chips enter the crack, you will have problems. If it is impossible to fit all slivers or the cracked surfaces back into their original position, then it's best to use a gap-filling epoxy glue. If all parts refit perfectly, use any appropriate glue.

The essential task is to get glue onto all of the separated or cracked surfaces. Illus. 532 shows fine thread or fish line being used to get the glue deeply into the "narrow" of the crack in a baseball bat. The edge of a piece of paper, air pressure, or a glue injector can also get this job done. When repaired properly, the reglued cracked or broken part will be surprisingly strong. I have repaired dozens and dozens of baseball bats over the years for the local high-school team. The repaired bats have been reused successfully.

Do not attempt to repair such breaks with glue and standard clamps. They give pressure only at one point. Do not use screws, nails, or dowels even with glue for pressure and holding power. The rubber-band wrap (Illus. 533) is the only functional way to get sufficient pressure, totally, in all directions and uniformly over the repair area.

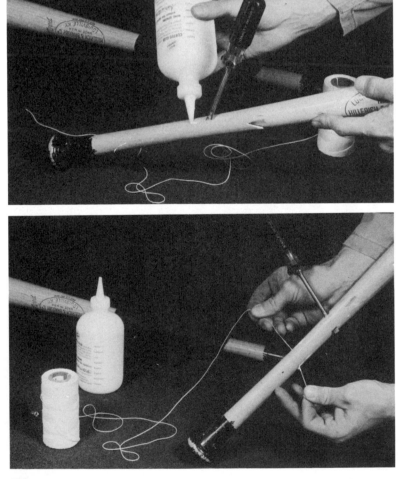

Illus. 531. Broken tool handles of all sorts and even baseball bats can be glued to repair the fracture. First, gently open the fracture to facilitate glue application.

Illus. 532. Work fishing line, fine thread, or the edge of a piece of paper back and forth to get the glue deeply into the narrow of the crack.

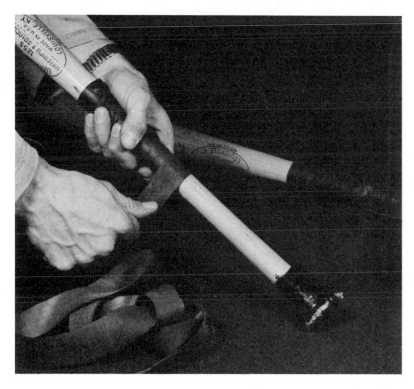

Illus. 533. Wrap heavy rubber bands (cut from inner tubes) to apply pressure from all directions around the fracture area.

Chair Repair

Chair repair is another common problem that often confronts the woodworker. Usually, it's loose dowel-type joints of the chair rung or stretchers that need to be repaired. They were either inappropriately glued, dried and shrunk from exposure to a dry environment, or they just worked loose by "racking" from use. Simply squirting glue into the hole will not correct the problem. However, a product called "Chair-loc" (Illus. 534) seems to penetrate into the joint. It is apparently water-solvent and swells the tenon or dowel, which results in a tight joint. The manufacturer's directions state that this product is not a glue and should not be used as an adhesive.

Simply reapplying glue is not a viable approach because the old glue has most likely sealed the tenon end and the inside of the hole. It's probably best to scrape the old glue off of the tenon; also drill the hole so that old glue is cut from the sides of the hole. The fit will now likely be too loose. To correct this, coat the tenon and hole with glue and stretch a small layer or two of nylon stocking over

the tenon before inserting the tenon back into the hole. Be sure the tenon is well-saturated with glue. Apply pressure, allow the glue to dry, and trim the excess around the rung (or whatever part is being repaired) with a sharp knife. Pressure can be applied using twine, cord, rope, or even wire in a tourniquet fashion as shown in Illus. 535. (See Illus. 536.)

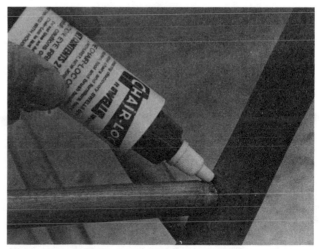

Illus. 534. "Chair Loc" swells and tightens loose joints.

Illus. 535. "Tourniquet"-type pressure works great for chair repairs.

Illus. 536. Clamps clamped to individual pieces can be drawn together with a third clamp; this sometimes solves difficult-to-clamp situations.

Clamping and Jig Projects

A Mitring Jig Project

A mitring jig project developed by the Adjustable Clamp Company is one of the best and most practical ways devised for framing jobs. As shown in Illus. 537, this jig can be adjusted to accommodate many different sizes, and equal pressure can be applied to all 4 corners simultaneously with just one clamp. The 4 legs or (arms) are 1 × 2 × 18 inch (or longer) hardwood. One-quarter-inch holes are drilled simultaneously through all 4 pieces at 1-inch intervals (See Illus. 538). The swivel bars and corner blocks are also cut from 1-inch thick-hardwood. One-quarter-inch holes are also drilled. Assemble with ¼ × 2¼-inch screws using washers and hex nuts or wing nuts.

Veneer Press Frames

Veneer press frames are another tool plan developed by the Adjustable Clamp Company to utilize their press screws. (See Illus. 539.) A minimum of two frames is required to make a press. More can be used in series to accommodate greater lengths of work. The plan calls for press screws to be located approximately 9½ inches from each other across the width of a single frame. One press frame is normally required for each 9 inches of length. However, spacing from frame to frame can be shifted one way or the other as circumstances dictate. (See Illus. 540 and 541.)

A Shop-Made Clamping System

A shop-made clamping system is a nut-and-bolt system that is easy to make. (See Illus. 542 and 543.) The system is developed essentially around the use of standard, continuously threaded rods, ⅜ inch in diameter, with washers, threaded hex nuts and couplings. All wood parts are cut out in your shop, the other parts are standard stock items at most good hardware dealers. T-nuts ⅜ inch in diameter are inserted into cut-out hand knobs (Illus. 543 and 544). The hand knobs speed up the threading adjustment, but they do not give as much pressure as the standard hex nuts that are turned tight with a wrench. (See Illus. 545–547.)

Illus. 537. The Adjustable Clamp Company's mitring jig project.

Illus. 538. Making the mitring jig.

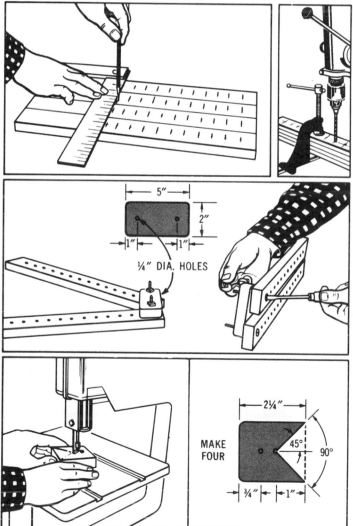

5″

2″

1″ 1″

¼″ DIA. HOLES

MAKE FOUR

2¼″

45°

90°

¾″ 1″

Illus. 539. These veneer press frames are another project that accommodates commercial press screws.

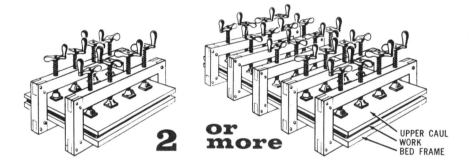

Illus. 540. These veneer frames are used in a series to accommodate any desired size.

UPPER CAUL
WORK
BED FRAME

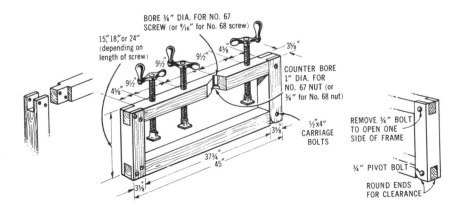

Illus. 541. Construction details for making veneer press frames designed to use "Jorgensen" brand press screws.

BORE ¾" DIA. FOR NO. 67
SCREW (or ⁹⁄₁₆" for No. 68 screw)

15", 18", or 24"
(depending on
length of screw)

9½"   9½"   4⅝"   3⅝"

4⅝"   9½"

COUNTER BORE
1" DIA. FOR
NO. 67 NUT (or
¾" for No. 68 nut)

REMOVE ¾" BOLT
TO OPEN ONE
SIDE OF FRAME

½"x4"
CARRIAGE
BOLTS

3⅝"

¾" PIVOT BOLT

37¾"
45

ROUND ENDS
FOR CLEARANCE

3⅝"

Illus. 542. A shop-made light-duty clamping system is comprised of parts easily available.

Illus. 543. A close-up look at the T-nuts used in the hand knobs. Note the grain direction and offset holes of the corner blocks.

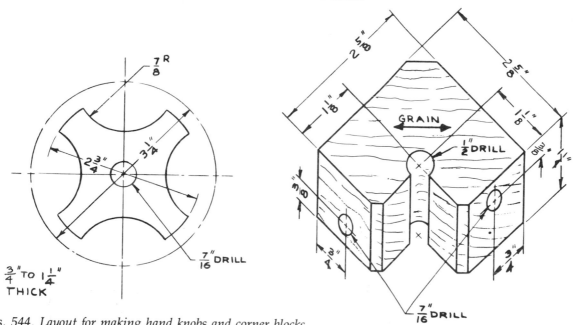

Illus. 544. Layout for making hand knobs and corner blocks.

217

Illus. 545. Assembly of a small box.

Illus. 546. Hardwood "straight" bars are cut slightly crowned to apply center pressure and to counter bending under load. See Illus. 547.

Illus. 547. Clamping the assembly of wide cabinet panels.

Deep-Reach C-Clamps

Deep-reach C-clamps are also homemade devices. They have the same parts as the shop-made clamping system. C-clamps are handy, but they do not provide great gluing pressure. The ones depicted in Illus. 548–550 have small jaw openings, but their shapes can be modified somewhat to increase the opening "bite." Note that a piece of leather (an old belt) or thick rubber serves as a hinge. One jaw (the lower one) has a T-nut that anchors the threaded rod. The other jaw has an elongated hole that the threaded rod passes through freely. Knobs or hex nuts provide the pressure. Illus. 550 will help you develop your own C-clamps.

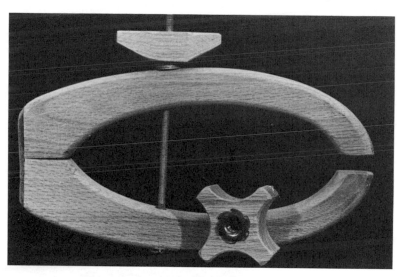

Illus. 548. Homemade, deep-reach "C" clamps.

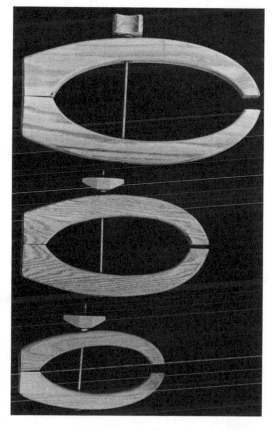

Illus. 549. Make clamps in any size desired.

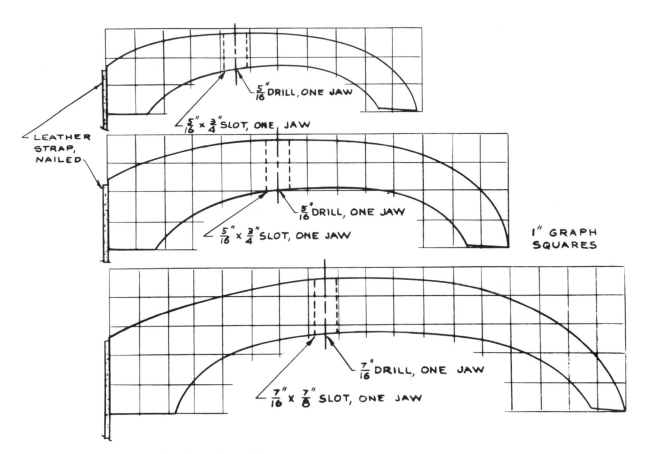

Illus. 550. Basic layout for three sizes of clamps.

Gluing in Wood Turning

This craft usually involves lots of gluing and clamping, as already discussed in Chapter 2. Illus. 551 and 552 depict two projects. One is a wood candle that uses interchangeable food warmer candles. The other project is a weed pot. Both projects involve face-to-face gluing.

The paper joint is a technique that allows joints to be separated cleanly when wedged open. This procedure is used by woodturners when making bowls. With this technique, a scrap block is glued to the bowl stock so the faceplate screws do not have to extend into the bottom of the turned bowl. Any piece of fairly heavy paper is glued between the scrap block and the turning blank. (See Illus. 553.) Glue is applied to both surfaces of the paper. The work is clamped and allowed to cure as usual. (See Illus. 554.) When the turning is completed, the scrap is

removed by splitting the paper joint gently with a chisel. (See Illus. 555.)

Illus. 551. Wood candle and weed pot.

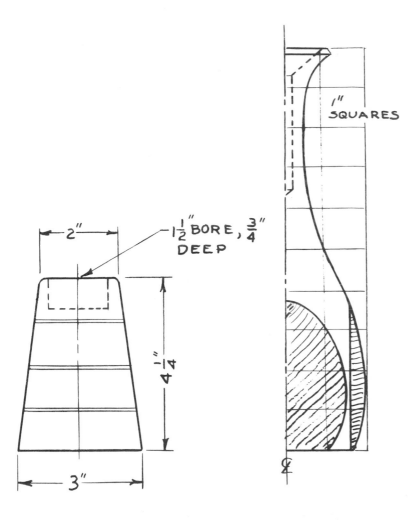

Illus. 552. Drawing of wood candle and weed pot.

1" SQUARES

2"

1½" BORE, ¾" DEEP

4¼"

3"

Illus. 553. The paper joint between the scrap and the bowl blank can be removed after the turning is completed.

Illus. 554. The face plate is screwed only into the scrap piece.

Illus. 555. With the turning completed, the paper joint is gently separated for a clean release.

The paper joint can also be applied to spindle turnings. The entire length of the turning or any parts of it can be split apart as desired. Illus. 556–558 show turnings that are partially split to make some unusual legs for a bookcase project. A bookcase and construction details for it are depicted in Illus. 559 and 560. A scale model (Illus. 561) was made to check the design. Balsa wood was used and the joints were held together with stick pins until the glue set.

Illus. 556. Here a spindle turning is being prepared for a partial separation with a paper glue joint.

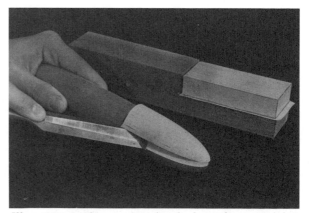

Illus. 557. Making a clean break along the paper joint area.

Illus. 558. A completed leg.

Illus. 559. Bookcase with turned legs.

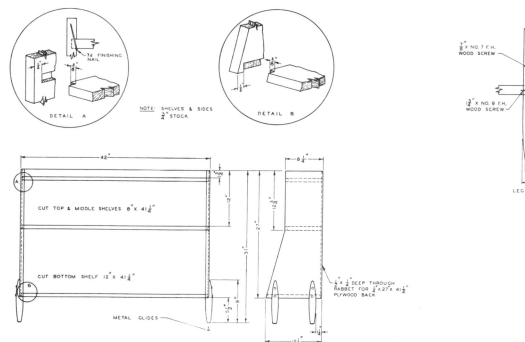

Illus. 560. Construction details.

Miscellaneous Projects

Illus. 562 shows a bookcase planter project with all its outer surfaces covered with plastic laminate. The project is 24 inches high, 25 inches wide, and 10 inches deep. The outside vertical dimension of the planter box is 8 inches and the base is 2 inches thick. Other interesting gluing projects are depicted in Illus. 563–567. Illus. 561 shows a scale-model bookcase!

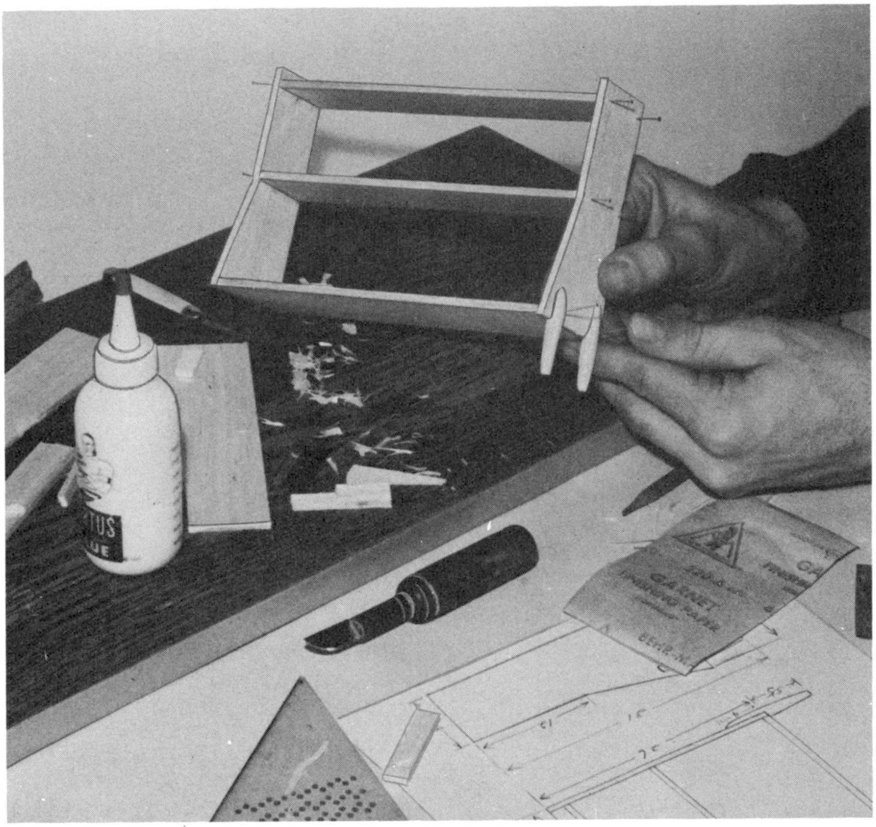

Illus. 561. Making a scale-model bookcase.

Illus. 562. Plastic laminate-faced bookcase planter crafted by Robert Cuellar.

Illus. 563. Clock of glued plywood by Jon Blahnik measures 11¼ inches square by 2¼ inches thick.

Illus. 564. Rolling pin and cutting boards.

Illus. 565. More cutting-board designs.

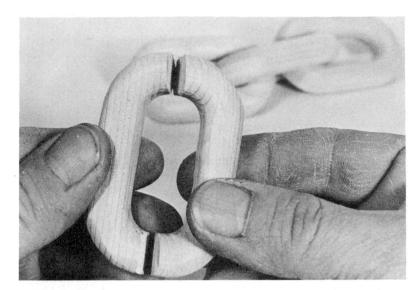

Illus. 566. Breaking and regluing a router-carved link is necessary for the assembly of wooden chain. (For all the how-to details refer to the Router Handbook.)

Illus. 567. Regluing connects the links.

Panelling a Room

Panelling a room with lumber is yet another type of gluing job for the handyman. Lumber panelling can be applied vertically, horizontally, or diagonally. Any number of different wood species is available in lap or tongue-and-groove edges. The use of band-

saw-textured redwood panelling applied vertically is shown in Illus. 568–571. Sometimes it is necessary to true uneven walls with firring strips. Otherwise panelling can be glued directly to the walls and/or nailed directly to the studding. Another important step is to condition the lumber to environmental moisture conditions. The best way to do this is to actually store the lumber in the room to be panelled for several days or more.

Arrange the pieces for a wall according to your choice of color and grain patterns. Place the least desirable pieces in areas where they are likely to be hidden behind furniture. In application, be sure to follow the manufacturer's instructions pertaining to the use of the panelling adhesive. This adhesive is usu-ally sold in tubes packaged for dispensing with a caulking gun (Illus. 569). Normally, the adhesive is applied to the prefit panelling board, then it's pressed against the wall to transfer some of the adhesive so both surfaces are coated. The board is immediately drawn away for a short period of time (Illus. 570), before it is tapped into its final position (Illus. 571). A finish nail is driven in at the top and bottom of the board as the adhesive sets.

Illus. 568. Condition the panelling and arrange the pieces for desired color and grain patterns before starting.

Illus. 569. Apply adhesive generously to the back of the panelling. Put newspapers on the carpet to protect it.

Illus. 570. Directions for using panelling adhesive should be carefully followed.

228

Illus. 571. Tapping a piece into place with a scrap block.

Appendices

Glossary

Adhere To cause two surfaces to be held together by adhesion.

Adherend A body which is held to another body by an adhesive.

Adherend failure Rupture of an adhesive bond, such that the separation appears to be within the adherend.

Adhesion The state in which two surfaces are held together by interfacial forces which may consist of valence forces or interlocking action or both.

> *mechanical.* Adhesion between surfaces in which the adhesive holds the parts together by interlocking action.

> *specific.* Adhesion between surfaces which are held together by valence forces of the same type as those which give rise to cohesion.

Adhesive A substance capable of holding materials together by surface attachment.

> *assembly.* An adhesive which can be used for bonding parts together, such as in the making of a boat, airplane, furniture, the like.

> *cold-setting.* An adhesive which sets at temperatures below 68°F (20°C).

> *construction.* Any adhesive used to assemble primary building materials into components during building construction; most commonly applied to elastomer mastic-type adhesives.

> *contact.* An adhesive which is apparently dry to the touch and which will adhere to itself instantaneously upon contact; also called contact bond adhesive or dry bond adhesive.

> *gap-filling.* Adhesive suitable for use where the surfaces to be joined may not be in close or continuous contact owing either to the impossibility of applying adequate pressure or to slight inaccuracies in matching mating surfaces.

heat-activated.   A dry adhesive film which is rendered tacky or fluid by application of heat or heat and pressure to the assembly.

hot-melt.   An adhesive that is applied in a molten state and forms a bond on cooling to a solid state.

hot-setting.   An adhesive which requires a temperature at or above 150°F (66°C) to set it.

room-temperature-setting.   An adhesive which sets in the temperature range of 68° to 86°F (20° to 30°C).

separate application.   A term used to describe an adhesive consisting of two parts; one part being applied to one adherend and the other part to the other adherend and the two brought together to form a joint.

solvent.   An adhesive having a volatile organic liquid as a vehicle. NOTE: This term excludes water-based adhesives.

Adhesive failure   Rupture of an adhesive bond, such that the plane of separation appears to be at the adhesive-adherend interface.

Air seasoning (air drying)   The process of drying green lumber or other wood products by exposure to prevailing atmospheric conditions outdoors or in an unheated shed.

Assembly time   Interval between spreading the adhesive on the surfaces to be joined and the application of pressure to the joint or joints. NOTE: For assemblies involving multiple layers or parts, the assembly time begins with the spreading of the adhesive on the first adherend.

open assembly time.   The time interval between the spreading of the adhesive on the adherend and the completion of assembly of the parts for bonding.

closed assembly time.   The time interval between completion of assembly of the parts for bonding and the application of pressure to the assembly.

Balanced construction   A construction such that the forces induced by uniformly distributed changes in moisture content will not cause warping. Also, symmetrical constructions in which the grain direction of the plies is either parallel or perpendicular to each other.

Bond (noun)   The union of materials by adhesives.

Bond (verb)   To unite materials by means of adhesive.

Bond failure   Rupture of adhesive bond.

Bondline   The layer of adhesive which attaches two adherends.

Bond strength   The unit load applied in tension, compression, flexure, peel, impact, cleavage, or shear required to break an adhesive assembly with failure occurring in or near the plane of the bond.

Book-matching   Matching veneer by turning over alternate sheets.

Bowing   Distortion whereby the faces of a wood product become concave or convex along the grain.

Burl   Burls come from a warty growth generally caused by some injury to the growing layer just under the bark. This injury, perhaps due to insects or bacteria, causes the growing cells to divide abnormally, creating excess wood that finds room for itself in many little humps. Succeeding growth follows these contours. Cutting across these humps by the half-round method brings them out as little swirl knots or eyes.

Burnished surface   A glazed surface with which it may be difficult to obtain a satisfactory bond.

Butt joint   An end joint formed by gluing together the squared ends of two pieces. Because of the inadequacy and variability in strength of butt joints when glued, such joints are generally not depended on for strength.

Catalyst   A substance which markedly speeds up the cure of an adhesive when added in minor quantity, as compared to the amounts of the primary reactants.

Check   In the case of wood, a separation along the grain, the greater part of which occurs across the rings of annual growth.

Clamping pressure   Pressure developed by clamps of various designs to bring joint surfaces into close contact for glue bond formation.

Cleavage   Splitting or dividing along the grain.

Closed assembly time   See Assembly time.

Coagulation   The process by which a liquid becomes a soft, semisolid mass.

Cohesion   The state in which the particles of a single substance are held together by primary or secondary valence forces. As used in the adhesive field, the state in which the particles of the adhesive (or the adherend) are held together.

Cohesive failure   Rupture of an adhesive bond, such that the separation appears to be within the adhesive.

Cold pressing Pressing panels or laminates without application of heat for curing the glue.

Composite A structural element consisting of wood and/or a combination of materials in which all pieces are attached together to act as a single unit.

Consistency That property of a liquid adhesive by virtue of which it tends to resist deformation.

Construction adhesive See Adhesive, construction.

Contact cement See Adhesive, contact.

Convex Curved like a section of the outside of a sphere.

Core A generally centrally located layer or composite component of a sandwich construction, usually low density, which separates facings and provides rigid construction.

Crazing Fine cracks which may extend in a network on or under the surface of or through a layer of adhesive.

Creep The dimensional change with time of a material under load, following the initial instantaneous elastic or rapid deformation. Creep at room temperature is sometimes called cold flow.

Crossband To place the grain of layers of wood at right angles in order to minimize shrinking and swelling; also, in plywood of three or more plies, a layer of veneer whose grain direction is at right angles to that of the face plies.

Cross grain A pattern in which the fibres and other longitudinal elements deviate from a line parallel to the sides of the piece. The term applies to either diagonal or spiral grain or a combination of the two.

Cross laminated A laminate in which some of the layers of material are oriented at right angles to the remaining layers with respect to the grain or strongest direction in tension. NOTE: Balanced construction of the laminations about the centerline of the thickness of the laminate is normally assumed.

Cup A distortion of a board in which there is a deviation flatwise from a straight line across the width of the board.

Cure To change the physical properties of an adhesive by chemical reaction, which may be condensation, polymerization, or vulcanization; usually accomplished by the action of heat and catalyst, alone or in combination, with or without pressure.

Curing time   The period of time during which an assembly is subjected to heat or pressure, or both, to cure the adhesive. NOTE: Further cure may take place after removal of the assembly from the conditions of heat or pressure, or both.

Dado   A rectangular groove across the width of a board or plank.

Decorative laminate   A dense multilayered panel made by compressing sheets of resin-impregnated paper together into a coherent solid mass with heat and pressure.

Defect   In the case of wood, any irregularity occurring in or on the wood that may lower its strength or appearance.

Delamination   The separation of layers in a laminate because of failure of the adhesive, either in the adhesive itself or at the interface between the adhesive and the adherend, or because of cohesive failure of the adherend.

Density   As usually applied to wood of normal cellular form, density is the mass of wood substance enclosed within the boundary surfaces of a wood-plus-voids complex having unit volume. It is variously expressed as pounds per cubic foot, kilograms per cubic metre, or grams per cubic centimeter at a specified moisture content.

Diagonal-grain wood   A form of cross grain where the longitudinal elements run obliquely but parallel to the surface; i.e., the growth layers are not parallel to the edge of the piece as viewed on a quarter-sawed surface.

Dimensional stability   Ability of a material to resist changes in dimensions due to changing environments that affect its size or volumes; i.e., metals in changing temperatures, wood in changing moisture conditions.

Door skins   Thin plywood, usually three-ply, used for faces of flush doors.

Double spreading   Application of adhesive to both mating surfaces of a joint.

Dovetail   Joint shaped like a dove's tail.

Dowel   Wood peg fitted into corresponding holes in two pieces to fasten them together.

Dressed size   The dimensions of lumber after being surfaced with a planing machine. The dressed size is usually ½ to ¾ inch less than the nominal or rough size. A 2 by 4-inch stud, for example, actually measures about 1½ by 3½ inches.

Dry   To change the physical state of an adhesive on an adherend by the loss of solvent constituents by evaporation or absorption, or both.

Drying time   The period of time during which an adhesive on an adherend or an assembly is allowed to dry with or without the application of heat or pressure, or both.

Dry kiln   A chamber having controlled air flow, temperature, and relative humidity for drying lumber, veneer, and other wood products.

Durability   As applied to glue lines, the life expectancy of the structural qualities of the adhesive under the anticipated service conditions of the structure.

Earlywood   The portion of the annual growth ring that is formed during the early part of the growing season. It is usually less dense and weaker mechanically than latewood.

Edge banding   A thin, flat strip of material bonded to edges of panels as a decorative and protective finish.

Edge gluing   Bonding veneers or boards edge to edge with glue.

Elasticity   The capacity of bodies to return to their original shape, dimensions, or positions on the removal of a deforming force.

Elastomer   A macromolecular material which, at room temperature, is capable of recovering substantially in size and shape after removal of a deforming force.

Electrodes   In radiofrequency heating, metal plates or other devices for applying the electric field to the material being heated.

Elevated-temperature-setting adhesive   An adhesive that requires a temperature at or above 87°F (31°C) to set. (See also room-temperature-setting adhesive.)

Emulsion   A mixture in which very small droplets of one liquid are suspended in another liquid.

End grain   The grain of a cross-section of a tree, or the surface of such a section.

End joint   A joint made by gluing two pieces of wood end to end, commonly by a scarf or finger joint.

Equilibrium moisture content   The moisture content at which wood neither gains nor loses moisture when surrounded by air at a given relative humidity and temperature.

Exothermic Characterized by or formed with evolution of heat.

Extender A substance, generally having some adhesive action, added to an adhesive to reduce the amount of the primary binder required per unit area.

Exterior service Service or use in the open (exposed to weather).

External stresses Stresses imposed by external load.

Extractives Substances in wood, not an integral part of the cellular structure, that can be removed by solution in hot or cold water, ether, benzene, or other solvents that do not react chemically with wood components.

Face The better side of a panel or board.

Facing The outermost layer or composite component of a sandwich construction, generally thin and of high density, which resists most of the edgewise loads and flatwise bending moments; synonymous with face and skin.

Fibreboard A broad generic term inclusive of sheet materials of widely varying densities manufactured of refined or partially refined wood (or other vegetable) fibres. Bonding agents and other materials may be added to increase strength, resistance to moisture, fire, or decay, or to improve some other property.

Fibre saturation point The stage in the drying or wetting of wood at which the cell walls are saturated and the cell cavities free from water. It applies to an individual cell or group of cells, not to whole boards. It is usually taken as approximately 30% moisture content, based on oven-dry weight.

Figured veneer General term for decorative veneer such as from crotches, burls, and stumps.

Filler A relatively nonadhesive substance added to an adhesive to improve its working properties, permanence, strength, or other qualities.

Fillet That portion of an adhesive which fills the corner or angle formed where two adherends are joined.

Finger joint An end joint made up of several meshing wedges or fingers of wood bonded together with an adhesive. Fingers are sloped and may be cut parallel to either the wide or edge faces of the piece.

Flakeboard A particle board composed of flakes.

Flat-grained lumber Lumber that has been sawed in a plane approximately perpendicular to a radius of the log. Lumber is considered flat-grained when the annual growth rings make an angle of less than 45° with the surface of the piece.

Flow Movement of an adhesive during the bonding process, before the adhesive is set.

Furring Strips of wood or metal applied to a wall or other surface to even it and normally to serve as a fastening base for finished material.

Gap-filling adhesive See Adhesive, gap-filling.

Glazed Worn shiny by rubbing.

Glossy finish Shiny finish, reflects light.

Gluability Term indicating ease or difficulty in bonding a material with adhesive.

Glue Originally, a hard gelatin obtained from hides, tendons, cartilage, bones, etc., of animals. Also, an adhesive prepared from this substance by heating with water. Through general use, the term is now synonymous with the term "adhesive."

Gluelam (Glue laminating) Parallel-laminations of two or more layers of wood bonded together with adhesive. See Wood, glue-laminated.

Glue line The layer of adhesive affecting union (bond) between any two adjoining wood pieces or layers in an assembly.

Green strength The strength of a bond line shortly after assembly and before full cure.

Growth rings, annual The layer of wood growth put on a tree during a single growing season. In the temperate zone, the annual growth rings of many species (i.e., oaks and pines) are readily distinguished because of differences in the cells formed during the early and late parts of the season. In some temperate zone species (black gum and sweet gum) and many tropical species, annual growth rings are not easily recognized.

Gusset A flat wood, plywood, or similar type member used to provide a connection at intersection of wood members. Most commonly used at joints of wood trusses. They are fastened by nails, screws, bolts, or adhesives.

Hardboard A generic term for a panel manufactured primarily from wood fibres consolidated under heat and pressure in a hot press to a density of 31 pounds per cubic foot or greater.

Hardener   A substance or mixture of substances added to an adhesive to promote or control the curing reaction by taking part in it. The term is also used to designate a substance added to control the degree of hardness of the cured film.

Hardwood   A conventional term for the timber of broad-leaves trees.

Heartwood   The wood extending from the pith to the sapwood, the cells of which no longer participate in the life processes of the tree. Heartwood may contain phenolic compounds, gums, resins, and other materials that usually make it darker and more decay resistant than sapwood.

High-frequency curing   Setting or curing adhesive with high-frequency electric currents.

High-pressure laminate   Laminates moulded and cured at pressures not lower than 1000 psi and more commonly in the range of 1200 to 2000 psi.

Hollow-core construction   A panel construction with facings of plywood, hardboard, or similar material bonded to a framed core assembly of wood lattice, paperboard rings, or the like, which support the facing at spaced intervals.

Honeycomb core   A sandwich core material constructed of thin sheet materials or ribbons formed to honeycomb-like configurations.

Hot press   A press in which the platens are heated to a prescribed temperature by steam, electricity, or hot water.

Humidify   To increase, by any process, the quantity of water vapor within a given space.

Hygroscopic   Term used to describe a substance, such as wood, that absorbs and looses moisture readily.

Interior service   Used in the interior (of a building) protected from outdoor weather.

Internal stress   Stress set up from internal conditions, such as differential shrinkage, aside from external loads applied to a member.

Jig   A device for holding an assembly in place during gluing or machining operations.

Joint   The junction of two pieces of wood or veneer.

> *butt joint.*   An end joint formed by abutting the squared ends of two pieces.

edge joint. The place where two pieces of wood are joined together edged to edge, commonly by gluing. The joints may be made by gluing two squared edges as in a plain edge joint or by using machined joints of various kinds, such as tongued-and-grooved joints.

end joint. The place where two pieces of wood are joined together end to end, commonly by scarf or finger jointing.

lap. A joint made by placing one member partly over another and bonding the overlapped portions.

scarf. An end joint formed by joining with glue the ends of two pieces that have been tapered or bevelled to form sloping plane surfaces, usually to a feather edge, and with the same slope of the plane with respect to the length in both pieces.

starved. A glue joint that is poorly bonded because an insufficient quantity of glue remained in the joint.

sunken. Depression in wood surface at glue joint caused by surfacing edge-glued material too soon after gluing. (Inadequate time allowed for moisture added with glue to diffuse away from the joint.)

tongue-and-groove. A kind of joint in which a tongue or rib on one board fits into a groove on another.

Jointer Machine equipped with rotary cutter and flat bed permitting surfacing of one side of a member at a time.

Kiln drying The process of drying wood products in a closed chamber in which the temperature and relative humidity of the circulated air can be controlled.

Laminate (noun) A product made by bonding together two or more layers of material or materials.

Laminate (verb) To unite layers of material with adhesive.

Laminated plastic (decorative) A dense, tough, solid produced by bonding together layers of kraft paper impregnated with a resin under heat and pressure.

Laminated wood An assembly made by bonding layers of veneer or lumber with an adhesive so that the grain of all laminations is essentially parallel.

horizontally laminated wood. Laminated wood in which the laminations are so arranged that the wider dimension of each lamination is horizontal.

vertically laminated wood. Laminated wood in which the laminations are so arranged that the wider dimension of each lamination is vertical.

Lamination The process of preparing a laminate. Also, any layer in a laminate.

Latewood The portion of the annual growth ring that is formed after the earlywood formation has ceased. It is usually denser and stronger mechanically than earlywood.

Layup Assembled parts placed in the position they occupy in final product.

Lignin The second most abundant constituent of wood.

Longitudinal Generally, parallel to the direction of the wood fibres or to the length of a board.

Lumber The product of the saw and planing mill not further manufactured than by sawing, resawing, passing lengthwise through a standard planing machine, crosscutting to length, and matching.

Manufactured unit A quantity of finished adhesive or finished adhesive component, processed at one time. NOTE: The manufactured unit may be a batch or a part thereof.

Marine plywood Plywood made of veneers of grades specified for marine use and bonded with waterproof adhesive (usually phenolic type).

Mastic A material with adhesive properties, usually used in relatively thick sections, that can be readily formed by application with trowel or spatula.

Mechanical adhesion See Adhesion, mechanical.

Mechanical fastener Nails, screws, bolts, and similar items.

Mitred joint Joint cut at a 45° angle with fibre direction.

Mixed grain Mixture of flat-sawed and quarter-sawed pieces.

Modifier Any chemically inert ingredient added to an adhesive formulation that changes its properties.

Mortise A slot cut in a board, plank, or timber, usually edgewise, to receive the tenon of another board, plank, or timber to form a joint.

Moisture content The amount of water contained in the wood, usually expressed as a percentage of the weight of the oven-dry wood.

Moisture resistance The ability of a material to resist absorbing moisture from the air or when immersed in water.

Moulding   Shaping or forming to desired pattern or form.

Nail bonding   Obtaining bonding pressure by nailing together the pieces spread with adhesive.

Nail popping   Protrusion of nailheads because of shrinking and swelling of wood.

Natural adhesive   Adhesive produced from naturally occurring products such as blood and casein.

Neoprene   Synthetic rubber.

Nominal size   As applied to timber or lumber, the size by which it is known and sold on the market; often differs from the actual size.

Open assembly   See Assembly time.

Oven-dry wood   Wood dried to a relatively constant weight in a ventilated oven at 214–221°F (101° to 105°C).

Overlay   A thin layer or object, functional or decorative, made of paper, plastic film, metal foil, or other material bonded to one or both faces of a panel or lumber.

Paper laminate   See Decorative laminate.

Parallel-laminated   A laminate in which all the layers of material are oriented approximately parallel with respect to the grain or strongest direction in tension.

Particle board   A generic term for a panel manufactured from wood essentially in the form of particles (as distinct from fibres) which are bonded together with synthetic resin or other suitable binder, under heat and pressure.

Penetration   The entering of an adhesive into an adherend. NOTE: This property of a system is measured by the depth of penetration of the adhesive into the adherend.

Permanence   See Durability.

Pith   The small, soft core occurring near the center of a tree trunk, branch, twig, or log.

Pith side   Side nearest to pith (and usually center of tree).

Planer   Machine equipped with cutter rolls and feed rolls for surfacing or planing wood.

Plank   A broad board, usually more than 1″ thick.

Plastic laminate   See Decorative laminate.

Platen   A flat plate, usually of metal, that exerts or receives pressure, as in a press used for gluing or veneering.

Pneumatic   Filled with compressed air.

Polymer   A compound formed by the reaction of simple molecules. Polymers may be formed by polymerization (addition polymer) or polycondensation (condensation polymer). When two or more monomers are involved, the product is called a copolymer.

Polymerization   A chemical reaction in which the molecules of a monomer are linked together.

Porosity   The ratio of the volume of a material's pores to that of its solid content.

Pot life   See Working life.

Precure   Condition of too much cure or set of the glue before pressure is applied, resulting in inadequate flow and glue bond.

Preservative   Any substance that, for a reasonable length of time, is effective in preventing the development and action of wood-rotting fungi, borers of various kinds, and harmful insects that deteriorate wood.

Quarter-sawed   Sawn so the annual rings are essentially perpendicular to the wide face of the board. Lumber is considered quarter-sawed when the annual growth rings form an angle of 45° to 90° with the wide surface of the piece.

Rabbet   A type of joint for fitting one wood member to another (for example, planking to keel and stem of a boat).

Radiofrequency (RF) curing   Curing of bond lines by the application of radiofrequency energy.

Radiofrequency energy   Electrical energy produced by electric fields alternating at radiofrequencies.

Relative humidity   Ratio of the amount of water vapor present in the air to that which the air would hold at saturation at the same temperature. It is usually considered on the basis of the weight of the vapor but, for accuracy, should be considered on the basis of vapor pressures.

Resin   A solid, semisolid, or pseudosolid organic material which has an indefinite and often high molecular weight, exhibits a tendency to flow when subjected to stress, and usually has a softening or melting range.

    liquid resin.   An organic polymeric liquid which when converted to its final state for use becomes a resin.

Resurfacing   Planing again to obtain a freshly clean surface for gluing.

Room-temperature-setting adhesive   An adhesive that sets at temperatures between 68° to 86°F.

Rotary cut   Veneer cut on a lathe which rotates a log or bolt, chucked in the center, against a fixed knife.

Sandwich panels   See Structural sandwich construction.

Sapwood   The wood of pale color near the outside of the log. Under most conditions, the sapwood is more susceptible to decay than heartwood.

Satin finish (plastic laminates)   The most common sheet finish, which has fine parallel brush lines running lengthwise to the sheet. Medium gloss.

Scarf joints   See Joint, scarf.

Sculptured finish   A three-dimensional surface of a decorative laminated plastic sheet.

Set   To convert an adhesive into a fixed or hardened state by chemical or physical action, such as condensation, polymerization, oxidation, vulcanization, gelation, hydration, or evaporation of volatile constituents.

Setting time   The period of time during which an assembly is subjected to heat or pressure or both, to set the adhesive.

Severe exposure   Exposure to harsh weather conditions or to harsh tests such as boiling and drying at low humidities.

Shear   A condition of stress or strain where parallel planes slide relative to one another.

Shear block test (also called block sheer test)   A means of testing a bond joint in shear.

Short grain   Term used for cross grain as when end grain is exposed on face of veneer.

Showthrough   Term used when effects of defects within a panel can be seen on the face.

Sizing   The process of applying an extra coat of adhesive for edge banding.

Spline   Thin piece of wood or plywood often used to reinforce a joint between two pieces of wood.

Spread   The quantity of adhesive per unit joint area applied to an adherend, usually expressed in pounds of adhesive per thousand square feet of joint area.

> *single spread*.   Refers to application of adhesive to only one adherend of a joint.

> *double spread*.   Refers to application of adhesive to both adherends of a joint.

Springwood   See Earlywood.

Squeeze-out   Bead of glue squeezed out of a joint when gluing pressure is applied.

Starved joint   See Joint, starved.

Storage life   The period of time during which a packaged adhesive can be stored under specific temperature conditions and remain suitable for use. Sometimes called shelf life.

Strength   The ability of a member to sustain stress without failure.

Stress   The force developed, under certain conditions, self-generated in the piece by internal variations of moisture content, temperature, or both.

Stressed-skin construction   A construction in which panels are separated from one another by a central partition of spaced strips with the whole assembly bonded so that when loaded it acts as a unit.

Structural adhesive   A bonding agent used for transferring required loads between adherends exposed to service environments typical for the structure involved.

Structural sandwich construction substrate   A material upon the surface of which an adhesive-containing substance is spread for any purpose, such as bonding or coating. A broader term than adherend. (See also Adherend.)

Summerwood See Latewood.

Sunken joint See Joint, sunken.

Surfaced lumber Lumber that is dressed by running it through a planer.

Synthetic adhesives Adhesives produced by chemical synthesis.

Synthetic rubber Any of various products (such as neoprene, butyl rubber, or nitril rubber) that resemble natural rubber more or less closely in their properties.

Tack The property of an adhesive that enables it to form a bond of measurable strength immediately after adhesive and adherend are brought into contact under low pressure.

> *dry.* The property of certain adhesives, particularly nonvulcanizing rubber adhesives, to adhere on contact to themselves at a stage in the evaporation of volatile constituents, even though they seem dry to the touch. Sometimes called "aggressive tack."

Tacky-dry Pertaining to the condition of an adhesive when the volatile constituents have evaporated or been absorbed sufficiently to leave it in a desired tacky state.

Telegraphing A condition in a laminate or other type of composite construction in which irregularities, imperfections, or patterns of an inner layer are visibly transmitted to the surface. NOTE: Telegraphing is occasionally referred to as photographing.

Temperature

> *curing.* The temperature to which an adhesive or an assembly is subjected to cure the adhesive.

> *drying.* The temperature to which an adhesive on an adherend or in an assembly or the assembly itself is subjected to dry the adhesive.

> *setting.* The temperature to which an adhesive or an assembly is subjected to set the adhesive.

Tempered hardboard A hardboard subjected to tempering or specially manufactured with other variation in usual process so that the resulting product has special properties of stiffness, strength, and water resistance.

Tensile strength The capacity of a body to sustain tensile loading (resistance to lengthwise stress). In wood, tensile strength is high along the grain and low across the grain.

Thermal softening Softens with heat.

Thermoplastic   A material which will repeatedly soften when heated and harden when cooled.

Thermoset   A material which will undergo or has undergone a chemical reaction by the action of heat, catalysts, ultraviolet light, etc., leading to a relatively infusible state.

Thermosetting   Having the property of undergoing a chemical reaction by the action of heat, catalysts, ultraviolet light, etc., leading to a relatively infusible state.

Thinner   A volatile liquid added to an adhesive to modify the consistency of other properties.

Tongue-and-groove joint   See Joints, tongue-and-groove.

Torque   The product of a force and a lever arm which tends to twist or rotate a body; for example, the action of a wrench turning a nut on a bolt.

Twist   A distortion caused by the turning or winding of the edges of a board so that the four corners of any face are no longer in the same plane.

Uncatalyzed   No catalyst employed or added.

Vehicle   The liquid portion of an adhesive or a finishing material; it consists of the binder (nonvolatile) and volatile thinners.

Veneer   A thin layer or sheet of wood.

   rotary-cut veneer.   Veneer cut in a lathe which rotates a log or bolt, chucked in the center, against a knife.

   sawed veneer.   Veneer produced by sawing.

   sliced veneer.   Veneer that is sliced off a log, bolt, or flitch with a knife.

Viscosity   The property of a fluid material by virtue of which when flow occurs inside it, forces arise in such a direction as to oppose flow.

Warp   A significant variation from the original, or plane surface.

Waterproof   The term is synonymous with exterior products bonded with highly resistant adhesives, which are capable of withstanding prolonged exposure to severe service conditions without failure in the glue bonds.

Water resistant   A moderately resistant adhesive capable of withstanding limited exposure to water or to severe conditions without failure.

Water soluble   Substance that can be dissolved in water.

Wood failure   The rupturing of wood fibres in strength tests on bonded specimens, usually expressed as the percentage of the total area involved which shows such failure.

Wood, glued-laminated   An assembly made by bonding layers of veneer or lumber with an adhesive so that the grain of all laminations is essentially parallel.

Working life   The period of time during which an adhesive, after mixing with catalyst, solvent, or other compounding ingredients, remains suitable for use. Also called pot life.

Working properties   The properties of an adhesive that affect or dictate the manner of application to the adherends to be bonded and the assembly of the joint before pressure application; i.e., viscosity, pot life, assembly time, setting time, etc.

Index

METRIC EQUIVALENCY CHART

MM—MILLIMETRES   CM—CENTIMETRES

INCHES TO MILLIMETRES AND CENTIMETRES

INCHES	MM	CM	INCHES	CM	INCHES	CM
⅛	3	0.3	9	22.9	30	76.2
¼	6	0.6	10	25.4	31	78.7
⅜	10	1.0	11	27.9	32	81.3
½	13	1.3	12	30.5	33	83.8
⅝	16	1.6	13	33.0	34	86.4
¾	19	1.9	14	35.6	35	88.9
⅞	22	2.2	15	38.1	36	91.4
1	25	2.5	16	40.6	37	94.0
1¼	32	3.2	17	43.2	38	96.5
1½	38	3.8	18	45.7	39	99.1
1¾	44	4.4	19	48.3	40	101.6
2	51	5.1	20	50.8	41	104.1
2½	64	6.4	21	53.3	42	106.7
3	76	7.6	22	55.9	43	109.2
3½	89	8.9	23	58.4	44	111.8
4	102	10.2	24	61.0	45	114.3
4½	114	11.4	25	63.5	46	116.8
5	127	12.7	26	66.0	47	119.4
6	152	15.2	27	68.6	48	121.9
7	178	17.8	28	71.1	49	124.5
8	203	20.3	29	73.7	50	127.0

YARDS TO METRES

YARDS	METRES	YARDS	METRES	YARDS	METRES	YARDS	METRES	YARDS	METRES
⅛	0.11	2⅛	1.94	4⅛	3.77	6⅛	5.60	8⅛	7.43
¼	0.23	2¼	2.06	4¼	3.89	6¼	5.72	8¼	7.54
⅜	0.34	2⅜	2.17	4⅜	4.00	6⅜	5.83	8⅜	7.66
½	0.46	2½	2.29	4½	4.11	6½	5.94	8½	7.77
⅝	0.57	2⅝	2.40	4⅝	4.23	6⅝	6.06	8⅝	7.89
¾	0.69	2¾	2.51	4¾	4.34	6¾	6.17	8¾	8.00
⅞	0.80	2⅞	2.63	4⅞	4.46	6⅞	6.29	8⅞	8.12
1	0.91	3	2.74	5	4.57	7	6.40	9	8.23
1⅛	1.03	3⅛	2.86	5⅛	4.69	7⅛	6.52	9⅛	8.34
1¼	1.14	3¼	2.97	5¼	4.80	7¼	6.63	9¼	8.46
1⅜	1.26	3⅜	3.09	5⅜	4.91	7⅜	6.74	9⅜	8.57
1½	1.37	3½	3.20	5½	5.03	7½	6.86	9½	8.69
1⅝	1.49	3⅝	3.31	5⅝	5.14	7⅝	6.97	9⅝	8.80
1¾	1.60	3¾	3.43	5¾	5.26	7¾	7.09	9¾	8.92
1⅞	1.71	3⅞	3.54	5⅞	5.37	7⅞	7.20	9⅞	9.03
2	1.83	4	3.66	6	5.49	8	7.32	10	9.14

About the Author

Patrick Spielman's love of wood began when, as a child, he transformed fruit crates into toys. Now this prolific and innovative woodworker is respected worldwide as a teacher and author.

His most famous contribution to the woodworking field has been his perfection of a method to season green wood with polyethylene glycol 1000 (PEG). He went on to invent, manufacture, and distribute the PEG-Thermovat chemical seasoning system.

During his many years as shop instructor in Wisconsin, Spielman published manuals, teaching guides, and more than 14 popular books, including *Modern Wood Technology*, a college text. He also wrote six educational series on wood technology, tool use, processing techniques, design, and wood-product planning.

Author of the best-selling *Router Handbook* (over 200,000 copies sold), Spielman has served as editorial consultant to a professional magazine, and his products, techniques, and many books have been featured in numerous periodicals.

This pioneer of new ideas and inventor of countless jigs, fixtures, and designs used throughout the world is a unique combination of expert woodworker and brilliant teacher—all of which endear him to his many readers and to his publisher.

At Spielman's Wood Works in the woods of northern Door County, Wisconsin, he and his family create and sell some of the most durable and popular furniture products and designs available.

Should you wish to write Pat, please forward your letters to Sterling Publishing Company.

CHARLES NURNBERG
STERLING PUBLISHING COMPANY

Current Books by Patrick Spielman

Working Green Wood with PEG. Covers every process for making beautiful, inexpensive projects from green wood without cracking, splitting, or warping. Hundreds of clear photos and drawings show every step from obtaining the raw wood through shaping, treating, and finishing your PEG-treated projects. 175 unusual project ideas. Lists supply sources. 160 pages.

Making Wood Signs. Designing, selecting woods, tools, and every process through finishing is clearly covered. Hand-carved, power-carved, routed, and sandblasted processes in small to huge signs are presented. Foolproof guides for professional letters and ornaments. Hundreds of photos (4 pages in full color). Lists sources for supplies and special tooling. 144 pages.

Making Wood Decoys. A clear step-by-step approach to the basics of decoy carving. This book is abundantly illustrated with closeup photos for designing, selecting, and obtaining woods; tools; feather detailing; painting; and finishing of decorative and working decoys. Six different professional decoy artists featured. Photo gallery (4 pages in full color) along with numerous detailed plans for various popular decoys. 160 pages.

Making Country-Rustic Furniture. Hundreds of photos, patterns, and detailed scaled drawings reveal construction methods, woodworking techniques, and Spielman's professional secrets for making indoor and outdoor furniture in the distinctly attractive Country-Rustic style. Covered are all aspects of furniture making from choosing the best wood for the job to texturing smooth boards. Among the dozens of projects are mailboxes, cabinets, shelves, coffee tables, weather vanes, doors, panelling, plant stands and many more durable and economical pieces. 400 illustrations. 4 pages in full color. 164 pages.

Alphabets and Designs for Wood Signs. 50 alphabet patterns, plans for many decorative designs, the latest on hand carving, routing, cutouts, and sandblasting. Pricing data. Photo gallery (4 pages in color) of wood signs by professionals from across the U.S. Over 200 illustrations. 128 pages.

Router Handbook. With nearly 600 illustrations of every conceivable bit, attachment, jig, and fixture, plus every possible operation, this definitive guide has revolutionized router applications. It begins with safety and maintenance tips, then forges ahead into all aspects of dovetailing, freehanding, advanced duplication, and more. Details for over 50 projects are included. 224 pages.

Realistic Decoys. Spielman and master carver Keith Bridenhagen reveal their successful techniques for carving, feather-texturing, painting, and finishing wood decoys. Details that you can't find elsewhere—anatomy, attitudes, markings, and the easy step-by-step approach to perfect delicate procedures—make this book invaluable. Includes listings for contests, shows, and sources of tools and supplies. 274 closeup photos, 28 in color. 224 pages.